Progressive Business Plan for a Background Check Company

Fourth Edition …..Last Update: June, 2018

Background Check
Business Plan
_____ (date)

Business Name: _____

Plan Time Period: 2018 - 2020

Founding Directors:

Name: _____

Name: _____

Contact Information:

Owner: _____

Address: _____

City/State/Zip: _____

Phone: _____

Cell: _____

Fax: _____

Website: _____

Email: _____

Submitted to: _____

Date: _____

Contact Info: _____

NON-DISCLOSURE AGREEMENT

_____ (Company)., and _____ (Person Name), agrees:

_____ (Company) Corp. may from time to time disclose to _____ (Person Name) certain confidential information or trade secrets generally regarding Business plan and financials of _____ (Company) corp.

_____ (Person Name) agrees that it shall not disclose the information so conveyed, unless in conformity with this agreement. _____ (Person Name) shall limit disclosure to the officers and employees of _____ (Person Name) with a reasonable "need to know" the information and shall protect the same from disclosure with reasonable diligence.

As to all information which _____ (Company) Corp. claims is confidential, _____ (Company) Corp. shall reduce the same to writing prior to disclosure and shall conspicuously mark the same as "confidential," "not to be disclosed" or with other clear indication of its status. If the information which _____ (Company) Corp. is disclosing is not in written form, for example, a machine or device, _____ (Company) Corp. shall be required prior to or at the same time that the disclosure is made to provide written notice of the secrecy claimed by _____ (Company) Corp. _____ (Person Name) agrees upon reasonable notice to return the confidential tangible material provided by it by _____ (Company) Corp. upon reasonable request.

The obligation of non-disclosure shall terminate when if any of the following occurs:
(a) The confidential information becomes known to the public without the fault of _____ (Person Name), or;
(b) The information is disclosed publicly by _____ (Company) Corp., or
(c) a period of 12 months passes from the disclosure, or;
(d) the information loses its status as confidential through no fault of _____ (Person Name).

In any event, the obligation of non-disclosure shall not apply to information which was known to _____ (Person Name) prior to the execution of this agreement.

Dated: _____

_____
_____ (Company) Corp.
_____(Person Name)

Business and Marketing Plan Instructions

1. If you need the digital file for this book, please send proof-of-purchase to probusconsult2@yahoo.com

2. Complete the Executive Summary section, as your final step, after you have completed the entire plan.

3. Feel free to edit the plan and make it more relevant to your strategic goals, objectives and business vision.

4. We have provided all the formulas needed to prepare the financial plan. Just plug in the numbers that are based on your particular situation. Excel spreadsheets for the financials are available on the microsoft.com website and www.simplebizplanning.com/forms.htm http://office.microsoft.com/en-us/templates/

5. Throughout the plan, we have provided prompts or suggestions as to what values to enter into blank spaces but use your best judgment and then delete the suggested values (?).

6. The plan also includes some separate worksheets for additional assistance in expanding some of the sections, if desired.

7. Additionally, some sections offer multiple choices and the word 'select' appears as a prompt to edit the contents of the plan.

8. Your feedback, referrals and business are always very much appreciated.

Thank you

Nat Chiaffarano, MBA
Progressive Business Consulting, Inc.
Pembroke Pines, FL 33027
ProBusConsult2@yahoo.com

Background Check Business Plan: Table of Contents

"Progressive Business Plan for a Background Check Company"

Limits of Liability / Disclaimer of Warranty

The author and the publisher of "Progressive Business Plan for a
Background Check Company", and all accompanying materials have used
their best efforts in preparing this program. The author and publisher make
no representations and warranties with respect to the accuracy, applicability,
fitness or completeness of the content of this program. The information
contained in this program is subject to change without notice and should not
be construed as a commitment by the author or publisher.

The authors and publisher shall in no event be held liable for any loss or
damages, including but not limited to special, incidental, consequential, or
other damages. The program makes no promises as to results or
consequences of applying the material herein: your business results may
vary in direct relation to your detailed planning, timing, availability of
capital and human resources, and implementation skills.

This publication is not intended for use as a source of legal, accounting, or
professional advice. As always, the advice of a competent legal, accounting,
tax, financial or other professional should be sought. If you have any
specific questions about your unique business situation, consider contacting
a qualified business consultant. The fact that an organization or website is
referred to as a 'resource' or potential source of information, does not mean
that the publisher or authors endorse the resource. Websites listed may also
have been changed since publication of the book.

1.0 Executive Summary

Industry Overview

It is increasingly common and necessary to conduct background checks on people who will hold positions of trust in an organization or business. Organizations owe it to themselves and to everyone with whom they come into contact to know everything they can about their employees and volunteers, and the most effective method to accomplish this is by conducting thorough background checks. Some 80 percent of employers now require background checks for all potential employees, according to the Privacy Rights Clearinghouse (PRC), a consumer rights advocacy group in San Diego. According to the US Small Business Administration, for every dollar an employer invests in employment screening, the return on investment ranges from $5-16, resulting from improved productivity, reduced absenteeism, lower turnover – and decreased employer liability. The United States Department of Commerce reports that 30% of all business failures result from theft or embezzlement.

A background check usually includes a search of civil and criminal court filings, credit information and personal history, including verification of degrees and past employment. Deeper background checks, such as those used for government security clearances, may even involve live interviews and inspection of the applicant's medical history. Ostensibly, the applicant gives his approval for this information, along with the data necessary to complete the check. This data includes full name, date of birth, Social Security number, past and present addresses and past employment information. Many background check forms also request driver's license or state ID numbers.

The Background Check Services industry has spent the better part of the past decade moving operations online, which sped up processes and attracted a huge number of new entrants to the new business model. As demand dropped during the recession, however, the market quickly became saturated, leading to slow growth and some industry exits. With favorable new regulation and a return to hiring in the United States, the industry is expected to grow steadily over the next five years.
Resource:
www.ibisworld.com/industry-trends/specialized-market-research-reports/advisory-financial-services/other-outsourced-functions/background-check-services.html

Business Overview

_____ (company name) will be a _____ (national/global?) background screening company in _____ (city), _____ (state). Our comprehensive research techniques will produce thorough, accurate background checks and screening reports that meet the unique needs of our clients and the standards of federal and international employment background check guidelines. We will offer scalability while maintaining our commitment to integrity, accuracy and timely results and will give clients the tools to make safer hiring decisions through comprehensive reports, interactive compliance services and intuitive, easy-to-use technology.

It will follow the best practices of its industry leaders, with particular emphasis on excellent customer service, innovative service offerings, a knowledgeable staff and competitive pricing.

The background check company will compete on the following basis:
1. Accurate and reliable background checks.
2. Exceptional customer service.
3. Quick report turnaround times.
4. Timely responses to questions and special requests.
5. One platform for the client's entire hiring process.

We believe that we can become the background screening company of choice in the _____ area for the following reasons:
1. We will develop a training program to create a competent staff, dedicated to continuously improving their skill sets to better assist our customers in making informed hiring decisions.
2. We will develop a questionnaire to survey changing customer needs and wants, build a comprehensive client profile and enable clients to express their level of satisfaction.
3. We will become a one-stop destination for customers in need of hiring related products and services.
4. We will offer quality background checking services, using the latest technological advances, at value-based prices with 24/7 convenient access hours.

In order to succeed, _____ (company name) will have to do the following:
1. Conduct extensive market research to demonstrate that there is a demand for a background checking company with our aforementioned differentiation strategy.
2. Make superior customer service our number one priority.
3. Stay abreast of developments in the background checking industry.
4. Precisely assess and then exceed the expectations of all clients.
5. Form long-term, trust-based relationships with clients to secure profitable repeat business and referrals.
6. Develop process efficiencies to achieve and maintain profitability.

Target Market

Our target market is businesses that hire 20 or more employees and landlords that process tenant applications that need to be pre-screened, as background screening has now become a standard practice of operating a successful business. We will also target businesses that service the needs of children, such as child care centers, tutors and babysitters. We also plan to work with staffing companies, airlines and trucking companies, financial services institutions, ride-sharing companies, and manufacturers.

Recap of Our Target Market:

Large companies	Small businesses
Schools and institutions	Medical facilities
Nursing homes	Childcare facilities
Domestic service companies	Dating services and singles

Security companies   Volunteer organizations
Churches, synagogues and mosques   Supermarkets
Movie theaters   Construction companies
Investors and investment clubs   Landlords
Real estate management companies
Source: www.backgroundscreenersofamerica.com/the_marketplace.php

Marketing Strategy

The foundation for this plan is a combination of primary and secondary research, upon which the marketing strategies are built. Discussions and interviews were held with a variety of businesses and landlords to develop financial and proforma detail. We consulted census data, county business patterns, and other directories to develop the market potential and assess the competitive situation.

Our market strategy will be based on a cost-effective approach to reach this defined target market. The basic approach to promote our products and services will be through establishing relationships with kcy influencers in the community and then through referral activities, once a significant client base has been established.

_____ (company name) will focus on developing loyal client relationships by offering background checking services based on the client's need for time-saving convenience and accuracy. The newest service offerings, staff accessibility and value-based pricing will all serve to differentiate our company from the other providers in the area. With the help of an aggressive marketing plan, _____ (company name) expects to experience steady growth. _____ (company name) also plans to attract its customers through the use of local business journal advertisements, circulating flyers, a systematic series of direct mailings, press releases in local newspapers, a website, and online directory listings. We will also become an active member of the local Chamber of Commerce.

Other marketing strategies will include:
1.   Conduct Free Value-Driven Webinars
2.   Create branded PDF reports
3.   Refer Service to Get Services in Return
4.   Give 100% Commission on a front-end service

Critical Risks

Management recognizes there are several internal and external risks inherent in our business concept. Quality, wraparound service selection, value pricing and convenience will be key factors in the consumers' decision to utilize our services. Clients must be willing to accept our one-stop services and become repeat and referral customers for the company to meet its sales projections. Building a loyal and trusting relationship with our clients and referral partners is a key component to the success of _____ (company name).

Customer Service

We will take every opportunity to help the client, regardless of what the revenue might be. We will outshine our competition by doing something "extra" and offering added-value services in a timely manner. We will take a long-term perspective and focus on the client's possible lifetime value to our business. By giving careful consideration to customer responsiveness, _____ (company name) goal will be to meet and exceed every service expectation. Quality service, accurate reporting and quick responsiveness will be the philosophy guiding a customer-centric approach to our background checking business.

Mission Statement   (optional)

Our Mission is to address the following customer pain points or unmet needs and wants, which will define the opportunity for our business: _____

To satisfy these unmet needs and wants, we will propose the following unique solutions, which will create better value for our customers:

_____

Business Plan Objectives

This business plan serves to detail the direction, vision, and planning necessary to achieve our goal of providing a superior background checking service. The purpose of this document is to provide a strategic business plan for our company and to support a request for a $ _____, five-year bank loan to purchase computer equipment and marketing support, as part of the financing for a start-up background checking business. The plan has been adjusted to reflect the particular strengths and weaknesses of _____ (company name). Actual financial performance will be closely tracked, and the business plan will be adjusted when necessary to ensure that full profit potential and loan repayment is realized on schedule. The plan will also help us to identify and quantify objectives, track and direct growth and create benchmarks for measuring success.

The Company

The business _____ (will be/was) incorporated on _____ (date) in the state of _____, as a _____ (Corporation/LLC), and intends to register for Sub-chapter 'S' status for federal tax purposes. This will effectively shield the owner(s) from personal liability and double taxation.

Business Goals

Our business goal is to continue to develop the _____ (company name) brand name. To do so, we plan to execute on the following:
1.   Offer quality background checking services, and timely customer support.
2.   Focus on quality controls and ongoing operational excellence.
3.   Recruit and train the very best ethical employees.
4.   Create a marketing campaign with a consistent look and message content.

Location

_____ (company name) will be located in the ___ (complex name) on _____ (address) in __ (city), __ (state). The __ (purchased/leased) space is easily accessible and provides ample parking for __ (#) visiting clients and staff. The location is attractive due to its reasonable rent, and space expanding and subletting options

Products and Services
We will offer the following services:

1.	Employment Screening	2.	Tenant Screening
3.	Custom Screening Solutions	4.	Drug Testing
5.	Fingerprinting	6.	DMV Driving Records
7.	DOT Drug and Alcohol Verification	8.	Employment Credit Reports
9.	Tenant Credit Reports	10.	SSN Verification
11.	Employment Verification	12.	Professional Reference Checks
13.	Prof. License & Credential Verify	14.	Education Verification
15.	Skills and Behavioral Testing	16.	Criminal County Court Check
17.	Form I-9 and E-Verify	18.	Electronic Application Process
19.	Employee Screening Consult Svcs	20.	Volunteer Background Checks
21.	Business Background Check Report		

Background Screening Services
We will cover both fundamental research components and specialized searches. All information gathered will be precisely tracked and monitored using built-in quality and accuracy controls and delivered in the format that best suit's the client's process.

Occupational Health Screening Services
We will offer integrated, national resources for drug and alcohol screening, physicals and other services, plus full program support through automatic forms supply, automated data reporting, medical reviews and more.

DOT Compliance Services
We will provide a turnkey approach to handling DOT driver drug and alcohol testing, driver qualification file maintenance, random pool administration and DOT-required reporting. All services will be managed through our consolidated, Web-based management system.

Competitive Edge
_____ (company name) will compete well in our market by offering competitive prices on an expanded line of reliable background checking services, knowledgeable and approachable staff, and by using the latest software to manage secure databases and enable convenient online ordering and report access. Furthermore, we will maintain an excellent reputation for trustworthiness and integrity with the community we serve.

Our plan is to achieve a competitive advantage in the following areas: (select)
- Cost
- Types of criminal searches conducted
- Types of verification services conducted
- Types of industry searches conducted

- Ease of use
- How easy the final reports are to access, read and understand
- How long the searches take
- Customer service
- The extra services the company offers, such as drug testing and I-9 verification management
- Better Business Bureau rating and complaint handling.
- National Association of Professional Background Screeners accreditation

Source:
https://www.businessnewsdaily.com/7638-best-background-check-services.html

The Management Team

_____ (company name) will be led by _____ (owner name) and _____ (co-owner name). ____ (owner name) has a _____ degree from _____ (institution name) and a _____ background within the industry, having spent ____ (#) years with ____ (former employer name or type of business). During this tenure, ___ (he/she) helped grow the business from $_____ in yearly revenue to over $___. ____ (co-owner name) has a ___ background, and while employed by __ was able to increase operating profit by __ percent. These acquired skills, work experiences and educational backgrounds will play a big role in the success of our background checking service business. Additionally, our president, _____ (name), has an extensive knowledge of the _____ area and has identified a niche market opportunity to make this venture highly successful, combining his ___ (#) years of work experience in a variety of businesses. _____ (owner name) will manage all aspects of the business to ensure effective customer responsiveness while monitoring day-to-day operations. Qualified and trained background check specialists personally trained by _____ (owner name) in customer service and record investigation skills will provide additional support services.

Recap of Past Successful Accomplishments

_____ (company name) is uniquely qualified to succeed due to the following past successes:

1. **Entrepreneurial Track Record**: The owners and management team have helped to launch numerous successful ventures, including a _____.

2. **Key Milestones Achieved**: The founders have invested $___ to-date to staff the company, build the core technology, acquire starting inventory, test market the _____ (product/service), realize sales of $_____ and launch the website.

Start-up Funding

_____ (owner name) will financially back the new business venture with an initial investment of $ _____ and will be the principal owner. Additional funding in the amount of $_____ will be sought from _____, a local commercial bank, with a SBA loan guarantee. This money will be needed to start the company. This loan will provide start-up capital, financing for a selected site lease, remodeling renovations, pay for permits and licensing, staff training and certification, computer equipment and working capital to cover expenses during the first year of operation.

Financial Projections

We plan to open for business on ___(date). __ (company name) is forecasted to gross in excess of $___ in sales in its first year of operation, ending ___ (month/ year). Profit margins are forecasted to be at about __ percent. Second year operations will produce a net profit of $__. This will be generated from an investment of $__ in initial capital. It is expected that payback of our total invested capital will be realized in less than __ (#) months of operation. It is further forecasted that cash flow becomes positive from operations in year __ (one?). We project that our net profits will increase from $___ to over $ __ over the next three years.

Financial Profile Summary

Key Indicator	2018	2019	2020
Total Revenue			
Expenses			
Gross Margin			
Operating Income			
Net Income			
EBITDA			

EBITDA = Revenue - Expenses (excluding tax, interest, depreciation and amortization) EBITDA is essentially net income with interest, taxes, depreciation, and amortization added back to it, and can be used to analyze and compare profitability between companies and industries because it eliminates the effects of financing and accounting decisions.

Gross Margin (%) = (Revenue - Cost of Goods Sold) / Revenue

Net Income = Total revenue - Cost of sales - Other expenses - Tax

Exit Strategy

If the business is very successful, ____ (owner name) may seek to sell the business to a third party for a significant, earnings multiple. Most likely, the Company will hire a qualified business broker to sell the business on behalf of _____ (company name). Based on historical numbers, the business could generate a sales premium of up to __(#) times earnings.

Summary

Through a combination of a proven business model and a strong management team to guide the organization, _____ (company name) will be a long lasting, profitable business. We believe our ability to create future product and service opportunities and growth will only be limited by our imagination and our ability to attract talented people who understand the concept of branding.

1.1.0   Tactical Objectives   (select - 3)

The following tactical objectives will specify quantifiable results and involve activities that can be easily tracked. They will also be realistic, tied to specific marketing strategies and serve as a good benchmark to evaluate our marketing plan success. (Select Choices)

1. Earn and maintain a rating as one of the best background checking service providers in the nation.
2. Establish and maintain ____ (30?)% minimum gross profit margins.
3. Achieve a profitable return on investment within _____ (two?) years.
4. Earn a ____ (15?)% internal rate of return for investors over the life of the lease.
5. Recruit talented and motivated staff.
6. Capture an increasing share of the new business development.
7. Offer our customers superior screening services at an affordable price.
8. Create a company whose primary goal is to exceed customer expectations.
9. To develop a cash flow that is capable of paying all salaries, as well as grow the business, by the end of the _____ (first?) year.
10. To be an active networking participant and productive member of the community by _____ (date).
11. Create over __ (30?) % of business revenues from repeat customers by ___ (date).
12. Achieve an overall customer satisfaction rate of ____ (98?) % by _____ (date).
13. Get a business website designed, built and operational by _____ (date), which will include an online shopping cart.
14. Achieve total sales revenues of $_____ in _____ (year).
15. Achieve net income more than ___ percent of net sales by the ____ (#) year.
16. Increase overall sales by _____ (20?) percent from prior year through superior service and word-of-mouth referrals.
17. Reduce the cost of new customer acquisition by ___ % to $ ___ by _____ (date).
18. Provide employees with continuing training, benefits and incentives to reduce the employee turnover rate to _____%.
19. To pursue a growth rate of ____ (20?) % per year for the first ____ (#) years.
20. Enable the owner to draw a salary of $ _____ by the end of year ____ (one?).
21. To reach cash break-even by the end of year ____ (one?).
22. Increase market share to ___ percent over the next ___ (#) months.
23. Become one of the top ___ (#) players in the emerging _____ category in __ (#) months.
24. Increase Operating Profit by ___ percent versus the previous year.
25. Achieve market share leadership in the ____ category by ____ (date).

1.1.1   Strategic Objectives

We will seek to work toward the accomplishment of the following strategic objectives, which relate back to our Mission and Vision Statements:
1. Improve the overall quality of our business services.
2. Make the buyer experience better, faster and more customer friendly.
3. Strengthen personal relationships with customers.

4. Enhance affordability and accessibility.
5. Promote creative thinking which introduces new services and delivers more effective processes, product enhancements, technology advancements and an overall improved customer experience.
6. Build a culture that encourages diverse ideas and creates evolving solutions for win/win relationships.

1.2.0   Mission Statement   (select)

Our Mission Statement is a written statement that spells out our organization's overall goal, provides a sense of direction and acts as a guide to decision making for all levels of management. In developing the following mission statement, we will encourage input from employees, volunteers, and other stakeholders, and publicize it broadly in our website and other marketing materials.

Our mission will be to deliver accurate and reliable background checks with unparalleled customer service. Our goal is to become a professional background screening company with the knowledge and ability to help a client design and access a screening program that is efficient, effective, and legal. Our Mission is to provide the tools, the experience, and the communication backbone needed to individualize the ideal employee-screening environment. As a background screening service provider, our mission will be to deliver exceptionally fast turnaround while ensuring accuracy to gain market share and grow our business. Our mission will be to deliver a highly personalized level of service while pushing the cutting edge of technology.

Our mission is to realize 100% customer satisfaction and generate long-term profits through referrals and repeat business. Our goal is to set ourselves apart from the competition by making customer satisfaction our number one priority and to provide customer service that is responsive, informed and respectful. Our Mission is to help potential employers, business persons and those relying on someone's trust, to verify that a person is who they say they are and uncover anything in their past that they are not divulging or inaccurately portraying.

1.2.1   Mantra

We will create a mantra for our organization that is three or four words long. Its purpose will be to help employees truly understand why the organization exists. Our mantra will serve as a framework through which to make decisions about product and business direction. It will boil the key drivers of our company down to a sentence that defines our most important areas of focus and resemble a statement of purpose or significance. Examples: Quality First / Low Prices Everyday
Our Mantra is _____

1.2.2   Core Values Statement

The following Core Values will help to define our organization, guide our behavior, underpin operational activity and shape the strategies we will pursue in the face of various challenges and opportunities:

Being respectful and ethical to our customers and employees.

Building enduring relationships with clients.

Seeking innovation in our industry.

Practicing accountability to our colleagues and stakeholders.

Pursuing continuous improvement as individuals and as a business entity.

Performing tasks on time to satisfy the needs of our internal and external clients.

Taking active part in the organization to meet the objectives and the establishment of continuous and lasting relationships.

Offering professional treatment to our clients, employees, shareholders, and the community.

Continuing pursuit of new technologies for the development of the projects that add value for our clients, employees, shareholders, and the community.

1.3 Vision Statement   (select)

The following Vision Statement will communicate both the purpose and values of our organization. For employees, it will give direction about how they are expected to behave and inspires them to give their best. Shared with customers, it will shape customers' understanding of why they should work with our organization.

We envision an employee screening environment that is client-directed and technology-enabled, a world where digital communication solutions are integral to improving the quality and value of client hired employees.

Our vision is to provide the best possible online access to the rapidly growing public record and to provide tools and resources to help people learn about, use, and manage public information more responsibly.

_____ (company name) will strive to become one of the most respected and favored background checking companies in the _____ area. It is our desire to become a landmark business in _____ (city), ____ (state), and become known not only for the quality of our background checking services, but also for our community and charity involvement.

_____ (company name) is dedicated to operating with a constant enthusiasm for learning about the background checking industry, being receptive to implementing new ideas, and maintaining a willingness to adapt to changing client needs and wants. To be an active and vocal member of the community, and to provide continual reinvestment through participation in community activities and financial contributions. To incorporate the use of more state-of-the-art technologies to provide high-quality background screening services, and thereby improve the effectiveness, efficiency and competitiveness of the client's business.

1.4   Keys to Success

In broad terms, the success factors relate to providing what our clients want and doing what is necessary to be better than our competitors. The following critical success factors are areas in which our organization must excel to operate successfully and achieve our objectives:

1. Make available audited financial statements to substantiate our viability, internal control environment, and reputation.
2. Develop a contract that contains language protecting the confidentiality of information obtained from applicants and clients.
3. Be ready to discuss our own hiring and employment processes.
4. Guarantee that any information obtained in the screening process is not provided to any other entities or persons or sold for profit.
5. Document the safeguards in place to prevent identity theft.
6. Express willingness and ability to review records in each and every local, state and federal jurisdiction where the applicant has previously lived and worked.
7. Develop the ability to steer clients through the legal requirements as well as federal and State regulations of background screening.
8. Publicize the fact that under FCRA, a small business can have limited legal immunity by using a third-party background pre-employment screening company.
9. Understand that background screening companies are regulated by the Federal Fair Credit Reporting Act, The Fair and Accurate Credit Transactions Act as enforced by the FTC, and the various state versions of these laws.
10. A screening company must be aware of all 51 state law versions as they pertain to background checks and maintain compliance with all of them, and clients must certify their compliance to the screening company.
11. Understand that the regulations and laws pertaining to screening are in constant motion, as they ride a political wave caused by each new data breach, theft, or lost laptop, and need to be monitored.
12. Play a major role in helping employer clients comply with new legal requirements and help them protect their employees and business assets.
13. Work with clients to develop a new hire application process that asks the applicant for permission to conduct a background check.
14. Consult with a labor attorney to make sure that job applications and releases are in legal compliance.
15. Before proceeding on conducting employee background checks, consult with an attorney or your Attorney General's office regarding privacy laws and background check procedures.
16. Read the Fair Credit Reporting Act, as this law requires job applicants give consent prior to the background check and receive a copy of the information obtained if an offer of employment is not offered because of information found.
17. Practice researching and locating skills and getting proof of permission from

client's job applicants prior to requesting reports.

18. Make effective use of social networking websites and browse LinkedIn and Facebook to view profiles of employees or applicants.

19. Make effective use of several different search engines and locate relevant blogs, forum and chat room posts.

20. Must ask client for a copy of signed release statement for each applicant that is processed.

21. Secure regular and ongoing customer feedback to make improvements and add in-demand services.

22. Provide excellent customer service to promote customer loyalty.

23. Launch a website to showcase services and customer testimonials, provide helpful information and facilitate online order placement.

24. Develop local community involvement and strategic business partnerships.

25. Conduct a targeted and cost-effective marketing campaign that seeks to differentiate our one-stop, convenient services from competitor offerings.

26. Institute a pay-for-performance component to the employee compensation plan.

27. Control costs and manage budgets at all times in accordance with company goals.

28. Institute management processes and controls to insure the consistent replication of operations.

29. Recruit screened employees with a passion for delivering exceptional service.

30. Institute an employee training to insure the best techniques are consistently practiced.

31. Network aggressively within the community, as word of mouth will be our most powerful advertising asset.

32. Develop retain client strategy to generate repeat purchases and initiate referrals.

33. Stay abreast of technological developments and new service offerings by competitors.

34. Build brand awareness, which will drive customers to increase their usage of our background screening services and make referrals.

35. Business planning with the flexibility to make changes based on gaining new insightful perspectives as we proceed.

36. Build trust by circulating to our Code of Ethics and Satisfaction Guarantees.

37. Set-up accounts with the credit bureaus (Experience, Equifax and TransUnion), state police department, DMV and court system.

38.   Specialize in one or more background investigations, such as pre-employment background checks, or tenant background checks.

39.   Know how to research original real estate documents or marriage licenses at county clerk and recorder offices, property tax records at county assessor offices. (Review record-search procedures with the County Clerk).
       Resource: www.inet-investigation.com/public-records-databases/how-to-use-
                 public-records-databases.htm

40.   Start by developing an expertise for servicing a niche industry, such as the hospitality industry.

50.   Subscribe to several legislative alert publications to keep abreast of the ever-changing FCRA rules and regulations.

51.   Must stay current on lawsuit dispositions, changing government regulations and supervision, industry trends, employment conditions, and new legislation.

52.   Make proper use of sales incentives and innovative compensation plans to motivate salespeople.

2.0 Company Summary

____ (company name) will be a service business that performs background checks for individuals and businesses. The company will be located at _____ (address) in the city of ___. ___ (company name) is a start-up ____ (Corporation/Limited Liability Company) consisting of __(#) principle officers with combined industry experience of ___(#) years.
Resources:
www.businessnewsdaily.com/8163-choose-legal-business-structure.html
www.nerdwallet.com/blog/small-business/online-legal-tools/

The owner of the company will be investing $ ___ of ____ (his/her) own capital into the company and will also be seeking a loan of $ __ to cover start-up costs and future growth. _____ (company name) will be located in a _____ (purchased/rented) _____ (suite/complex) in the ____ on _____ (address) in _____ (city), __ (state). The owner, _____ has ___ (#) years of experience in managing _____ (type of business?).

The company plans to use its existing contacts and customer base to generate short-term revenues. Its long-term profitability will rely on focusing on referrals, networking within community and business organizations, and a comprehensive marketing program that includes public relations activities and a structured referral program.

Sales are expected to reach $_____ within the first year and to grow at a conservative rate of _____ (20?) percent during the next two to five years.

Facilities Renovations

The necessary renovations are itemized as follows:	Estimate
Partition of space into functional cubicles.	_____
Build storage areas.	_____
Painting and other general cosmetic repairs	_____
Create combination conference and classroom.	_____
Install computer equipment and software.	_____
Install communications and DSL lines.	_____
Other _____	_____
Total:	_____

Hours of Operations

_____ (company name) will open for business on _____ (date) and will maintain the following office business hours:

Monday through Thursday:	_____	(9 AM to 7 PM?)
Friday:	_____	
Saturday:	_____	
Sunday:	_____	

The company will invest in customer relationship management software (CRM) to track real-time sales data and collect customer information, including names, email addresses, key reminder dates and preferences. This information will be used with email, e-newsletter and direct mail campaigns to build personalized fulfillment programs, establish customer loyalty and drive revenue growth.

2.0.1   Traction (optional)

We will include this section because investors expect to see some traction, both before and after a funding event and investors tend to judge past results as a good indicator of future projections. It will also show that we can manage our operations and develop a business model capable of funding inventory purchases. Traction will be the best form of market research and present evidence of customer acceptance.

Period	_____
Product/Service Focus	_____
Our Sales to Date:	_____
Our Number of Users to Date:	_____
Number of Repeat Users	_____
Number of Pending Orders:	_____
Value of Pending Orders:	_____
Reorder Cycle Period:	_____
Key Reference Sites	_____
Mailing List Subscriptions	_____
Competitions/Awards Won	_____
Notable Product Reviews	_____
Actual Percent Gross Profit Margin	_____
Industry Average: GPM	_____
Actual B/(W) Industry Average	_____

Note: Percent Gross Profit Margin equals the sales receipts less the cost of goods sold divided by sales receipts multiplied by 100.

2.1 Company Ownership

_____ (company name) is a _____ (Sole-proprietorship /Corporation/ Limited Liability Corporation (LLC)) and is registered to the principal owner, _____ (owner name). The company was formed in _____ (month) of _____ (year). It will be registered as a Subchapter S to avoid double taxation, with ownership allocated as follows: _____ (owner name) _____ % and _____ (owner name) _____ %.

The owner is a _____ (year) graduate of _____ (institution name), in _____ (city, _____ (state), with a _____ degree. He/she _____ has a second degree in _____ and certification as a _____ . He/she also has _____ years of executive experience in the _____ (?) industry as a _____ , performing the following roles: _____ .
His/her major accomplishments include: _____

Ownership Breakdown:

Shareholder Name	Responsibilities	Number and Class of Shares	Percent Ownership

The remainder of the issued and outstanding common shares are retained by the Company for ___(future distribution / allocation under the Company's employee stock option plan).

Shareholder Loans

The Company currently has outstanding shareholder loans in the aggregate sum of $_____. The following table sets out the details of the shareholder loans.

Shareholder Name	Loan Amount	Loan Date	Balance Outstanding

Directors

The Company's Board of Directors, which is made up of highly qualified business and industry professionals, will be a valuable asset to the Company and be instrumental to its development. The following persons will make up the Board of Directors of the Company:

Name of Person	Educational Background	Past Industry Experience	Other Companies Served

2.2 Company Licensing & Liability Protection

We plan to hire a legal consultant to help us work through all the various legal issues that will surface, including what kind of legal entity to use for our business, how to best protect against liability problems and negligence lawsuits, how to meet government hiring, disclosure and interviewing rules and regulations, what rules apply to advertising, and so forth. We will contact an insurance agent to find out what types of insurance to carry and how much insurance will cost.

After we have established our company from a legal perspective, we will apply for a business license for that company, at the address of the building that we have _____ (purchased/leased). It is our goal to eventually purchase the property.

The process of applying for a business license varies from state to state. We will contact the City Clerk's office in the town where you wish to do business for more information on how to apply for a business license in our area.

Our business will consider the need to acquire the following types of insurances. This will require extensive comparison shopping, through several insurance brokers, listed with our state's insurance department:

1. Workers' Compensation Insurance,
2. Business Policy: Property & Liability Insurance
3. Health insurance.
4. Commercial Auto Insurance
5. State Unemployment Insurance
6. Business Interruption Insurance (Business Income Insurance)
7. Disability Insurance
8. Life Insurance
9. Errors and Omissions Insurance
10. Professional Liability Insurance
11. Cyber Liability Insurance
12. Inland Marine Insurance

We will carry business liability and property insurance and any other insurance we deem necessary after receiving counsel from our lawyer and insurance agent. Health insurance and workers' compensation will be provided for our full-time employees as part of their benefit package. We feel that this is mandatory to ensure that they do not leave the company for one that does offer these benefits. Workers' Compensation covers employees in case of harm attributed to the workplace. The Property and Liability Insurance protects the building from theft, fire, natural disasters, and being sued by a third party.   Life and Disability Insurance may be required if a bank loan is obtained.

Liability Insurance includes protection in the face of day-to-day accidents, unforeseen results of normal business activities, and allegations of abuse or molestation, food poisoning, or exposure to infectious disease.

Property Insurance - Property Insurance should take care of the repairs less whatever deductible you have chosen.

Loss of Income Insurance will replace our income during the time the business is shut-down. Generally, this coverage is written for a fixed amount of monthly income for a fixed number of months.

Professional Liability/Errors and Omissions Insurance: Coverage includes "Resulting Financial Loss". Professional Liability Insurance (EO insurance) protects company from claims if client holds you responsible for errors, or the failure of your work to perform as promised in your contract. Coverage includes legal defense costs - no matter how baseless the allegations. Professional Liability insurance will pay for any resulting judgments against the company, including court costs, up to the coverage limits on the policy. Professional Liability Insurance coverage extends to both W2 employees and 1099 subcontractors and can be worldwide in scope.

To help save on insurance cost and claims, management will do the following:

1. Stress employee safety in our employee handbook.
2. Screen employees with interview questionnaires and will institute pre-employment drug tests and comprehensive background checks.
3. Videotape our equipment and inventory for insurance purposes.
4. Create an operations manual that shares safe techniques.
5. Limit the responsibilities that we choose to accept in our contracts.
6. Consider the financial impact of assuming the exposure ourselves.
7. Establish loss prevention programs to reduce the hazards that cause losses.
8. Consider taking higher deductibles on anything but that which involves liability insurance because of third-party involvement.
9. Stop offering services that require expensive insurance coverage or require signed releases from clients using those services.
10. Improve employee training and initiate training sessions for safety.
11. Require Certificate of Insurance from all subcontractors.
12. Make staff responsible for a portion of any damages they cause.
13. We will investigate the setting-up of a partial self-insurance plan.
14. Convince underwriters that our past low claims are the result of our ongoing safety programs and there is reason to expect our claims will be lower than industry averages in the future.
15. At each renewal, we will develop a service agreement with our broker and get their commitment to our goals, such as a specific reduction in the number of incidents.
16. We will assemble a risk control team, with people from both sides of our business, and broker representatives will serve on the committee as well.
17. When an employee is involved in an accident, we will insist on getting to the root cause of the incident and do everything possible to prevent similar incidents from re-occurring.
18. At renewal, we will consult with our brokers to develop a cost-saving strategy and decide whether to bid out our coverage for competitive quotes or stick with our current carrier.
19. We will set-up a captive insurance program, as a risk management technique, where our business will form its own insurance company subsidiary to finance its retained losses in a formal structure.
20. Review named assets (autos and equipment), drivers and/or key employees identified on policies to make sure these assets and people are still with our company.
21. As a portion of our business changes, that is, closes, operations change, or outsourcing occurs, we will eliminate unnecessary coverage.
22. We will make sure our workforce is correctly classified by our workers' compensation insurer and liability insurer because our premiums are based on the type of workers used.
23. We will become active in Trade Organizations or Professional Associations, because as a benefit of membership, our business may receive substantial insurance discounts.

24. We will adopt health specific changes to our work place, such as adopting a no smoking policy at our company and allow yoga or weight loss classes to be held in our break room.
25. We will consider a partial reimbursement of health club membership as a benefit.
26. We will find out what employee training will reduce rates and get our employees involved in these programs.

The required business insurance package will be provided by _____ (insurance carrier name) . The business will open with a ____ (#) million dollar liability insurance policy, with an annual premium cost of $ _____.

The business will need to acquire the following special licenses, accreditations, certifications and permits:
1. A Sales Tax License is required through the State Department of Revenue.
2. Use Tax Registration Certificate
3. A County and/or City Occupational License.
4. Business License from State Licensing Agency
5. Permits from the Fire Department and State Health Department.
6. Building Code Inspections by the County Building Department.
7. State Identification Service Section to get rules and regulations for running this type of business

We will consider acquiring the following professional certifications to boost business and increase our cooperate identity:
1. Association of Professional Background Screeners
2. Certified Background
3. ESR Online Safe Hiring Certification
4. Professional License & Certificate Verification

Other Certifications:
ISO 9001:2008 Quality Management Certification
Verizon Cybertrust Security Enterprise Certification
HR-XML Certification of Data Exchange Standards
Safe Harbor Certification
EI3PA Compliant

National Association of Professional Background Screeners (NAPBS) certifies companies as earning the distinction of an NAPBS Accredited organization.

The NAPBS Background Screeners Credentialing Council (BSCC) will affirm that our company has successfully proved compliance with the Background Screening Agency Accreditation Program (BSAAP) and will be formally recognized as BSCC Accredited. This accreditation will be viewed as a major achievement, as it will signify our commitment to the background screening industry and our valued clients. It will mean that our background screening best practices, high principles for data integrity and commitment to high ethical standards and service excellence adhere to strict measures and operational guidelines.

Note: Must fulfill the investigative licensing or certification requirements for your state. Private Investigator Magazine lists each state and its licensing or certification requirements. As of February 2010, five states have no licensing requirements to practice investigations (Colorado, Idaho, Mississippi, South Dakota and Wyoming).
Resource: http://pursuitmag.com/resources/investigator-licensing/

Example: An investigator in Arkansas must be licensed. The Arkansas Private Investigators and Private Security Agencies Act designates the Arkansas State Police (www.asp.arkansas.gov/divisions/rs/rs_index.html#private) as an administering agency to regulate private investigators, private security agencies and individuals or businesses offering security or investigative services.

Note: In most states, you are legally required to obtain a business license, and a dba certificate. A business license is usually a flat tax assessment and a percentage of your gross income. A dba stands for Doing Business As, and it is the registration of your trade name if you have one. You will be required to register your trade name within 30 days of starting your business. Instead of registering a dba, you can simply form an LLC or Corporation and it will have the same effect, namely register your business name.

Resources:
Workers Compensation Regulations
          http://www.dol.gov/owcp/dfec/regs/compliance/wc.htm#IL
New Hire Registration and Reporting
          www.homeworksolutions.com/new-hire-reporting-information/
State Tax Obligations
          www.sba.gov/content/learn-about-your-state-and-local-tax-obligations

Resource:
www/sba.gov/content/what-state-licenses-and-permits-does-your-business-need

Note: Check with your local County Clerk and state offices or Chamber of Commerce to make sure you follow all legal protocols for setting up and running your business.
Note: To find out about your local business licensing office, visit SBA.gov. This government website compiles information on business licenses and permits at the state level.

Resources:
Insurance Information Institute   www.iii.org/individuals/business/
National License Directory   www.sba.gov/licenses-and-permits
National Association of Surety Bond Producers   www.nasbp.org
Independent Insurance Agents & Brokers of America   www.iiaa.org
Century Surety Group   www.centurysurety.com
The Mechanic Group Inc.   www.mechanicgroup.com
Find Law   http://smallbusiness.findlaw.com/starting-business/starting-business-licenses-permits/starting-business-licenses-permits-guide.html
Business Licenses   www.iabusnet.org/business-licenses

Legal Zoom   www.legalzoom.com
Bizfilings   www.bizfilings.com

2.3   Start-up To-Do Checklist

1. Describe your business concept and model, with special emphasis on planned multiple revenue streams and services to be offered.
2. Create Business Plan and Opening Menu of Products and Services.
3. Determine startup costs of Background Check business, and operating capital and capital budget needs.
4. Seek and evaluate alternative financing options, including SBA guaranteed loan, equipment leasing, social networking loan (www.prosper.com) and/or a family loan (www.virginmoney.com).
5. Do a name search: Check with County Clerk Office or Department of Revenue and Secretary of State to see if the proposed name of business is available.
6. Decide on a legal structure for business.
    Common legal structure options include Sole Proprietorship, Partnership, Corporation or Limited Liability Corporation (LLC).
7. Make sure you contact your State Department of Revenue, Secretary of State, and the Internal Revenue Service to secure EIN Number and file appropriate paperwork. Also consider filing for Sub-Chapter S status with the Federal government to avoid the double taxation of business profits.
8. Protect name and logo with trademarks, if plan is to go national.
9. Find a suitable location with proper zoning.
10. Research necessary permits and requirements your local government imposes on your type of business. (Refer to: www.business.gov & www.ttb.gov)
11. Call for initial inspections to determine what must be done to satisfy Fire Marshall and Building Inspector requirements.
12. Adjust our budget based on build-out requirements.
13. Negotiate lease or property purchase contract.
14. Obtain a building permit.
15. Obtain Federal Employee Identification Number (FEIN).
16. Obtain State Sales Tax ID/Exempt Certificate.
17. Open a Business Checking Account.
18. Obtain Merchant Credit Card /PayPal Account.
19. Obtain City and County Business Licenses
20. Create a prioritized list for equipment, furniture and décor items.
21. Comparison shop and arrange for appropriate insurance coverage with product liability insurance, public liability insurance, commercial property insurance and worker's compensation insurance.
22. Locate and purchase all necessary equipment and furniture prior to final inspections.
23. Get contractor quotes for required alterations.
24 Manage the alterations process.
25. Obtain information and price quotes from possible supply distributors.
26. Set a tentative opening date.

27. Install 'Coming Soon' sign in front of building and begin word-of-mouth advertising campaign.
28. Document the preparation, project and payment process flows.
29. Create your accounting, purchasing, payroll, marketing, loss prevention, employee screening and other management systems.
30. Start the employee interview process based on established job descriptions and interview criteria.
31. Contact and interview the following service providers: uniform service, security service, trash service, utilities, telephone, credit card processing, bookkeeping, cleaning services, etc.
32. Schedule final inspections for premises.
33. Correct inspection problems and schedule another inspection.
34. Set a Grand Opening date after a month of regular operations to get the bugs out of the processes.
35. Make arrangements for website design.
36. Train staff.
37. Schedule a couple of practice lessons for friends and interested prospects.
38. Be accessible for direct customer feedback.
39. Distribute comment cards and surveys to solicit more constructive feedback.
40. Remain ready and willing to change your business concept and offerings to suit the needs of your actual customer base.

2.3.1   EMPLOYER RESPONSIBILITIES CHECKLIST

1. Apply for your SS-4 Federal Employer Identification Number (EIN) from the Internal Revenue Service. An EIN can be obtained via telephone, mail or online.
2. Register with the State's Department of Labor (DOL) as a new employer. State Employer Registration for Unemployment Insurance, Withholding, and Wage Reporting should be completed and sent to the address that appears on the form. This registration is required of all employers for the purpose of determining whether the applicants are subject to state unemployment insurance taxes.
3. Obtain Workers Compensation and Disability Insurance from an insurer. The insurance company will provide the required certificates that should be displayed.
4. Order Federal Tax Deposit Coupons – Form 8109 – if you didn't order these when you received your EIN. To order, call the IRS at 1-800-829-1040; you will need to give your EIN. You may want to order some blanks sent for immediate use until the pre-printed ones are complete. Also ask for the current Federal Withholding Tax Tables (Circular A) – this will explain how to withhold and remit payroll taxes, and file reports.
5. Order State Withholding Tax Payment Coupons. Also ask for the current Withholding Tax Tables.
6. Have new employees complete an I-9 Employment Eligibility Verification form. You should have all employees complete this form prior to beginning work. Do not send it to Immigration and Naturalization Service – just keep it with other employee records in your files.

7.   Have employees complete aW-4 Employees Withholding Allowance Certificate.

2.4.0   Company Location

_____ (company name) will be located in the _____ area in ____ (city). The site is one of the densest business markets in the state. Our offices will be prime commercial space in the _____ (northeast?) corner of the ____ Avenue building. The building is centered within a cluster of ____ (#) commercial _____ (buildings?), with ___ (#) office suites.

_____ (company name) will be located in the _____ (complex name) in _____ (city), ___ (state). It is situated on a _____ (turnpike/street/avenue) just minutes from _____ (benchmark location), in the neighborhood of _____. It borders a large parking lot which is shared by all the businesses therein. Important considerations relative to practice location are competition, visibility, accessibility, community growth trends, demographics, and drive by traffic patterns.

The location has the following advantages: (Select Choices)
1.   It is easy to locate and accessible to a number of major roadways.
2.   Easy access from public transportation and high-speed internet service.
3.   Good traffic flow.
5.   Plentiful parking.
6.   Proximity to _____ and _____ business growth areas.
7.   Proximity to businesses in same affinity class with same ideal client profiles.
8.   Reasonable rent.
9.   Conveniently located to client base.
10.   Proximity to the growing residential community of _____.
11.   Low crime rate with good police and fire protection.
12.   Good security system.
13.   Flexible wall partitions and computer cabling.

2.4.1   Company Facilities

_____ (company name) signed a _____ (#) year lease for _____ (#) square foot of space. The cost is very reasonable at $____ /sq. foot. We also have the option of expanding into an additional _____ sq. ft. of space and subletting the space. A leasehold improvement allowance of $___ /sq. ft. would be given. Consolidated area maintenance fees would be $___ /month initially. _____ (company name) has obtained a _____ (three) month option on this office space effective _____ (date), the submission date of this business plan, and has deposited refundable first and last lease payments, plus a $ _____ security deposit with the leasing agent.

The facilities will incorporate the following room parameters into the layout:

		Percentage	Square Footage
1.	Specialist Cubicles	_____	_____

2.	Supplies Storage	_____	_____
3.	Inventory Storage	_____	_____
4.	Staff Break Room	_____	_____
5.	Admin Office	_____	_____
6.	Conference Room	_____	_____
7.	Utility/Computer/Copy Room	_____	_____
8.	Restroom	_____	_____
Totals:		_____	_____

2.5.0   Start-up Summary

The start-up costs for the background check business will be financed through a combination of an owner investment of $ _____ and a short-term bank loan of $ _____. The total start-up costs for this business are approximately $ _____ and can be broken down in the following major categories:

1.	Land, Building and Improvements	$ _____
2.	Computer Equipment and Installation Expenses	$ _____
3.	Business Development Expense	$ _____
4.	Office Furniture: Work Tables and Cabinets	$ _____
5.	Research Database Accounts Link Access	$ _____
6.	Working Capital (6 months)	$ _____
	For day-to-day operations, including payroll, etc.	
7.	Renovate Office Space	$ _____
	Includes architect, lighting update, flooring, etc.	
8.	Marketing/Advertising Expenses	$ _____
	Includes sales brochures, direct mail, opening expenses.	
8.	Utility/ (Rent?) Deposits	$ _____
9.	Licenses and Permits	$ _____
10.	Other (Includes training, legal expenses, etc.)	$ _____

The company will require $_____ in initial cash reserves and additional $_____ in assets. The start-up costs are to be financed by the equity contributions of the owner in the amount of $ _____ , as well as by a _____ (#) year commercial loan in the amount of $ _____. The funds will be repaid through earnings.
These start-up expenses and funding requirements are summarized in the tables below.

2.5.1   Inventory

Inventory:	Supplier	Qty	Unit Cost	Total
Cleaning Supplies				
Office Supplies				
Computer Supplies				
Marketing Materials				
Business Forms/Releases				

Misc. Supplies _____
Totals: _____

2.5.2   Supply Sourcing

We will search for and contact several wholesale suppliers for our company. We will first contact the National Association of Wholesaler-Distributors and ask our contact person if they can supply a list of _____ wholesalers. We will also visit the Tradepub.com website and order some free trade publications on retailing. We will read through the classified ads for potential _____ wholesalers. We will consider the wholesalers that offer the best mix of lowest unit cost of _____ products, the fastest re-order turnaround service, and the best open credit terms. We will meet up with suppliers and inquire if we can avail discounted prices if we buy in bulk.

Initially, ____ (company name) will purchase all its computer equipment from _____ and supplies from _____, the _____ (second/third?) largest supplier in _____ (state), because of the discount given for bulk purchases. However, we will also maintain back-up relationships with two smaller suppliers, namely _____ and _____. These two suppliers have competitive prices on certain products.

Resources:
Business Forms   www.socrates.com
NYS Criminal Justice Svcs   www.criminaljustice.ny.gov/ojis/recordreview.htm
NY Background Check Links www.diligentiagroup.com/background-
                                investigations/new-york-background-check-links/
NYS Rules   www.employeescreen.com/Background-Checks-NewYork.asp

Input Products	Description	Source	Back-up	Cost

2.5.3   Supplier Assessments

We will use the following form to compare and evaluate suppliers, because they will play a major role in our procurement strategies and significantly contribute to our profitability.

	Supplier #1	Supplier #2	Compare
Supplier Name			
Website			
Address			
Contacts			
Annual Sales			
Distribution Channels			

Memberships/Certifications   _____
Quality System   _____
Positioning   _____
Pricing Strategy   _____
Payment Terms   _____
Discounts   _____
Delivery Lead-time   _____
Return Policy   _____
Rebate Program   _____
Technical Support   _____
Core Competencies   _____
Primary Product   _____
Primary Service   _____
New Products/Services   _____
Innovative Applications/Uses   _____
Competitive Advantage   _____
Capital Intensity   _____
State of Technology   _____
Capacity Utilization   _____
Price Volatility   _____
Vertical Integration   _____
References   _____
Overall Rating   _____

2.5.4   Equipment Leasing

Equipment Leasing will be the smarter solution allowing our business to upgrade our equipment needs at the end of the term rather than being overly invested in outdated equipment through traditional bank financing and equipment purchase. We also intend to explore the following benefits of leasing some of the required equipment:

1. Frees Up Capital for other uses.
2. Tax Benefits
3. Improves Balance Sheet
4. Easy to add-on or trade-up
5. Improves Cash Flow
6. Preserves Credit Lines
7. Protects against obsolescence
8. Application Process Simpler

List Any Leases:

Leasing Company	Equipment Description	Monthly Payment	Lease Period	Final Disposition

Resource:

LeaseQ   www.leaseq.com

An online market place that connects businesses, equipment dealers, and leasing companies to make selling and financing equipment fast and easy. The LeaseQ Platform is a free, cloud-based SaaS solution with a suite of on-demand software and data solutions for the equipment leasing industry. Utilizes the Internet to provide business process optimization (BPO) and information services that streamline the purchase and financing of business equipment across a broad array of vertical industry segments.

Innovative Lease Services   http://www.ilslease.com/equipment-leasing/
This company was founded in 1986 and is headquartered in Carlsbad, California. It is accredited by the Better Business Bureau, a longstanding member of the National Equipment Finance Association and the National Association of Equipment Leasing Brokers and is the official equipment financing partner of Biocom.

2.5.5   Funding Source Matrix

Funds Source	Amount	Interest Rate	Repayment Terms	Use

2.5.6   Distribution or Licensing Agreements (if any)

Note: These are some of the key factors that investors will use to determine if we have a competitive advantage that is not easily copied.

Licensor	License Rights	License Term	Fee or Royalty

2.5.7   Trademarks, Patents and Copyrights (if any)

Our trademark will be virtually our branding for life. Our choice of a name for our business is very important. Not only will we brand our business and services forever, but what may be worthless today will become our most valuable asset in the years to come. A trademark search by our Lawyer will be a must, because to be told down the road that we must give up our name because we did not bother to conduct a trademark search would be a devastating blow to our business. It is also essential that the name that we choose suit the expanding product or service offerings that we plan to introduce.

Note: These are some of the key factors that investors will use to determine if we have a competitive advantage that is not easily copied.

Resources:
Patents/Trademarks   www.uspto.gov
Copyright   www.copyright.gov

2.5.8   Innovation Strategy   (optional)

_____ (company name) will create an innovation strategy that is aligned with not only our firm's core mission and values, but also with our future technology, supplier, and manufacturing strategies. The objective of our innovation strategy will be to create a sustainable competitive advantage. Our education and training systems will be designed to equip our staff with the foundations to learn and develop the broad range of skills needed for innovation in all its forms, and with the flexibility to upgrade skills and adapt to changing market conditions. To foster an innovative workplace, we will ensure that employment policies facilitate efficient organizational change and encourage the expression of creativity, engage in mutually beneficial strategic alliances and allocate adequate funds for research and development. Our radical innovation strategies include _____ to achieve first mover status. Our incremental innovation strategies will include modifying the following _____ (products/services/processes) to give our customers added value for their money.
Resource:
https://hbr.org/2015/04/the-5-requirements-of-a-truly-innovative-company

2.5.9   Summary of Sources and Use of Funds

Sources:

Owner's Equity Investment	$ _____
Requested Bank Loans	$ _____
Total:	$ _____

Uses:

Capital Equipment	$ _____
Beginning Inventory	$ _____
Start-up Costs	$ _____
Working Capital	$ _____
Total:	$ _____

2.5.9.1   Funding to Date   (optional)

To date, _____'s (company name) founders have invested $_____ in _____ (company name), with which we have accomplished the following:
1.   _____ (Designed/Built) the company's website
2.   Developed content, in the form of ___ (#) articles, for the website.
3.   Hired and trained our core staff of __(#) full-time people and ___ (#) part-time people.
4.   Generated brand awareness by driving ___ (#) visitors to our website in a ___(#) month period.
5.   Successfully _____ (Developed/Test Marketed) ___ (#) new _____

(products/services), which compete on the basis of _____.

6. _____ (Purchased/Developed) and installed the software needed to _____ (manage _____ operations?)
7. Purchased $ _____ worth of _____ (supplies)
8. Purchased $ _____ worth of _____ equipment.

2.6 Start-up Requirements

Start-up Expenses:		Estimates
Legal	_____	15000
Accountant	_____	300
Accounting Software Package	_____	300
State Licenses & Permits	_____	40000?
Store Set-up	_____	25000
Unforeseen Contingency	_____	3000
Market Research Survey	_____	300
Office Supplies	_____	300
Sales Brochures	_____	300
Direct Mailing	_____	500
Other Marketing Materials	_____	2000
Logo Design		500
Advertising (2 months)	_____	2000
Consultants	_____	5000
Insurance	_____	
Rent (2 months security)	_____	3000
Rent Deposit	_____	1500
Utility Deposit	_____	1000
DSL Installation/Activation	_____	100
Telecommunications Installation	_____	3000
Telephone Deposit	_____	200
Expensed Equipment	_____	1000
Website Design/Hosting	_____	2000
Computer System	_____	12000
Used Office Equipment/Furniture	_____	2000
Organization Memberships	_____	300
Cleaning Supplies	_____	200
Staff Training	_____	5000
Promotional Signs	_____	7000
Security System	_____	8000
Other	_____	
Total Start-up Expenses	_____ **(A)**	

Start-up Assets:		
Cash Balance Required	_____ **(T)**	15000

Start-up Equipment	_____	See schedule
Start-up Inventory	_____	See schedule
Other Current Assets	_____	
Long-term Assets	_____	
Total Assets	_____	**(B)**
Total Requirements	_____	(A+B)

Start-up Funding

Start-up Expenses to Fund	_____	(A)
Start-ups Assets to Fund	_____	(B)
Total Funding Required:	_____	**(A+B)**

Assets

Non-cash Assets from Start-up	_____	
Cash Requirements from Start-up	_____	(T)
Additional Cash Raised	_____	(S)
Cash Balance on Starting Date	_____	(T+S=U)
Total Assets:	_____	**(B)**

Liabilities and Capital

Short-term Liabilities:

Current Borrowing	_____	
Unpaid Expenses	_____	
Accounts Payable	_____	
Interest-free Short-term Loans	_____	
Other Short-term Loans	_____	
Total Short-term Liabilities	_____	**(Z)**

Long-term Liabilities:

Commercial Bank Loan	_____	
Other Long-term Liabilities	_____	
Total Long-term Liabilities	_____	**(Y)**
Total Liabilities	_____	**(Z+Y = C)**

Capital

Planned Investment

Owner	_____	
Family	_____	
Other	_____	
Additional Investment Requirement	_____	
Total Planned Investment	_____	**(F)**
Loss at Start-up (Start-up Expenses) (-)	_____	**(A)**
Total Capital (=)	_____	**(F+A=D)**
Total Capital and Liabilities	_____	**(C+D)**
Total Funding	_____	(C+F)

2.6.1 Capital Equipment List

Equipment Type	Model No.	New/ Used	Lifespan	Quantity	Unit Cost	Total Cost
Security System						
Electronic Safe						
Computer System						
Remote Printers						
Fax Machine						
Copy Machine						
Scanner						
Digital Camera						
Video Surveillance System						
Answering Machine						
Phone System						
TV and DVD Player						
Office Furniture						
Background Check Software						
Accounting Software						
Shelving Units						
Lockers						
Assorted Signs						
Telephone headsets						
Calculator						
Filing & Storage Cabinets						
Credit Card Verification Machine						
Surveillance Equipment						
Lunchroom Equipment						
Paper Shredder						
Drug Screening Equipment						
Fingerprint Identification Equip.						
Other						

Total Capital Equipment _____

Note: Equipment costs are dependent on whether purchased new or used or leased. All items that are assets to be used for more than one year will be considered a long-term asset and will be depreciated using the straight-line method.

2.7.0 SBA Loan Key Requirements

In order to be considered for an SBA loan, we must meet the basic requirements:
1. Must have been turned down for a loan by a bank or other lender to qualify for most

SBA Business Loan Programs. 2. Required to submit a guaranty, both personal and business, to qualify for the loans. 3. Must operate for profit; be engaged in, or propose to do business in, the United States or its possessions; 4. Have reasonable owner equity to invest; 5. Use alternative financial resources first including personal assets.

All businesses must meet eligibility criteria to be considered for financing under the SBA's 7(a) Loan Program, including: size; type of business; operating in the U.S. or its possessions; use of available of funds from other sources; use of proceeds; and repayment. The repayment term of an SBA loan is between five and 25 years, depending on the lift of the assets being financed and the cash needs of the business. Working capital loans (accounts receivable and inventory) should be repaid in five to 10 years. The SBA also has short-term loan guarantee programs with shorter repayment terms.

A Business Owner Cannot Use an SBA Loan:

To purchase real estate where the participant has issued a forward commitment to the developer or where the real estate will be held primarily for investment purposes. To finance floor plan needs. To make payments to owners or to pay delinquent withholding taxes. To pay existing debt, unless it can be shown that the refinancing will benefit the small business and that the need to refinance is not indicative of poor management.

SBA Loan Programs:
Low Doc: www.sba.gov/financing/lendinvest/lowdoc.html
SBA Express www.sba,gov/financing/lendinvest/sbaexpress.html
Basic 7(a) Loan Guarantee Program
   For businesses unable to obtain loans through standard loan programs.
   Funds can be used for general business purposes, including working
    capital, leasehold improvements and debt refinancing.
   www.sba.gov/financing/sbaloan/7a.html
Certified Development Company 504 Loan Program
   Used for fixed asset financing such as purchase of real estate or
   machinery.
  www. Sba.gov/gopher/Local-Information/Certified-Development-Companies/
MicroLoan 7(m) Loan Program
   Provides short-term loans up to $35,000.00 for working capital or
    purchase of fixtures.
   www.sba.gov/financing/sbaloan/microloans.html

2.7.1   Other Financing Options

1.   Grants:
       Health care grants, along with education grants, represent the largest percentage

of grant giving in the United States. The federal government, state, county and city governments, as well as private and corporate foundations all award grants. The largest percentage of grants are awarded to non-profit organizations, health care agencies, colleges and universities, local government agencies, tribal institutions, and schools. For profit organizations are generally not eligible for grants unless they are conducting research or creating jobs.

A. Contact your state licensing office.
B. Foundation Grants to Individuals: www.fdncenter.org
C. US Grants   www.grants.gov
D. Foundation Center   www.foundationcemter.org
E. The Grantsmanship Center   www.tgci.com
F. Contact local Chamber of Commerce
G. The Catalog of Federal Domestic Assistance is a government-wide compendium of Federal programs, projects, services, and activities that provide assistance or benefits to the American public. It contains financial and nonfinancial assistance programs administered by departments and establishments of the Federal government. https://www.cfda.gov/
H. The Federal Register is a good source to keep current with the continually changing federal grants offered.
I. FedBizOpps is a resource, as all federal agencies must use FedBizOpps to notify the public about contract opportunities worth over $25,000.
J. Fundsnet Services   http://www.fundsnetservices.com/
K. SBA Women Business Center www.sba.gov/content/womens-business-center-grant-opportunities
L. http://usgovinfo.about.com/od/smallbusiness/a/stategrants.htm

Local Business Grants
Check with local businesses for grant opportunities and eligibility requirements. For example, Bank of America sponsors community grants for businesses that endeavor to improve the community, protect the environment or preserve the neighborhood.
Resource:
www.bankofamerica.com/foundation/index.cfm?template=fd_localgrants

Green Technology Grants
If you install green technology in the business as a way to reduce waste and make the business more energy efficient, you may be eligible for grant funding. Check your state's Economic Development Commission. This grant program was developed as part of the American Recovery and Reinvestment Act.
Resource: www.recovery.gov/Opportunities/Pages/Opportunities.aspx

2. Friends and Family Lending   www.virginmoney.com
3. National Business Incubator Association   www.nbia.org/
4. Women's Business Associations   www.nawbo.org/
5. Minority Business Development Agency   www.mbda.gov/

6.   Social Networking Loans   www.prosper.com
7.   Peer-to-Peer Programs   www.lendingclub.com
8.   Extended Credit Terms from Suppliers   30/60/90 days.
9.   Consignment Terms from Suppliers   Contract statements.
10.   Community Bank
11.   Prepayments from Customers
12.   Seller Financing: When purchasing an existing background checking service.
13.   Business Funding Directory   www.businessfinance.com
14.   FinanceNet   www.financenet.gov
15.   SBA Financing   www.sbaonline.sba.gov
16.   Micro-Loans   www.accionusa.org/
17.   Private Investors   http://ActiveCapital.org
18.   Use retirement funds to open a business without taxes or penalty. First, establish a C-corporation for the new business. Next, the C-corporation establishes a new retirement plan. Then, the owner's current retirement funds are rolled over into the C-corporation's new plan. And last, the new retirement plan invests in stock of the C-corporation. Warning: Check with your accountant or financial planner. Resource: http://www.benetrends.com/
19.   Business Plan Competition Prizes
www.nytimes.com/interactive/2009/11/11/business/smallbusiness/Competitions-table.html?ref=smallbusiness
20.   Unsecured Business Cash Advance based on future credit card transactions.
www.merchantcreditadvance.com
21.   Kick Starter   www.kickstarter.com
22.   Tech Stars   www.techstars.org
23.   Capital Source   www.capitalsource.com
www.msl.com/index.cfm?event=page.sba504
Participates in the SBA's 504 loan program. This program is for the purchase of fixed assets such as commercial real estate and machinery and equipment of a capital nature, which are defined as assets that have a minimum useful life of ten years. Proceeds cannot be used for working capital.
24.   Commercial Loan Applications   www.c-loans.com/onlineapp/
www.wellsfargo.com/com/bus_finance/commercial_loans
25.   Sharing assets and resources with other non-competing businesses.
26.   Angel Investors   www.angelcapitaleducation.org
https://gust.com/entrepreneurs
27.   The Receivables Exchange   http://receivablesxchange.com/
28.   Bootstrap Methods: Personal Savings/Credit Card/Second Mortgages
29.   Community-based Crowd-funding   www.profounder.com
These platforms include GoBigNetwork, Kickstarter, IndieGogo, RocketHub and PeerBackers. A funding option designed to link small businesses and entrepreneurs with pools of prospective investors. Crowdfunding lenders are often repaid with goods.
30.   On Deck Capital   www.ondeckcapital.com/
Created the Short-Term Business Loan (up to $100,000.00) for small businesses to get quick access to capital that fits their cash flow, with convenient daily

payments.

31. Royalty Lending   www.launch-capital.com/
   With royalty lending, financing is granted in return for future revenue or company performance, and payback can prove exceedingly expensive if a company flourishes.

32. Stock Loans   Southern Lending Solutions, Atlanta. GA.
                                   Custom Commercial Finance, Bartlesville, OK
   A stock loan is based on the quality of stocks, Treasuries and other kinds of investments in a businessperson's personal portfolio. Possession of the company's stock is transferred to the lender's custodial bank during the loan period.

33. Lender Compatibility Searcher   www.BoeFly.com

34. Strategic Investors
   Strategic investing is more for a large company that identifies promising technologies, and for whatever reason, that company may not want to build up the research and development department in-house to produce that product, so they buy a percentage of the company with the existing technology.

35. Bartering

36. Small Business Investment Companies   www.sba.gov/INV

37. Cash-Value Life Insurance

38. Employee Stock Option Plans   www.nceo.org

39. Venture Capitalists   www.nvca.org

40. Initial Public Offering (IPO)

41. Meet investors through online sites, including LinkedIn (group discussions), Facebook (BranchOut sorts Facebook connections by profession), and CapLinked (enables search for investment-related professionals by industry and role).

42. SBA Community Advantage Approved Lenders
               www.sba.gov/content/community-advantage-approved-lenders

43. Small Business Lending Specialists
   https://www.wellsfargo.com/biz/loans_lines/compare_lines
   http://www.bankofamerica.com/small_business/business_financing/
   https://online.citibank.com/US/JRS/pands/detail.do?ID=CitiBizOverview
   https://www.chase.com/ccp/index.jsp?pg_name=ccpmapp/smallbusiness/home/pa
           ge/bb_business_bBanking_programs

44. Startup America Partnership   www.s.co/about
   Based on a simple premise: young companies that grow create jobs. Once startups apply and become a Startup America Firm, they can access and manage many types of resources through a personalized dashboard.

45. United States Economic Development Administration   www.eda.gov/

46. Small Business Loans   http://www.iabusnet.org/small-business-loans

47. Tax Increment Financing (TIF)
   A public financing method that is used for subsidizing redevelopment, infrastructure, and other community-improvement projects. TIF is a method to use future gains in taxes to subsidize current improvements, which are projected to create the conditions for said gains. The completion of a public project often results in an increase in the value of surrounding real estate, which generates additional tax revenue. Tax Increment Financing dedicates tax increments within

a certain defined district to finance the debt that is issued to pay for the project. TIF is often designed to channel funding toward improvements in distressed, underdeveloped, or underutilized parts of a jurisdiction where development might otherwise not occur. TIF creates funding for public or private projects by borrowing against the future increase in these property-tax revenues.

48.   Gust   https://gust.com/entrepreneurs
Provides the global platform for the sourcing and management of early-stage investments. Gust enables skilled entrepreneurs to collaborate with the smartest investors by virtually supporting all aspects of the investment relationship, from initial pitch to successful exit.

49.   Goldman Sachs 10,000 Small Businesses   http://sites.hccs.edu/10ksb/

50.   Earnest Loans   www.meetearnest.com

51.   Biz2Credit   www.biz2credit.com

52.   Funding Circle   www.fundingcircle.com
A peer-to-peer lending service which allows savers to lend money directly to small and medium sized businesses

53.   Lending Club   www.lendingclub.com

54.   Equity-based Crowdfunding   www.Indiegogo.com
                                    www.StartEngine.com
                                    www.SeedInvest.com

55.   National Funding   www.nationalfunding.com
Their customers can to get working capital, merchant cash advances, credit card processing, and, equipment leasing.

56.   Quick Bridge Funding   www.quickbridgefunding.com
Offers a flexible and timely financing program to help assist small and medium sized businesses achieve their goals.

57.   Kabbage   www.kabbage.com
The industry leader in providing working capital online.

Resource: www.sba.gov/category/navigation-structure/starting-managing-business/starting-business/local-resources

http://usgovinfo.about.com/od/moneymatters/a/Finding-Business-Loans-Grants-Incentives-And-Financing.htm

3.0 Products and Services   (Select)

In this section, we will not only list all our planned products and services, but also describe how our proposed products and services will be differentiated from those of our competitors and solve a real problem or fill an unmet need in the marketplace.

Services:

1. Employment Screening
2. Tenant Screening
3. Custom Screening Solutions
4. Drug Testing
5. Fingerprinting
6. DMV Driving Records
7. DOT Drug and Alcohol Verification
8. Employment Credit Reports
9. Tenant Credit Reports
10. SSN Verification
11. Employment Verification
12. Professional Reference Checks
13. Professional License and Credential Verification
14. Education Verification
15. Skills and Behavioral Testing
16. On-premise Criminal County Court Check
17. Form I-9 and E-Verify
18. Electronic Application Process (EAP)
19. Employee Screening Consulting Services
20. Volunteer Background Checks
21. Business Background Check Report
22. Litigation Support Services

3.1 Service Descriptions

In creating our service descriptions, we will provide answers to the following types of questions:

1. What does the service do or help the customer to accomplish?
2. Why will people decide to buy it?
3. What makes it unique or a superior value?
4. How expensive or difficult is it to make or copy by a competitor?
5. How much will the service be sold for?

Employment Screening
This service will include county and state criminal records, SSN verification, address history, sexual offender registry. Employee background checks are used to locate potentially negative information, such as a criminal record or poor credit history. They are also used to verify prior employment, educational accomplishments and personal

reputation. State and federal law limit the specific information on an employee background check, as well as the consent the employee provides to obtain information.

Employment Verification
This service will be for pre-employment screening purposes only. The client will be required to fax a signed applicant release form before we process the request. The client will receive instructions on how to send in this information after their purchase. After we receive the signed applicant release, turnaround time is 1 to 4 business days. The client will receive email notification when their report is available. This service will be very important because nearly 45 percent of all resumes contain falsified information. Checks for employers outside the U.S. will be available for an additional cost.

Form I-9 & E-Verify
It is suggested that a thorough background check be followed with a verification of employment eligibility. This will be performed by utilizing the Form I-9 & E-Verify feature. The purpose of this form is to document that each new employee (both citizen and non-citizen) hired after November 6, 1986 is authorized to work in the United States. Employers are required to complete Form I-9 for each new employee within 3 days of the hire date. This electronic version of Form I-9 will use information already contained in the client's account to populate most of the data fields, saving time and streamlining the hiring process. Associated with the Form I-9 is E-Verify, which is a service provided by the Department of Homeland Security and the Social Security Administration. We will integrate with E-Verify to confirm the employees' eligibility to work in the United States. Employers in some states and most companies that work on Federal Contracts are required to use E-Verify.

Employment Nationwide Check
This report includes an instant, paperless search of criminal records in 43 states, plus a nationwide sex offender registry check. If the client provides an SSN for the applicant, the report will also include an SSN verification and address history. Federal criminal records and employee monitoring will be made available for an additional charge.

Tenant Screening
This service will include county and state criminal records, SSN verification, address history, sexual offender registry. Other parts of the service include the following:
1.   Address History/SSN Trace:
This will help identify historical addresses and is helpful in revealing any addresses the potential tenant may have withheld. It also helps confirm the identity of the individual, as names associated with the provided SSN will be produced.
2.   County Criminal Record Searches:
This search is conducted at the county courts identified by the Address History search and produces the most up to date information available on criminal offenses.
3.   Multi-State Criminal Database Search:
Our Multi-State search includes all states that offer records with name and date-of-birth data and will be an excellent supplement to the County level searches, casting a wider scope of coverage. It is not intended to be used exclusively.
4.   Employment Verification:

Information provided by the candidate will be verified by our contacting the employer directly. Verifications typically include the employer's information, start and end dates, title upon departure, and eligibility for rehire. We will also try to verify compensation if it's provided – companies have varying policies on compensation verification.

5.   Tenant Reference Verification:

Prior landlords or property management firms will be contacted to confirm lease location and dates, monthly rent, payment history and eligibility to rent again.

6.   Nationwide Sex Offender Search:

This search includes data from all 50 states and the District of Columbia. Sources vary and may include Sex Offender Registries, court records and proprietary databases of sex offender records.

7.   Eviction Search:

Using the specific location where the prospective tenant resided, this address will be compared to a database of eviction records. While this is data does not include all eviction information, it is a very beneficial resource for increasing the likelihood of a successful tenancy.

Tenant Nationwide Check

This report will include an instant, paperless search of criminal records in 43 states, plus a nationwide sex offender registry check. If the client provides an SSN for the applicant, the report also includes an SSN verification and address history. Federal criminal records and tenant monitoring will be available for an additional charge.

Criminal Checks

Our criminal checks will include an examination of the following records: State and County Criminal Records, Multi-State Instant Criminal and Sex Offender Registry Check Federal Criminal Records, Canadian Criminal Records, Other International Criminal Searches, Medical Fraud and Abuse Checks (OIG, GSA, FDA Debarment) and OFAC Terrorist Watch List Check

On-Premise Criminal County Court Check

This will be an on-premise criminal check at the county level. Our network of court researchers will conduct the client's search as quickly as possible. The average turnaround time is two business days; however, processing times vary by county and state. For all states other than New York, Criminal County Checks are priced at $____ (49.95?). New York searches are against the statewide New York OCA Database and are priced at $____ (99.95?).

Fingerprinting Services

_____ (company name) will establish contacts with fingerprinting services nationwide. All providers use live-scan imaging equipment for accuracy. In many cases, applicants can be screened right in the client's office. Our providers are often able to return results within 72 hours.

Drug Testing

_____ (company name) will offer drug testing through more than 10,000 collection sites across the U.S. Tests are highly customizable and can include other medical reviews including lift, vision, and hearing testing. Integration with e-Screen Drug Testing is also available.

1. Five Panel Drug Test

_____ (company name) will contract with LabCorp and Quest laboratories to provide nationwide collection site coverage. Tests with negative results are typically complete the next business day. Tests that produce non-negative results may take a day or two longer; allowing for secondary testing, review and contact with the Medical Review Officer (MRO). The five-panel test includes Amphetamines (speed), Cannabinoids/THC (Marijuana), Cocaine (Crack), Opiates (Heroin, Morphine) and Phencyclidine (Angel Dust/PCP).

2. Ten Panel Drug Test

_____ (company name) will contract with LabCorp and Quest laboratories to provide nationwide collection site coverage. Tests with negative results are typically complete the next business day. Tests that produce non-negative results may take a day or two longer; allowing for secondary testing, review and contact with the Medical Review Officer (MRO). The ten-panel test includes Amphetamines (speed), Barbiturates, Benzodiazepines, Cannabinoids/THC (Marijuana), Cocaine (Crack), Methadone, Opiates (Heroin, Morphine), Phencyclidine (Angel Dust/PCP), Propoxyphene and Methaqualone (Quaaludes).

DOT Drug and Alcohol Verification

The Department of Transportation (DOT) Drug and Alcohol Verification is used to find previous drug or alcohol use on the part of an applicant. Our agent will phone the applicant's past supervisors and take them through a standard questionnaire.

DMV Driving Records

_____ (company name) will offer driving records for all 50 U.S. states, the District of Columbia, and most Canadian provinces. DMV checks are an effective way to identify unsafe drivers. In some states, certain kinds of driving offenses (including DUIs) can appear only in DMV records and not in criminal background reports, making the DMV check especially critical.

Employment Credit Reports

Employment credit reports will include credit history and credit-related legal actions or bankruptcies. There will be a nonrefundable $____ (125?) fee to set up a credit report account. An onsite visit and business verification will be required.

Tenant Credit Reports

Tenant credit reports will include credit history, credit-related legal actions or bankruptcies, and FICO scores. There will be a nonrefundable $____ (125?) fee to set up a credit report account. An onsite visit and business verification will be required.

SSN Verification

Social Security Number (SSN) Verification is essential for U.S. applicants. Our check will verify that an SSN was issued by the Social Security Administration and is in the name provided by the applicant. Also, SSN verification may reveal alternate names associated with the SSN and additional addresses the applicant may not have reported.

Professional Reference Checks
Our agents will contact the applicant's professional references to verify their past work performance, using either a standard set of reference questions or custom questions provided by the client.

Professional License and Credential Verification
For industries and positions where special licenses are required, _____ (company name) will verify a valid license with any state or issuing agency. We will particularly specialize in Department of Transportation (DOT) and medical verifications.

Education Verification
Our agents will check the applicant's educational claims, from high-school diplomas and GEDs to college and graduate degrees. This check will identify falsified schools or padded credentials. This service will be for pre-employment screening purposes only. The client will be required to fax a signed applicant release form before we process the request. After we receive the signed applicant release, turnaround time will be 1 to 4 business days. The client will receive email notification when their report is available.

Skills Testing and Behavioral Assessment
Skills Tests will measure a candidate's actual competencies through performance- and knowledge-based tests, while Behavioral Assessments will demonstrate the attitudes and aptitudes of a candidate, such as trustworthiness, rules compliance, reliability and a violence-free attitude, helping employers determine their fit within an organization.

Electronic Application Process (EAP)
Our EAP module will allow applicants to easily and conveniently enter the information needed for pre-employment screening via the internet. At home, applicants have convenient access to reference materials they may need and data legibility and integrity are ensured through online submission. The EAP module will be customizable to ensure that only the data needed for the client's screening program is captured. EAP will utilize the strongest SSL encryption available to securely transfer personal information. Applicants can request a copy of the background check report from within the application, helping to ensure compliance in states that require such access.

Employee Screening Consulting Services
We will work with businesses to develop consistent background screening procedures that can be used at all levels of the organization, from entry-level cashiers to top executives. The policy will define what is needed for each position level in accordance with organizational goals and objectives. Furthermore, the policies developed will address periodic background check procedures in addition to pre-employment screening. Consulting to establish a consistent background screening policy across all employment

levels is fundamental for organizations to help keep shrinkage to a minimum and curtail violence and other inappropriate behavior in the workplace, resulting in reduced liability concerns. It will also be important to educate clients to that the fact that they do not have unlimited rights to dig into an employee's background or personal life.

Volunteer Background Checks
Child abuse within volunteer organizations has become an issue of national importance. With the passage of the Volunteers for Children Act, volunteer organizations have the potential of being held liable for negligent hiring if their volunteers sexually molest a child, elderly or disabled person in their care and if the volunteer has been previously convicted of a relevant crime. _____ (company name) will proudly support volunteer organizations by offering very low-cost access to our criminal database searches. We will offer a Volunteer Screen, that is, a quick and affordable solution for identifying sex offenders on a multi-jurisdictional scale.

Business Background Check Report
Our Business Background Check Report will return all available records pertaining to a business, including business assets and pertinent details about principals. We will access the big national business databases and our court reps will search county records for the lowdown on professional licenses, plus business and personal assets. Involves checking into OSHA violations, litigation, credit check, liens and judgments, SEC records if a publicly traded company, Better Business Bureau, Chamber of Commerce in the business's city, consumer complaints, products and services, business reputation, legal status, industry, major competitor and finally a criminal check or the owners or officers of the company.

Litigation Support Services
Our Litigation Support services will include:
1.   Discreet Fact-Finding Investigations
2   Identification and Interviews with Potential Witnesses
3.   "Test" Purchases and Notary Purchases
4.   Asset and Person Tracing
5.   Market Research for Loss Valuation
6.   Background Checks on Expert Witnesses

3.1.2   Our Service Benefits

Among the many economic benefits of our service will be the following:
1.   Reduce the economic costs of redeeming image among your employees and dishonest people.
2.   Reduced labor costs by reducing the dismissal of problematic employees. Improve the profitability of the company by avoiding these costs.
3.   Immediate deterrent effect on those candidates who want to distort their resume or having a problematic history.

The benefits of using background screenings to hire were identified as:
1.   Improved quality of hires at 53%, which means only correctly-qualified applicants end up in that firm's key roles.
2.   A safer and more secure workplace (49%).
3.   Better regulatory compliance (36%), which is critical in an ever-shifting regulatory environment.
4.   Better company reputation
5.   Greater employee retention.

Our background checks will potentially raise red flags on the following types of issues that should be addressed before proceeding any further:

1.   **Financial Issues:**
      Bankruptcy, tax liens, poor credit, and other financial problems should raise a red flag, even if your potential employee, partner, buyer or supplier will not be contributing financially to the business. Someone in a financial crisis may have grossly mismanaged his or her personal or business finances and may lack the skills or discipline to be successful. Worst-case scenario: he or she may look for ways to steal from the business to solve their own personal problems.

2.   **Ethical Issues:**
      Bad press, pending litigation, or possible ethical problems may signal your potential employee or partner is not trustworthy. Furthermore, anyone who misrepresents his academic history, references, or employment information on his résumé immediately demonstrates a lack of honesty. Look for a candidate who values integrity and practices good personal and business ethics. An unethical business associate may steal ideas or clients from the company or involve the business in their legal troubles.

3.   **Personal Issues:**
      Serious personal challenges or problems may keep your potential candidates from committing fully to a business. Running a business takes focus, time, and energy. If a team member is dealing with one personal crisis after another, the weight of the corporate responsibility may not be carried fairly.

4.   **Academic Records and Performance:**
      Academic performance will be important if there is an academic requirement for the business venture, such as working as a doctor, lawyer, or architect.

3.2   Alternative Revenue Streams

1.   Classified Ads in our Newsletter
2.   Vending Machine Sales
3.   Product Rentals.
4.   Website Banner Ads
4.   Content Area Sponsorship Fees
5.   Online Survey Report Fees
6.   Consulting Services
7.   Facilities Sub-leases

3.3   Production of Products and Services

We will use the following methods to locate the best suppliers for our business:
- Attend association trade shows and seminars to spot upcoming trends, realize
      networking opportunities and compare prices.

- Subscribe to appropriate trade magazines, journals, newsletters and blogs.

Workforce Magazine
Upsize Magazine   www.upsizemag.com
Business Partner Magazine   www.businesspartnermagazine.com
Social Media Today   www.socialmediatoday.com

- Join our trade association to make valuable contacts, get listed in any online
      directories, and secure training and marketing materials.

National Association of Professional Background Screeners   www.napbs.com
Exists to promote ethical business practices, promote compliance with the Fair Credit
Reporting Act and foster awareness of issues related to consumer protection and privacy
rights within the background screening industry. The NAPBS Accreditation was
established after the Federal Trade Commission (FTC) indicated that it desired standards
by which background screening companies could be objectively evaluated. The
Background Screening Accreditation Program (BSAP) is a rigorous process through
which organizations have to undergo in order to receive NAPBS Accreditation.
The BSAP represents the gold standard in background screening processes. For an
organization to successfully complete BSAP, it must be able to meet the highest industry
standards in all aspects including legal compliance, customer service, data protection,
client education, consumer protection and general business practices.

Society of Human Resource Management (SHRM)

Staffing Management Association (SMA)

Electronic Privacy Information Center   **http://epic.org/**
A public interest research center in Washington, D.C. It was established in 1994 to focus
public attention on emerging civil liberties issues and to protect privacy, the First
Amendment, and constitutional values. EPIC publishes an award-winning e-mail and
online newsletter on civil liberties in the information age - the EPIC Alert.

Expungement Clearinghouse   **www.expungementclearinghouse.org**

The American Society for Industrial Security
ASIS has updated their guidelines on background screening.

3.4   Competitive Comparison

There are only ____ (#) other background check service providers in the _____ area. _____ (company name) will differentiate itself from its local competitors by offering a broader range of background check services, maintaining a database of client preferences, searches and transaction history, guaranteeing customer satisfaction, offering membership club benefits to qualifying volume users, using a monthly newsletter to stay-in-touch with customers and offering an array of innovative packaged service options.

We will also place a heavy emphasis on the development of a staff training program to meet client information and background screening demands, while also serving to control operational costs.

We will use occasional surveys to solicit customer feedback and provide new service concepts to local businesses and individuals. We will also encourage clients to make special screening requests.

_____ (company name) does not have to pay for under-utilized staff. Our flexible employee scheduling procedures and use of part-timers ensure that the business is never overstaffed during slow times. We will also adopt a pay-for-performance compensation plan, and use referral incentives to generate new business.

We will reinvest major dollars every year in professional and educational materials. We will participate in online webinars to bring clients the finest selection of seminars related to our background screening services, and industry trend information.

Our prices will be competitive with other businesses that offer far less in the way of benefits, innovative services, and packaged options

3.5   Sales Literature

____ (company name) has developed sales literature that illustrates a professional organization with vision. ____ (company name) plans to constantly refine its marketing mix through a number of different literature packets. These include the following:
- direct mail with introduction letter and product price sheet.
- product information brochures
- press releases
- new product/service information literature
- email marketing campaigns
- website content

- corporate brochures

A copy of our informational brochure is attached in the appendix of this document. This brochure will be available to provide referral sources, leave at seminars, and use for direct mail purposes.

3.6 Fulfillment

The key fulfillment and delivery of services will be provided by our director/owner, and certified background investigators and screening specialists. The real core value is the industry expertise of the founder, and staff experience and company training programs.

3.7 Technology

We will combine innovative technology with experienced professional and industry insight to provide the following kinds of information and security systems:
1.   Our web ordering systems will provide unmatched functionality and flexibility in ordering reports, retrieving results and managing client screening process.
2.   We will use technology to place the highest priority on protecting both the client's and the applicants' personal information and maintaining the highest levels of privacy.
3.   We will allow users to seamlessly integrate our screening platform with their talent management systems.
4.   _____ (company name) will employ and maintain the latest technology to enhance its office management, inventory management, payment processing, customer profiling and record keeping systems.

We plan to integrate with PeopleSoft, Taleo, Kenexa, iCIMS and VirtualEdge. We will also seamlessly interface with the HR technology of the client's choice and we will continue to build our strategic partner network.

Deverus   **www.deverus.com**
Their platform delivers up-to-date criminal and sex offender information to their clients.

Tazworks   **https://www.tazworks.com/**
They released a lot of new software features in 2017, especially in drug screening and compliance areas like the QA Workflow. Thy provide a total solution for simple, powerful, and user-friendly background screening software.

Accio Data   **http://www.acciodata.com/**
Their software automates or augments the client's screening process from order entry all the way to results delivery and billing. Clients can log into our server, place orders, and retrieve results 24/7/365. Features configurability for almost any industry.

The SME Toolkit   **http://us.smetoolkit.org/**

A free program that enables entrepreneurs and small businesses to learn how to implement the sustainable business management practices needed for growth in areas such as finance, accounting, international business, marketing, human resources or legal.

E-Verifile

Develops workforce management software that allows midsized to large companies to run background checks, credit history reports, and criminal background investigations on vendors and their employees.

Mobile Phone Credit Card Reader   https://squareup.com/

Square, Inc. is a financial services, merchant services aggregator and mobile payments company based in San Francisco, California. The company markets several software and hardware products and services, including Square Register and Square Order. Square Register allows individuals and merchants in the United States, Canada, and Japan to accept offline debit and credit cards on their iOS or Android smartphone or tablet computer. The app supports manually entering the card details or swiping the card through the Square Reader, a small plastic device which plugs into the audio jack of a supported smartphone or tablet and reads the magnetic stripe. On the iPad version of the Square Register app, the interface resembles a traditional cash register.

Google Wallet   https://www.google.com/wallet/

A mobile payment system developed by Google that allows its users to store debit cards, credit cards, loyalty cards, and gift cards among other things, as well as redeeming sales promotions on their mobile phone. Google Wallet can be used NFC to make secure payments fast and convenient by simply tapping the phone on any PayPass-enabled terminal at checkout.

Apple Pay   http://www.apple.com/apple-pay/

A mobile payment and digital wallet service by Apple Inc. that lets users make payments using the iPhone 6, iPhone 6 Plus, Apple Watch-compatible devices (iPhone 5and later models), iPad Air 2, and iPad Mini 3. Apple Pay does not require Apple-specific contactless payment terminals and will work with Visa's PayWave, MasterCard's PayPass, and American Express's ExpressPay terminals. The service has begun initially only for use in the US, with international roll-out planned for the future. Resource: www.wired.com/2018/01/shadow-apple-pay-google-wallet-expands-online-reach/

WePay   https://www.wepay.com/

An online payment service provider in the United States. WePay's payment API focuses exclusively on platform businesses such as crowdfunding sites, marketplaces and small business software. Through this API, WePay allows these platforms to access its payments capabilities and process credit cards for the platform's users.

Chirpify

Connects a user's PayPal account with their Twitter account in order to enable payments through tweeting.

Article: www.prnewswire.com/news-releases/tips-to-leverage-mobile-payments-in-your-marketing-strategy-300155855.html

3.8 Future Products and Services

_____ (company name) will continually expand our offering of services based on industry trends and changing client needs. We will not only solicit feedback via surveys and comments cards from clients on what they need in the future, but will also work to develop strong relationships with all of our clients and vendors. We also plan to open _____ (#) additional locations in the _____ region starting in _____ (year).

We plan to expand our offering of services to include the following:
1. Ordering via our website and fax transmissions.
2. Mobile Consulting Services
3. Database record repair services for individuals wanting to clean or repair their profiles.
4. Drug testing
5. Education and professional reference verification.
6. Executive Job Applicant Comprehensive Review
7. Potential romantic partner screenings.
8. Expand the selection of HR management consulting services.
9. DIY online database access via our website.

Executive Job Applicant Comprehensive Review
This will be a personalized service that requires a network of ground agents to provide a more comprehensive picture of an applicant's background and credentials. This service is needed to address the increasing level of falsified information by applicants in the business and educational sectors. This service will seek to verify the applicants claims about their prior job responsibilities and remuneration packages, academic credentials, and past achievements.

Company Reports
These company reports will include the following types of information:
1. Operating address and contact details
2. Profile and history of subject company
3. Company activities, products and services, operations and Industry Classification with NACE code
4. Operational figures, financial and banking information
5. Registration information and date of establishment: registry and official information - name and location of official source, registry, (tax)authority, Chamber of Commerce

6.   Ownership and management - with group linkages (to parent, subsidiaries, associates), where possible
7.   Legal status and payment information
8.   Credit rating and opinion, payment experience and commentary

Note: The credit rating will be a 1-20 score, generally calculated from the following factors:

- Age of company	- Legal form
- Size	- Activities
- Financial strength (if available)	- Link to parent company (if any)
- Payment history	- Director/Shareholder structure
- Assets owned, leased or rented	

Bespoke Investigations

These will include commissioned, special customized investigations that include services such as photography, to illustrate how a company's registered premises looks, as well as the number of people who work there. Tailored Business Investigation pricing will be available on request.

Competitive Intelligence Service

Our intelligence service will allow our clients to adjust services that match and beat their closest competitors. This service may lead to the discovery of patent infringement, theft of trade secrets and dumping. Our Competitive Intelligence services will include:

1.   Market research and surveys
2.   Identification of unmet customer needs
3.   Product and price comparisons
4.   Assessing competitor perceptions and capabilities
5.   Discovery and response to market trends
6.   Counterintelligence training for trade secrets

Corporate Documents

These documents will include: Annual Accounts, Certificates of Incorporation, Articles or Statues and extracts from different countries' Company Registers, where available.

Company Name Search

We will provide the client with confirmation of whether a Company Name exists at a Corporate Registry in a particular country or jurisdiction. If the client is unsure in which country a particular company name is registered, we will provide a Worldwide Company Name Search.

Wholesale Accounts

We will market our Wholesale Service Partner Program to resellers who need to offer an array of screening products to their clients. They will gain access to cost-effective screening products backed by our industry-leading data. Our powerful and flexible technology will provide them with secure, streamlined XML gateway site integrations.

The underlying mechanics will be behind the scenes, giving a smooth, consistent appearance. The customers of our Service Partner clients will submit their requests to us through the client company's online interface. We will make it easy for our wholesale clients and seamless for their customers. The advantages to our wholesale clients will be as follows:

1. Industry-leading criminal data
2. Frequent data updates
3. Strict data-management procedures
4. Competitive pricing
5. Easy integration

Customized Background Checks

We will offer customized programs that consider the client's unique risks, compliance issues, budget, time frame, and business needs. We will not charge clients for information they don't need. We will be a screening company that listens to the client's needs and tailors a screening program appropriately. We will ask the following types of insightful questions about the client's company, including the exact position titles they are hiring for, company job descriptions, reporting matrix, financial exposure, their organizational risk appetite, current employment policies, business objectives, lessons learned from prior hires, need for access to background screening experts, record of employment compliance, and other questions that will affect the composition of the screening program.

4.0 Market Analysis Summary

Our Market Analysis will serve to accomplish the following goals:
1.   Define the characteristics and needs and wants of the target market.
2.   Serve as a basis for developing sales, marketing and promotional strategies.
3.   Influence the e-commerce website design.

Background checks are most often used by employers as a means of objectively evaluating a job candidate's qualifications and to identify potential hiring risks

Research indicates that larger companies are more likely to outsource the background check function than smaller companies. The average staff size of the companies who outsource is 3,313 compared to 2,162 for those who carry out in-house checks. Financial services firms had the highest proportion of respondents who outsource the service, with over a quarter (26%) doing so, compared to an overall average of 16% who outsource vetting to a third-party provider. The construction and property industry showed the lowest level of outsourcing, with 89% of such firms in the sample carrying out checks in-house, making the overall average 16%.

The following represents the most common types of checks performed:
1.   Employment References
2.   Education Verification: School degrees and professional qualifications obtained.
3.   Character Reference Check
4.   Gaps in employment history
5.   Identity and Address Verification
6.   Whether an applicant holds a directorship
7.   Credit History - bankruptcies
8.   Criminal History Report

_____ (company name) has a defined target market of mid-sized companies that will be the basis of this business. Effective marketing combined with an optimal packaged service offering mix is critical to our success. The owner possesses solid information about the market and knows a great deal about the common attributes of those that are expected to be loyal clients. This information will be leveraged to better understand who we will serve, their specific needs, and how to better communicate with them. The owner strongly believes that as more and more products become commodities that require highly competitive pricing, it will be increasingly important to focus on the development of innovative HR services, that can be structured, managed and possibly outsourced.

4.1 Secondary Market Research

We will research demographic information for the following reasons:
1.   To determine which segments of the population, such as Hispanics and the elderly, have been growing and may now be underserved.

2. To determine if there is a sufficient population base in the designated service area to realize the company's business objectives.
3. To consider what products and services to add in the future, given the changing demographic profile and needs of our service area.

We will pay special attention to the following general demographic trends:
1. Population growth has reached a plateau and market share will most likely be increased through innovation and excellent customer service.
2. Because incomes are not growing, and unemployment is high, process efficiencies and sourcing advantages must be developed to keep prices competitive.
3. The rise of non-traditional households, such as single working mothers, means developing more innovative and personalized programs.
4. As the population shifts toward more young to middle aged adults, ages 30 to 44, and the elderly, aged 65 and older, there will be a greater need for child-rearing and geriatric mobile support services.
5. Because of the aging population, rising pollution and high unemployment, new 'green' ways of dealing with the resulting stress levels will need to be developed.

We will collect the demographic statistics for the following zip code(s):

_____

We will use the following sources: www.census.gov, www.zipskinny.com, www.brainyzip.com, www.city-data.com, www.demographicsnow.com, www.freedemographics.com, www.ffiec.gov/geocode, www.esri.com/data/esri_data/tapestry and www.claritas.com/claritas/demographics.jsp. This information will be used to decide upon which targeted programs to offer and to make business growth projections.
Resource: www.sbdcnet.org/index.php/demographics.html

Snapshots of consumer data by zip code are also available online:
http://factfinder.census.gov/home/saff/main.html?_lang=en
http://www.esri.com/data/esri_data/tapestry.html
http://www.claritas.com/MyBestSegments/Default.jsp?ID=20

1.	**Total Population**	_____
2.	**Number of Households**	_____
3.	**Population by Race:**	White ____% Black ___%
		Asian Pacific Islander ___% Other ____%
4.	**Population by Gender**	Male ____% Female ____%
5.	**Income Figures:**	Median Household Income $_____
		Household Income Under $50K ____%
		Household Income $50K-$100K ____%
		Household Income Over $100K ____%
6.	**Housing Figures**	Average Home Value - $_____
		Average Rent $_____
7.	**Homeownership:**	Homeowners % _____
		Renters % _____

8.	**Education Achievement**	High School Diploma	% _____
		College Degree	% _____
		Graduate Degree	% _____
9.	**Stability/Newcomers**	Longer than 5 years	% _____
10.	**Marital Status**	___% Married ___% Divorced ___% Single	
		___% Never Married ___% Widowed ___% Separated	
11.	**Occupations**	___%Service ___% Sales ___% Management	
		___% Construction ___% Production	
		___% Unemployed ___% Below Poverty Level	
12.	**Age Distribution**	___%Under 5 years ___%5-9 yrs ___%10-12 yrs	
		___% 13-17 yrs ___%18-years	
		___% 20-29 ___% 30-39 ___% 40-49 ___% 50-59	
		___% 60-69 ___% 70-79 ___% 80+ years	
13.	**Prior Growth Rate**	_____ % from _____ (year)	
14.	**Projected Population Growth Rate**	_____ %	
15.	**Employment Trend**	_____	
16.	**Business Failure Rate**	_____	

Secondary Market Research Conclusions:
This area will be demographically favorable for our business for the following reasons:

_____

_____

Resource:
www.allbusiness.com/marketing/segmentation-targeting/848-1.html

4.1.1   Primary Market Research

We plan to develop a survey for primary research purposes and mail it to a list of local home magazine subscribers, purchased from the publishers by zip code. We will also post a copy of the survey on our website and encourage visitors to take the survey. We will use the following survey questions to develop an Ideal Customer Profile of our potential client base, so that we can better target our marketing communications. To improve the response rate, we will include an attention-grabbing _____ (discount coupon/ dollar?) as a thank you for taking the time to return the questionnaire.

1.   What is your zip-code? _____
2.   What is your company's target market? _____
3.   What is your company's primary product/service? _____
4.   What is your age? _____
5.   What has been the sales trend in the last 3 years? _____
6.   What is your company's annual sales? _____
7.   What is your educational level? _____
8.   What is your profession? _____

9. How many people are employed by your company?

10. What are your hobbies/other entertainment forms? _____

11. How many years has the business been established? _____

12. What are your favorite trade magazines? _____

13. What is your favorite local newspaper? _____

14. What is your favorite radio station? _____

15. What are your favorite cable television programs? _____

16. What are your favorite websites? _____

17. What trade organizations are you a member of? _____

18. Does the area have an adequate number of background check companies?

19. Does your company currently patronize a screening company? Yes / No

20. Are you satisfied with your current screening company? Yes / No

21. How many times per month do you use a screening company? _____

22. What HR services do you typically outsource? _____

23. On average, how much do you spend on screening services per month? ____

25. What is the name of your currently patronized background screening company?

26. What are their strengths as service providers?

27. What are their weaknesses or shortcomings?

28. What would it take for us to earn your background screening business?

29. What is the best way for us to market our background check business?

30. Do you think you will be in need of screening services in the near future?

31. Would you be interested in joining a Screening Club that would offer special Membership benefits?

32. Describe your experience with other background screening establishments.

33. Please rank (1 to 14) the importance of the following factors when choosing a Background Screening company:

   ___ Quality of Screening Services   ___ Services Selection
   ___ Reputation   ___ Staff Courtesy/Friendliness
   ___ Service Speed   ___ Staff Professionalism
   ___ Convenient location   ___ Value
   ___ Referral/References   ___ Complaint Handling
   ___ Privacy/Security Measures   ___ Government Compliance
   ___ Price   ___ Satisfaction Guarantee
   ___ Other _____

34. What method of payment do you prefer?
   ___ Cash ___ Credit Card ___ Debit Card ___ Check ___ Other _____

35. Has your background check/ATS/JBS provider suffered any breaches in data privacy or data security involving PII in the last 5 years?

36. Does your background check/ATS/JBS provider "offshore" (send outside of the United States) PII data to a foreign land to be processed in any way beyond the jurisdiction of U.S. Privacy laws?

37. Does your background check/ATS/JBS provider repurpose (convert for use as another format or product) PII data for other uses such as marketing purposes?

38. Does your background check/ATS/JBS provider resell PII to skip tracers, collection agencies, lawyers, or marketing lists?

39. Does the parent company or any subsidiaries of your background check/ATS/JBS

provider resell information for marketing purposes or sell information for profit?

40. Do you have any special screening requirements that need to be addressed?
41. What information would you like to see in our company newsletter?
42. Which online social groups have you joined? Choose the ones you access.

    ___ Facebook   ___ MySpace

    ___ Twitter   ___ LinkedIn

    ___ Ryze   ___ Ning

43. What types of new background screening services would most interest you?
44. What is your general need for a background screening service?

Circle Months: J F M A M J J A S O N D (All)

Circle Days: S M T W T F S (All)

Indicate Hours: _____ or (24 hours)

45. What are your suggestions for realizing a better background screening experience?
46. Are you on our mailing list? Yes/No   If No, can we add you?   Yes / No
47. Would you be interested in attending a free seminar on preventing negligent hiring?
48. Can you supply the name and contact info of person who might be interested in our background checking services?

Please note any comments or concerns about background screening companies in general.

We very much appreciate your participation in this survey. If you provide your name, address and email address, we will sign you up for our e-newsletter, inform you of our survey results, advise you of any new screening companies opening in your area and enter you into our monthly drawing for a free _____.

Name   Address

Email   Phone

4.1.2   Voice of the Customer

To develop a better understanding of the needs and wants of our Background Check clients, we will institute the following ongoing listening practices:

1. Focus Groups
   Small groups of customers (6 to 8) will be invited to meet with a facilitator to answer open-ended questions about priority of needs and wants, and our company, its products or other given issues. These focus groups will provide useful insight into the decisions and the decision-making process of target consumers.
2. Individual Interviews
   We will conduct face-to-face personal interviews to understand customer thought processes, selection criteria and service preferences.

3. Customer Panels
   A small number of customers will be invited to answer open-ended questions on a regular basis.
4. Customer Tours
   We will invite customers to visit our facilities to discuss how our processes can better serve them.
5. Visit Customers
   We will observe customers as they actually use our services to uncover the pains and problems they are experiencing during usage.
6. Trade Show Meetings
   Our trade show booth will be used to hear the concerns of our customers.
7. Toll-free Numbers
   We will attach our phone number to all products and sales literature to encourage the customer to call with problems or positive feedback.
8. Surveys
   We will use surveys to obtain opinions on closed-ended questions, referrals and improvement suggestions.
9. Mystery Shoppers
   We will use mystery shoppers to report on how our employees treat our customers.
10. Salesperson Debriefing
    We will ask our salespeople to report on their customer experiences to obtain insights into what the customer faces, what they want and why they failed to make a sale.
11. Customer Contact Logs
    We will ask our sales personnel to record interesting customer revelations and insights.
12. Customer Serviceperson's Hotline
    We will use this dedicated phone line for service people to report problems.
13. Discussions with competitors.
14. Installation of suggestion boxes to encourage constructive feedback. The suggestion card will have several statements customers are asked to rate in terms of a given scale. There are also several open-ended questions that allow the customer to freely offer constructive criticism or praise. We will work hard to implement reasonable suggestions in order to improve our service offerings as well as show our commitment to the customer that their suggestions are valued.

4.2 Market Segmentation

Market segmentation is a technique that recognizes that the potential universe of users may be divided into definable sub-groups with different characteristics. Segmentation enables organizations to target messages to the needs and concerns of these subgroups. We will segment the market based on the needs and wants of select customer groups. We will develop a composite customer profile and a value proposition for each of these segments. The purpose for segmenting the market is to allow our marketing/sales program to focus on the subset of prospects that are "most likely" to purchase our background checking services. If done properly this will help to insure the highest return for our marketing/sales expenditures.

_____ (company name) will provide small- to medium-sized businesses with a comprehensive, integrated and easy-to-use set of applicant background screening services across the following major market segments:
1.   Employment screening
2.   Volunteer screening
3.   Tenant screening
4.   Security screening

Federal and State Law Mandated Background Checks
Employers are legally required to conduct background checks for certain jobs. Depending on the company's industry, there may be a need to conduct background checks and may be prevented by statute from hiring employees convicted of particular offenses. For instance, almost every state requires a background check for anyone who works with children or in a healthcare facility.

Prevention of Negligent Hiring Lawsuits
Conducting background checks can prevent negligent hiring lawsuits. Most states recognize the tort of negligent hiring, where employers are held liable for hiring an employee whose actions harm someone else.

Flagging False or Inflated Information
Conducting background checks allows employers to confirm the accuracy of information in a prospective employee's job application. Replacing an unsatisfactory employee or providing additional training is more expensive than the cost of a background check. A recent study showed that almost half of all job applicants submitted inaccurate information to their potential employer.

The total potential market in units is shown in the following table and chart.
1.   There are approximately ___ (#) businesses in ___ (state) that could potentially be our customers.
2.   There are ____ (#) landlords in ____ (city), according to the 2000 U.S. Census, with __ (5) % projected growth over the next ten years.
3.   There are ____ (#) Public Service Organization that could potentially be our customers in the state of _____.

Composite Customer Profile:
By assembling this composite customer profile, we will know what needs and wants to focus on and how best to reach our target market. We will use the information gathered from our customer research survey to assemble the following composite customer profile:

Ideal Customer Profile

Who are they? _____

Location of business headquarters (city) _____

Type of Business _____

Number of employees _____

Approximate annual revenues _____

Years in business _____

Company growth stage _____

Publications subscribed to _____

Trade associations the company belongs to? _____

What is the total sq/ft. of the facility? _____

Where are they located (zip codes)? _____

Trend Preferences? Trendsetter/Trend follower/Other _____

How often do they buy? _____

What are most important purchase factors? Price/Brand Name/Quality/Terms/Service/ Convenience/Green/Other_____

What is their key buying motivator? _____

How do they buy it? Cash/Credit/Terms/Other_____

Where do they buy it from (locations)? _____

What problem do they want to solve? _____

What are the key frustrations/pains that these customers have when buying? _____

What info search methods do they use? _____

What is preferred problem solution? _____

Table: Market Analysis

Potential Customers	Growth	Number of Potential Customers		
		2018	2019	2020
Public Corporations	10%			
Private Corporations	10%			
Government Agencies	10%			
Public Service Organizations	10%			
Landlords	10%			
Other	10%			
Totals:	10%			

4.3   Target Market Segment Strategy

Our target marketing strategy will involve identifying a group of customers to which to direct our background checking services. Our strategy will be the result of intently listening to and understanding customer needs, representing customers' needs to those responsible for product production and service delivery, and giving them what they want. In developing our targeted customer messages, we will strive to understand things like: where they work, worship, party and play, where they shop and go to school, how they spend their leisure time, what magazines they read and organizations they belong to, and where they volunteer their time. We will use research, surveys and observation to uncover this wealth of information to get our product details and brand name in front of our customers and prospects when they are most receptive to receiving our messaging.

Target Market Worksheet   (optional)

Product Benefits: Actual factor (cost effectiveness, design, performance, etc.) or perceived factor (image, popularity, reputation, etc.) that satisfies what a customer needs or wants. An advantage or value that the product will offer its buyer.

Products Features: One of the distinguishing characteristics of a product or service that helps boost its appeal to potential buyers. A characteristic of a product that describes its appearance, its components, and its capabilities. Typical features include size and color.

Product or Service	Product/ Service Benefits	Product/ Service Features	Potential Target Markets

Background checks will be performed for the following market segments:

1. Employers.

   Due to identity theft and the prevalence of falsifying information, various companies and smaller businesses like to perform background checks on potential employees to determine whether or not they are honest and reliable, not to mention qualified for the job they are applying for.

2. Local and national government.

   Most government employees receive mandatory background checks, the extensiveness of the checks determined by their seniority level or their security clearance. The government also performs checks on those they are investigating or those they believe to be a risk to national security.

3. Parents

   Parents conduct background checks because they are concerned about the company their children are keeping.

4. Concerned Citizens

   They may perform background checks on people they meet that they perceive to be a threat to themselves or others. This mainly stems from online dating.

5. Private Investigators

   Investigators will perform background checks related to their cases.

6. Law enforcement

   They perform background checks as part of their investigations.

7. Lawyers

   Defense lawyers conduct background checks to uncover information that they can use to weaken the credibility of the plaintiff.

Many companies realize that the most important step in the hiring process may be the pre-employment background check. Depending on the industry, some companies have screening requirements mandated by Federal and State agencies. As an example, transportation companies, must perform drug tests and check the status of employee's commercial drivers' licenses and hazardous materials endorsements. Companies in the securities industry also must perform background checks, professionals from casino workers to insurance agents are screened for a criminal history. All states have passed legislations requiring background checks in jobs that serve the vulnerable or at risk, such as the elderly, children, and disabled. These mandatory checks are usually performed by state agencies using the applicant's fingerprints to check state and federal records.

We will focus on the following well-defined target market segments and emphasize our good value, high quality, varied service selections and packages, and prompt service.

Target Independent Rental Owners (IRO)
We will target independent rental owners because a recent national survey of IROs shows a sharp decline in the quality of rental applicants over the last few years, underscoring the need for more comprehensive background screening. Property owners and managers can't afford to rent to individuals or businesses with a history of nonpayment, property damage, or criminal activity. Landlords need to fill vacancies with tenants who will pay their rent on time, be respectful of their neighbors, and keep the property in good shape. To weed out prospects likely to become headaches in the future, property owners and managers will sign-up for our reliable tenant screening programs.

Target Real Estate Agents and Brokers
We will target real estate agents because they are often required to do background checks on prospective renters. The American Apartment Owner's Association (AAOA) says the best way to insure a tenant applicant doesn't have a history of bad tenant behavior is through a tenant background check.
Resources:
www.zillow.com/blog/pro/finding-trustworthy-renters-using-credit-and-background-checks-108629/
www.RentecDirect.com
http://realtytimes.com/investoradvice1/item/27045-20180106-why-a-tenant-background-check-is-so-important-htm

Target Mid-sized Companies
We will target midsized corporations who are looking for a reliable background check company. In these cases, we will contact the human resource department directly and set-up a meeting to discuss our background check services. Businesses want to receive a return on their investment and mitigate potential legal and financial exposures. Conducting background checks on potential employees utilizing a background check service has become a major part of the business process. It's important for businesses to have a solid and consistent program in place to run pre-employment background checks on candidates. We will also provide consulting services because businesses do not have unlimited rights to dig into an employee's background or personal life.

Target the Hospitality Industry

In the hospitality industry customer service is the foundation of repeat business, and it is important to hire individuals who can interact successfully with clients. Front-desk and wait staff must provide quality service, handle complaints, and process payments. Many of the positions are often unsupervised, so it will be especially important to hire trustworthy, loyal, and emotionally stable employees. We will offer employment screening products for the hospitality industry, which include, but are not limited to: criminal searches, employment and education verification, Social Security number and address-history verification, drug testing and credit reports. This industry also has a high employee turnover rate, which will be good for our business.

Target Hospitals

We will become members of the following trade associations to engage in networking opportunities:

American Hospital Association (AHA)

American Society for Healthcare Human Resources Association (ASHHRA)

Target Pediatricians

A new policy statement from the American Academy of Pediatrics urges adding a drug screening to adolescent office visits.

Target Retailers

Retailers look for honest, reliable, and friendly employees, but most stores are struggling with the same issues: stock shrinkage, employee absenteeism and turnover, and workplace violence. We will offer pre-employment retail background checks for substance-abuse problems and criminal histories that can help the retailer to select the right person for the job.

Target Federal and State Agencies

Federal and state laws require that background checks be conducted for certain jobs. For example, most states require criminal background checks for anyone who works with children, the elderly, or disabled. The federal National Child Protection Act authorizes state officials to access the FBI's National Crime Information Center (NCIC) database for some positions. Many state and federal government jobs require a background check, and depending on the kind of job, may require an extensive investigation for a security clearance. We will also target adoption agencies and volunteer fire departments.

Target Community Centers

We will target community centers because they require background checks on everyone who performs services for their centers, including seminar and workshop presenters.

Target Non-Profit Organizations

Nonprofit organizations provide valuable services to millions of people nationwide. Because so many nonprofits are service-based organizations, they tend to work with members of society who are vulnerable and not able to protect themselves - the infirm,

the elderly, and children. And most nonprofit organizations rely heavily on the services of volunteers. The public relies on nonprofit organizations to be trustworthy and dependable. A staff member or volunteer who commits a crime can expose the non-profit organization to intense public scrutiny and damage its reputation. We will work with non-profit organizations to screen volunteers as carefully as employees performing similar duties. Additionally, charities and voluntary organizations may wish to partner with businesses to deliver services or purchase goods. Given that the reputation of a charity is important in maintaining public trust, it will also be useful to check out a business before joining forces. This will help to avoid conflicts of interest, poor value for money and shady or reputation destroying dealings.
Resource:
https://knowhownonprofit.org/how-to/how-to-do-a-background-check-on-local-
        businesses-guide

Target Ride-sharing Companies
We will target ride-sharing companies because they also look closely at driving records, which aren't included in fingerprint checks through the FBI. Among driver candidates who aren't accepted by Uber, 97% are turned away because of a poor driving record. Ridesharing organizations like Uber and Lyft, have been using FBI fingerprinting for background checks, which is a method that is inaccurate and incomplete and does not meet Fair Credit Reporting Act (FCRA) standards for maximum possible accuracy. Thus, companies must establish a strong internal screening policy, ideally consistent with Equal Employment Opportunity Commission (EEOC) guidance, and partner with a thorough background screening provider that can scale alongside the growing independent workforce.
Resources:
www.chicagonow.com/chicago-on-the-radar/2018/06/chicago-city-council-considers-fbi-
        background-checks-for-uber-lyft/
https://easybackgrounds.com/five-background-screening-trends-that-will-impact-hiring-
        in-2018/

Target Churches
Many churches now have a policy that everyone who works in the children and youth areas must have a current background check on file. They also run background checks on all volunteers for their children and youth camps.

Target Schools
Many schools are now requiring their school bus drivers and cafeteria workers to have background checks and be fingerprinted.

Target Colleges
We will target colleges because an increasing number of colleges have mandated background screenings for students, particularly those enrolled in health science programs. There is a growing interest in background queries, if not full screenings, for all college-bound students—and for annual checks while the student is enrolled on campus. This need was highlighted by the Virginia Tech massacre in April of 2007.

Resources:
www.universitybusiness.com/article/background-checks-college-students-rising
Examples;
www.corporatescreening.com/services/background-screening/verifystudents-2/

Target Nanny Agencies
These agencies have a great interest in only placing nannies with clean backgrounds to avoid down-the-road litigation battles.
Ex: NannyCare.com has partnered with USSearch.com to offer affordable nanny
         background checks.

Target Mobile Tutoring Services
These businesses perform background checks on all tutors before they are dispatched to a client's home. they also conduct annual background checks to determine if anything has changed.

Target Babysitters
We will target families that use babysitters and agencies that recruit babysitters. They will require the babysitter to sign a background check release form. As a potential employer, they are not legally able to obtain a background check, unless the potential employee consents, according to Backgroundcheck.org. If we plan to obtain a credit check, we must provide the candidate with a copy of the Fair Credit Report Act. On the form, we will ask the babysitter candidate to list his birth date, social security number, address, previous addresses and any aliases or names he might have previously used.
Resource: http://www.care4hire.com/tips/17-babysitter-background-checks/

Target Online Dating Sites
Some dating sites are taking some initiative to help make singles safer with required background checks.

Target Gun Dealers
Research indicates that most gun dealers support expanded background checks.

Target Nursing Homes
We will target nursing homes because states are changing their laws to mandate background checks on all job applicants.
Resource: www.ctpost.com/local/article/Background-check-for-nursing-home-
                   applicants-a-3969236.php

Target Home Healthcare Agencies
Many states now require home healthcare agencies to conduct employee background checks and provide five (5) hours of entry level training.

Target Child Care Centers and Family Child Care Homes
We will target child care centers and family child care homes because more state governments are increasingly requiring all child care staff members to submit to

background checks. In the United States alone, more than 32 million children are in some kind of child care while their parents work outside the home, according to the Census Bureau's latest figures, from 2011. Families spend an average of $179 a week on child care for young children, according to the agency, and for many households, it's the biggest single expense.

Resources: http://childcareaware.org/child-care-centers-state-by-state-regulations
        http://childcareaware.org/family-child-care-home-state-be-state-regulations

Ex: www.care.com
Care.com was launched to fill a void between free online classified ad services such as Craigslist — still its biggest competitor on the Web, and high-end nanny placement companies. It would offer many of the same screenings, background checks, and a la carte expert-finder options as premium services but charge much less because it spread out the cost of those services to a larger network of users. Its subscriptions today range from $37 to $147, depending on the duration of the membership (one month to 12 months).

Target Local Ethnic Businesses
Ongoing demographic trends suggest that, in the coming decades, programs will be serving a population of people which is increasingly diverse in economic resources, racial and ethnic background, and family structure. Our plan is to reach out to consumers of various ethnic backgrounds, especially Hispanics, who comprise nearly 13 percent of the country's total population. In addition to embarking on an aggressive media campaign of advertising with ethnic newspapers and radio stations, we will set up programs to actively recruit bilingual employees and make our store more accessible via signage printed in various languages based on the store's community. We will accurately translate our marketing materials into other languages. We will enlist the support of our bilingual employees to assist in reaching the ethnic people in our surrounding area through a referral program. We will join the nearest _____ (predominate ethnic group) Chamber of Commerce and partner with _____ (Hispanic/Chinese/Other?) Advocacy Agencies. We will also develop programs that reflect cultural influences and brand preferences.

Target Employers in China
We will target employers in China because the latest Q4 Hudson Report on Employment and HR trends in China surveyed over 1,500 employers across Asia and found that more than two-thirds (68%) of business respondents across all sectors had encountered candidates being dishonest about their background or experience in their resumes in China, a far higher proportion than in the other markets surveyed in Asia.

Source:
www.huffingtonpost.com/richard-powell/background-checks-busines_b_825882.html

Target Dating Services and Matchmakers
These companies are very concerned about the safety of the people who participate in their programs. Intelius has created an application for mobile devices that allows users to do a quick background check on a potential date.

Target Engaged Couples
We will target couples because a woman or man using the services of a matchmaker might request a premarital background check on the future lifetime partner. We will also offer our services through wedding consultants and marriage counselors.

Target Law Firms
We will target law firms because they frequently have clients that may be in need of background checks. As an example, people entering into business partnerships or seeking investors, should do back ground checks on their partners and/or potential investors. Law firms also help their real estate owning clients to perform background checks on new tenants and property management company executives.

Helpful Resources:

U.S. census Bureau Statistics	www.census.gov
U.S. Dept. of Labor/Bureau of Labor Statistics	www.bls.gov/data/home.htm
National Hispanic Medical Association	

4.3.1   Market Needs

Our business will be created to address chronic and growing deficiencies in the industry's response to unmet customer demand, particularly with respect to long turn-around times, poor customer service, and incomplete and inaccurate reports that are often hard to understand and use by hiring managers at different levels of the client's organization.

Over 96% of HR professionals report that their companies do background checks of new hires, up from 66% in 1996, according to The Society for Human Resource Management Workplace Violence Survey.

A new study shows 64% of small companies in the United States have discovered inaccuracies during employment background checks, while experts warn firms who fail to identify them risk prolonged financial pain.

There are several reasons why employers voluntarily conduct pre and post-employment (current employee) checks. Background screening reduces the risk of negligent hiring and retention lawsuits. Two thirds of negligent hiring cases brought to court have received jury awards with an average award of $600,000. According to the Workplace Violence Research Institute, the average award in these suits is $3 million. Employers must exercise due diligence in determining if the applicant has a criminal history that may be relevant to the position and are obligated to protect their employees, customers and the general public from other employees with violent histories and are held liable because they know or should have known of the risk posed by an employee.

Background checks not only help to prevent workplace violence but are a defense against liability claims. Add to this an estimate by the U.S. Department of Commerce that one third of business failures are caused by employee theft. On top of this are studies that show 50% of resumes contain false information and overstated qualifications.

According to the Workplace Violence Research Institute, negligent-hiring lawsuits cost U.S. businesses $18 billion each year. Additionally, the Food Marketing Institute's "Supermarket Security and Loss Prevention 2007" report estimates that nearly 40% of total shrink comes from employees stealing money or merchandise, with checkout and service departments accounting for 75% of employee theft.

Risk management is one of the best defenses against lost revenue, growing shrink and workplace violence, especially when it comes to hiring reliable and trustworthy workers. Employee background screening can be used at all levels of the organization to help maintain the company's overall integrity and reputation and potentially save thousands of dollars, or more, by avoiding one bad hire.

It's estimated that up to 40% of resumes can contain false or tweaked information, so, employers want to ensure that what they are getting in an employee is what they were promised. The employer may perform a background check to find out whether the applicant actually graduated from the college they said they did or to confirm that they worked for a previous employer(s) during the time stated on the resume or job application.

Moreover, if your applicant will have contact with other employees or with customers, an important reason to do that checking is to avoid negligent hiring claims. If the employer has an employee who turns violent and harms either a customer or another employee, the employer could be slapped with a lawsuit if reference checking would have kept the company from hiring that person.

Additionally, with the recent corporate scandals of Enron and WorldCom, the popularity and necessity of executive background checks has greatly increased. In order to protect themselves from potential disasters later on, many companies are now requiring extensive investigation on prospective executives to verify their employment and educational history as well as information regarding any past wrongdoings.

A 2005 survey found that 2.3% of all businesses experience some form of co-worker violence, ranging from .6% to 8.1% for businesses with up to 250 employees and up to 34.1% for businesses with 1000+ total employees. In addition, a 2006 survey discovered that 13% of all workplace fatalities were caused by assaults and violent acts.

4.4 Buying Patterns

A Buying Pattern is the typical manner in which /buyers consumers purchase goods or services or firms place their purchase orders in terms of amount, frequency, timing, etc. In determining buying patterns, we will need to understand the following:
- Why consumers make the purchases that they make?
- What factors influence consumer purchases?
- The changing factors in our society.

Due in large part to the shocking terrorist attacks that unfolded on September 11, 2001 and led to increased security on all fronts in the United States, the background check industry has increasingly helped employers keep criminals, terrorists, and imposters out of their workplaces. Other factors behind the increased use of background checks include well publicized incidents of workplace violence, multi-million-dollar negligent hiring verdicts, a sharp rise in cases of resume fraud including some well publicized examples of fake degrees, and a national awareness of the dangers to children and other vulnerable groups when unqualified or dangerous persons are allowed access to them. A study last year by the Society for Human Resource Management showed that 87% of employers today conduct criminal-background checks, up hugely in the past 20 years.

In most cases, clients make the purchase decision on the basis of the following criteria:
1. Referrals and relationship with other clients.
2. Personality and expected relationship with the company personnel.
3. Internet-based information gathering.

Background checks are most often performed for the following reasons:

When Hiring Employees:
Pre-employment screening and employee background checks are more common these days than ever before. Employers need to know who they are hiring, and they have duty to their shareholders, stakeholders and co-workers to keep everyone as safe as possible.

As Part of Investment Due Diligence:
When buying a business one should always conduct a complete and detailed background check of the person or people selling the business as well as a background check on the business itself. A due diligence background check may also be used in cases where an investment is being considered in some type of project or venture.

For Litigation Purposes:
Often, when litigation is commenced, an attorney will want as much ammunition as possible to try and attack the opponent. A background check can reveal all sorts of things about people that can be used to attack their credibility, truthfulness and to verify or refute the testimony that they provide.

Whenever Children are Involved:
People will conduct a background of their children's care givers, people they may be traveling with, people that live in the neighborhood who may appear suspicious, etc. etc. A background check is an excellent way to get information that a parent may need to protect their child.

Before a Relationship Gets Legal:
People who are in a relationship and are pondering moving into marriage often want to conduct a background check of the soon to be spouse. There is also a pattern that shows that the more well off you are, the more likely you are to conduct this type of background check, with the obvious idea behind it being that it will help to insulate our client from being taken advantage of by the other person.

_____ (company name) will gear its offerings, marketing, and pricing policies to establish a loyal client base. Our value-based pricing, easy database access, preferred membership programs, and innovative service package options will be welcomed in _____ (city) and contribute to our success.

4.5   Market Growth

We will assess the following general factors that affect market growth:

Current Assessment

1. Interest Rates   _____
2. Government Regulations   _____
3. Perceived Environment Impact   _____
4. Consumer Confidence Level   _____
5. Population Growth Rate   _____
6. Unemployment Rate   _____
7. Political Stability   _____
8. Currency Exchange Rate   _____
9. Innovation Rate   _____
10. Home Sales   _____
11. Trend Linkage   _____
12. Overall Economic Health   _____

Industry revenue returned to growth in 2011, after a period of contraction in the wake of the economic downturn. Background checks are often submitted by potential employers and landlords, therefore high unemployment at this time reduced demand from businesses because fewer employees were getting hired. The Background Check Services industry has grown over the past five years, although it has experienced some variability. As macroeconomic conditions improved, industry revenue grew, and posted good results overall for the five-year period. IBISWorld expects industry revenue to grow at an annualized rate of 1.3% in the five years to 2016. In 2016 alone, industry revenue is expected to increase 0.3% to $1.8 billion.

The United States Department of Justice statistics for 2002 reveal that 6.7 million people (one in every 32 adults) are jailed, in prison, or are released on probation or parole. 67.5% of all prisoners released are subsequently re-arrested for a serious misdemeanor or felony within three years. Additionally, twenty to thirty percent of job applications contain false information. A study performed by the Society for Human Resource Management found that fifty three percent of the study sample had given false information about length of employment, fifty one percent about past salaries and forty five percent falsely said they had no criminal records.

Moreover, employee theft is a $400 billion industry, estimated to take over 6% of all revenue. The recidivism rate for criminals is reported to be 67.5%, so the odds are likely that convicted felons will come through your doors seeking employment. Only by responsible screening practices can companies and the public protect themselves from those seeking to prey on the vulnerabilities of the unsuspecting. Research indicates that about half of all companies, based on government and private surveys, now use credit reports as part of the hiring process, except in those states that limit or restrict their use.

The general industry analysis shows that _____ (city) is expected to experience _____ (double digit?) population, housing and commercial business growth. This suggests that as more families continue to move into the _____ area, there will be an increasing demand for quality background check services by employers and landlords, and this makes it a prime location for a background check company that is willing to think outside-of-the-box.

4.6.0   Service Business Analysis

The reasons for checking a person's background will most likely determine what information is checked. Types of information that may be investigated include:

1.	Criminal records	2.	Credit reports
3.	Driving records	4.	Marriage records
5.	Divorce records	6.	Employment or personal references
7.	Birth records	8.	Education records
9.	Medical history	10.	Psychiatric history
11.	Home ownership	12.	Military history, if applicable

Some general ways to obtain information include:
1. Online research.
   There are free databases online that provide public information, as well as paid services that allow access to information on a person's driver's license, their marriage records or divorce records, as well as their criminal history.

2. Courthouse research.
   It is possible to obtain many records from county courthouses if the person being

investigated is from the area in which the background check is being performed.

Several popular websites are available for background checks online. A few of the most popular are E-Background Check, U.S. Search, Net Detective Plus and Best People Search. These websites offer a variety of levels of investigation, depending upon the employer's needs.

The main reasons employers are increasingly checking into employment backgrounds and performing drug screening today are to:
1.   Mitigate or practice risk management.
2.   Improve the quality of new hires
3.   Promote workplace safety
4.   Meet regulatory compliance requirements.

Background checks are also recommended for all employees in high-risk areas, such as those who drive company vehicles, visit customer locations, handle money, or work with children, elderly or the impaired.

4.7   Barriers to Entry   (select)

_____ (company name) will benefit from the following combination of barriers to entry, which cumulatively present a moderate degree of entry difficulty or obstacles in the path of other background check businesses wanting to enter our market.

1.   Business Experience.   2.   Community Networking
3.   Referral Program   4.   People Skills
5.   Marketing Skills   6.   Supplier Relationships
7.   Operations Management   8.   Cash Flow Management
9.   Website Design   10.   Start-up Capital Investment
11. Technical Expertise

4.7.1   Porter's Five Forces Analysis

We will use Porter's five forces analysis as a framework for the industry analysis and business strategy development. It will be used to derive the five forces which determine the competitive intensity and therefore attractiveness of our market. Attractiveness in this context refers to the overall industry profitability.

Competitors The degree of rivalry is high in this segment, but less when compared to the overall category. There are _____ (#) major competitors in the _____ area and they include: _____
Threat of Substitutes
            Substitutes are high for this industry. These include other background checking companies, online search providers, etc.
Bargaining Power of Buyers

Buyer power is moderate in the business. Buyers are sensitive to quality, Integrity, privacy, legality, and pricing as the segment attempts to capitalize on the pricing and quality advantage.

Bargaining Power of Suppliers

Supplier power is moderate in the industry. Resource can be obtained from a number of vendors. A high level of operational efficiency for managing resources and supplies can be achieved.

Threat of New Entrants

Relatively high in this segment. The business model can be easily copied.

Conclusions: _____ (company name) is in a competitive field and has to move fast to retain its competitive advantage. The key success factors are to develop operational efficiencies, innovative programs, cost-effective marketing and customer service excellence.

4.8   Competitive Analysis

Competitor analysis in marketing and strategic management is an assessment of the strengths and weaknesses of current and potential competitors. This analysis will provide both an offensive and defensive strategic context through which to identify our business opportunities and threats. We will carry out continual competitive analysis to ensure our market is not being eroded by developments in other firms. This analysis needs to be matched with the target segment needs to ensure that our products and services continue to provide better value than the competitors. The competitive analysis needs to be able to show very clearly why our products and services are preferred in some market segments to other offerings and to be able to offer reasonable proof of that assertion.

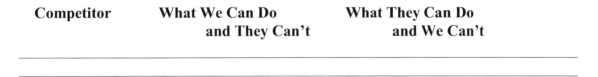

Competitor	What We Can Do and They Can't	What They Can Do and We Can't

Competition in this industry is very high, because the majority of industry operators provide similar services. The U.S. Background check industry is forecast to earn $2 billion in yearly revenue with an annual growth of 2.2 percent over the next 10 to 15 years.

Competitive factors include industry knowledge, customer service, expense management, marketing programs, employee training and productivity, management of information databases, extended hours of operation, turnaround speed, service packaging, customer loyalty programs, pricing, and branded reputation.

We will conduct good market intelligence for the following reasons:
1.   To forecast competitors' strategies.
2.   To predict competitor likely reactions to our own strategies.
3.   To consider how competitors' behavior can be influenced in our own favor.

Overall competition in the area is _____ (weak/moderate/strong).

Competitive analysis conducted by the company owners has shown that there are _____ (# or no other?) background check service providers currently offering the same combination of products and services in the _____ (city) area. However, the existing competitors offer only a limited range of traditional services. In fact, of these, _____ (# or none) of the competitors offered a range of services and packaged offerings comparable with what _____ (company name) plans to offer to its clients.

Self-assessment

Competitive Rating Assessment: **1 = Weak ....5 = Strong**

	Our Company	Prime Competitor	Compare
Our Location	_____	_____	_____
Our Facilities	_____	_____	_____
Our Services and Amenities	_____	_____	_____
Our Management Skills	_____	_____	_____
Our Training Programs	_____	_____	_____
Our Research & Development	_____	_____	_____
Our Company Culture	_____	_____	_____
Our Business Model	_____	_____	_____
Overall Rating	_____	_____	_____

Rationale: _____

The following businesses are considered direct competitors:

Competitor	Address	Market Share	Primary Focus	Secondary Prod/Svcs	Strengths	Weaknesses

Indirect Competitors include the following:

_____

_____

Alternative Competitive Matrix

Competitor Name:	Us	_____	_____	_____
Location:		_____	_____	_____

Comparison Items:

Sales Revenue	_____
Growth Rate	_____
Product Focus	_____
Product Range	_____
Membership Programs	_____
Profitability	_____

Market Share _____

Brand Names _____

Specialty _____

Services _____

Capitalization _____

Target Markets _____

Service Area _____

Open Days _____

Operating Hours _____

Operating Policies _____

Turnaround Time _____

Payment Options _____

Other Financing _____

Pricing Strategy _____

Price Level L/M/H _____

Economies of Scale _____

Volume Discounts _____

Yrs in Business _____

Reputation _____

Customer Loyalty _____

Reliability _____

Quality _____

Marketing Strategy _____

Marketing Goals _____

Innovation Strategy _____

Methods of Promotion _____

Alliances _____

Brochure/Catalog _____

Website _____

Sales Revenues _____

No. of Staff _____

Key Competitive Advantage _____

Credit Policies _____

Comments _____

Competitor Profile Matrix

Critical Success Factors	Our Score	Competitor 1 Rating	Score	Competitor 2 Rating	Score	Competitor 3 Rating	Score
Advertising							
Product Quality							
Price Competition							
Management							
Financial Position							
Customer Loyalty							
Brand Identity							
Market Share							

Total _____

We will use the following sources of info to conduct our competition analysis:
1.   Competitor company websites.
2.   Mystery shopper visits.
3.   Annual Reports   (www.annual reports.com)
4.   Thomas Net   (www.thomasnet.com)
5.   Trade Journals
6.   Trade Associations
7.   Sales representative interviews
8.   Research & Development may come across new patents.
9.   Market research can give feedback on the customer's perspective
10. Monitoring services will track a company or industry you select for news.
     Resources: www.portfolionews.com   www.Office.com
11. Hoover's   www.hoovers.com
12. www.zapdata.com   (Dun and Bradstreet) You can buy one-off lists here.
13. www.infousa.com   (The largest, and they resell to many other vendors)
14. www.onesource.com (By subscription, pull information from many sources)
15. www.capitaliq.com   (Standard and Poors).
16. Obtain industry specific information from First Research
     (www.firstresearch.com) or IBISWorld, both are by subscription only,
     although you may be able to buy just one report.
17. Get industry financial ratios and industry norms from RMA or by using
     ProfitCents.com software.
18. Company newsletters
19. Industry Consultants
20. Local Suppliers and Distributors
21. Customer interviews regarding competitors.
22. Analyze competitors' ads for their target audience, market position, product
     features, benefits, prices, etc.
23. Attend speeches or presentations made by representatives of your competitors.
24. View competitor's trade show display from potential customer's point of view.
25. Search computer databases (available at many public libraries).
26. Review competitor Yellow Book Ads.
27. www.bls.gov/cex/ (site provides information on consumer expenditures
     nationally, regionally, and by selected metropolitan areas).
28. www.sizeup.com
29. Business Statistics and Financial Ratios   www.bizstats.com

4.9 Market Revenue Projection

For each of our chosen target markets, we will estimate our market share in number of customers, and based on consumer behavior, how often do they buy per year? What is the average dollar amount of each purchase? We will then multiply these three numbers to project sales volume for each target market.

Target Market	Number of Customers		No. of Purchases per Year	Average Dollar Amount per Purchase		Total Sales Volume
	A	x	B	x	C	=	D

_____

_____

Using the target market number identified in this section, and the local demographics, we have made the following assessments regarding market opportunity and revenue potential in our area: **Potential Revenue Opportunity** =

	_____	Local No. of Businesses
(x)	_____	Expected ___% Market Share
(=)	_____	Number of likely local customers
(x)	$ _____	Average annual sales dollar amount per customer
(=)	$ _____	Annual Revenue Opportunity.

Or

	No. of Clients Per Day	(x)	Avg. Sale	(=)	Daily Income
Services	_____		_____		_____
Product Sales	_____		_____		_____
Other	_____		_____		_____
Total:					
Annualized:				(x)	250
Annual Revenue Potential:					_____

Recap:

Month   Jan Feb Mar Apr May Jun Jul Aug Sep Oct Nov Dec   Total

Products/Services

_____

_____

_____

Gross Sales: _____

(-) Returns   _____

Net Sales   _____

Revenue Assumptions:

1. The sources of information for our revenue projection are:

_____

2. If the total market demand for our product/service = 100%, our projected sales volume represents _____% of this total market.

3. The following factors might lower our revenue projections:

_____

5.0   Industry Analysis

SIC Code:	7375	Information Retrieval Services
NAICS Code:	514199	Computer Systems Design Services

The $4 billion business of background screening is booming. Companies large and small are sorting mostly mid- and lower-level job applicants based on information compiled by hundreds of background checking companies. Background screening has become a highly profitable corner of the HR world.

Some employers have grown more vigilant about hiring since the September 11 terrorist attacks. Others like the efficiency and cost-effectiveness of outsourcing tasks once handled by in-house human resources departments. Whatever their motives, employers are becoming more dependent on mass-produced background reports.

In a 2004 study by the Society for Human Resource Management, 96% of personnel executives said their companies conduct background checks on job candidates, up from 51% in 1996. Two-thirds of larger companies say they outsource screening, and many now vet current employees in addition to applicants.

Over the last three years, there have been over 50 publicized transactions in the background screening industry. There are a number of active, "willing" buyers and the industry is poised for continued consolidation. A few characteristics that are driving the consolidation include: high growth, fragmentation, and the inherent competitive advantages of a larger company.

Most background screening companies are bullish on the future growth of the industry. In a recent KPMG Corporate Finance LLC survey of companies in the background screening industry, nearly all respondents expected revenue to increase over the next 12 months, and 40% expect revenue to increase more than 25%. Over the past few years, the awareness of the value of screening has increased substantially and more companies are requiring screening as part of the new hiring process.

The industry is highly fragmented and can be characterized by a barbell shape. There are a small number of larger providers (only four companies have screening revenue in excess of $100 million), a limited number of mid-size companies (less than 30 companies have revenue over $10 million in screening revenue) and a large number of small companies. In fact, the majority of companies have screening revenues less than $2 million.

Larger and mid-sized screening companies have a competitive advantage over the smaller companies. Larger and mid-sized firms have the ability to leverage investments in technology, infrastructure, personnel, compliance, and marketing and can compete more effectively for the larger corporate clients. These firms have a proven track record and are considered the "safer" vendor choice. As a result, to be successful, smaller companies will increasingly focus on a core group of customer relationships or become a niche service provider.

Current acquisition activity is being driven by firms trying to:
1.   Expand and bundle complementary software and other HR services with screening services.
2.   Expand the range of existing business footprint via geography, services, or customer base.

The positive outlook for the industry, the fragmented nature of the industry and the competitive benefits of being a larger company, will result in continued consolidation.

In the five years to 2018, IBISWorld estimates that revenue for the Background Check Services industry will decrease at an average rate of 0.2% per year to $3.7 billion. The decline is largely the result poor performance during the recession, with revenue falling 7.6% and 2.6% in 2009 and 2010, respectively. According to IBISWorld, "Rising unemployment reduced the need for businesses to screen for job candidates while an increase in rental vacancy rates diminished demand from apartment leasing companies." Luckily for industry operators, slow improvement in the labor market and a decline in rental vacancy rates have since boosted demand for background check services. As a result, IBISWorld estimates that industry revenue will increase 3.3% in 2018.

Over the past decade, the internet has been the primary driver for the industry's growth. Traditionally, background check services were largely manual. However, the internet has streamlined and automated many of the processes performed by hand. This factor caused a significant number of firms to enter the industry during the past decade. However, this market saturation, coupled with the fall in demand from the recession, caused industry profit to decline, prompting a period of consolidation within the industry. IBISWorld estimates that the number of firms operating in the industry will decline at an annualized rate of 0.1% to 3,635 in the five years to 2018.

In 2018, the four largest firms are expected to account for about 10.0% of the Background Check Services industry's revenue, indicating a low level of market share concentration. Historically, industry operators required considerable expertise to conduct investigations and detailed background checks. However, the growth of online technology over the past decade has provided an opportunity for firms to enter this industry. According to the National Association of Professional Background Screeners, most industry operators are small firms focused on aggregating public records. Less than 2.0% of industry firms are large background screening providers that operate at a national or international level. Over the past five years, market share concentration has marginally increased due to some consolidation among leading industry firms. For instance, Sterling Infosystems' 2011 acquisition of Axciom's background screening business doubled the market share of one of the larger firms in this industry.

IBISWorld expects that industry revenue will increase in the five years to 2020. During that time, industry operators will benefit from slow but steady improvement in the labor market. Businesses will turn to industry operators as they hire more employees. This factor will be bolstered by an increasing number of cities and counties that have enacted laws banning companies from asking applicants whether or not they have been convicted of a crime. However, strong growth will be mitigated by an increase in vacancy rates, which will diminish demand from apartment leasing companies.

Source: http://www.prweb.com/releases/2018/2/prweb10481030.htm

5.1   Industry Leaders

We plan to study the best practices of industry leaders and adapt certain selected practices to our business model concept. Best practices are those methods or techniques resulting in increased customer satisfaction when incorporated into the operation.

ChoicePoint   **www.choicepoint.com**
The largest screening firm for corporate employers in the U.S. Based in Atlanta, ChoicePoint checks applicants for more than half of the country's 100 biggest companies, including Bank of America, UnitedHealth Group, and United Parcel Service. The company conducts 10 million background checks annually and estimates it has about 20% of the U.S. market.

USIS   **www.usis.com**
It screens government workers and runs an employment-history database used by 2,500 transport companies called Drive-A-Check, or DAC. Serves Pentagon and other federal agencies as well as transportation and retail companies. Providence Equity Partners bought USIS for $1.5 billion.

First Advantage   **www.fadv.com**
Has major clients in manufacturing and financial services. In February it acquired a screening firm in Malaysia to serve multinationals in Asia.

Kroll Background Screening   **www.kroll.com**
Has clients in the health-care, energy, and entertainment industries. Formed in 1999 after Kroll bought a firm called Background America.

SentryLink   **www.sentrylink.com**
Provides criminal background checks, employment screening, driving records and other information to help businesses hire safely. We are FCRA compliant and offer instant results for criminal records, MVRs and credit reports. Please contact us for help with your employee background checks.

Advanced Background Check, Inc.   **www.abcheck.com**
Meeting the wholesale needs of the employment screening industry, Advanced Background Check is a timely, accurate and cost-effective provider of nationwide courthouse information. In addition to criminal searches, offers a wide array of services.

IntelliCorp Records, Inc.   **www.intellicorp.net**
IntelliCorp's Service Partner division provides wholesale instant criminal data, flexible integration solutions, and a dedicated account team. With IntelliCorp's breadth and depth of data, you get what you pay for.

KnowX   **www.knowx.com/index.jsp**
Owned by research behemoth LexisNexis, KnowX was established in 1997. Offering individual and commercial consumers a myriad of services, a basic background check

from this firm, costs $24.95. All information is available to customers via its web portal.

US Search
Founded in 1994, US Search calls itself the leader in people search and background check service. Background checks from this provider are initiated through its website. The organization guarantees that results are emailed to the purchaser within 24 hours. Available to both businesses and corporations, a basic background screening costs, according to TopTenReview.com in 2010, $39.95. US Search is headquartered in Culver City, California.

CrimCheck   https://crimcheck.net/
Based in Berea, Ohio, more than 3,500 companies have engaged their background check services since 1991. Allowing companies and individuals to order background screenings via the web or over the telephone, this organization announced in 2010 that it has partnered with business software provider TALEO. The goal of the partnership is for the company's services to be usable on a computer interface that is used by many firms across the country. According to TopTenReview.com in 2010, CrimCheck's services start at a rate of $29.95. Specializes in background screening for the Advertising, Marketing and Public Relations industries. Major advertising and marketing firms as well as those in the PR industry utilize Crimcheck to screen their employees, film candidates, vendors and contract workers.
Source:
https://crimcheck.net/industries/advertising-marketing-and-public-relations-industry-
        background-checks

eFindOuttheTruth
Established in 2002, the company bills itself as the "Background Check Superstore." Offering a variety of background screening packages to corporate and individual clients via the web, TopTenReview.com reported in 2010 that the firm's service fee starts as $14.95. In June 2010, however, eFindOuttheTruth offered customers a special low rate of $10 for a basic screening. In addition to background checks, this organization also sells various spy gadgets, including voice changers and vehicle GPS tracking devices.

Intelius
A Bellevue, Washington-based corporation, whose mission is to intelligently integrate information online for personal security and to inform the decision-making process." Offering a multitude of background screening solutions geared toward both individuals and businesses, TopTenReview.com indicated in 2010 that the starting rate for this organization's services is $49.95. Each of the products offered by Intelius is available through its online portal.

Criminal Searches   www.CriminalSearches.com

Search Systems   http://publicrecords.searchsystems.net/
Resource: http://background-check-services-review.toptenreviews.com/

Social Intelligence   www.socialintel.com/

A Riv Data Corp. company, this is the leading provider of social media screening and research solutions to a wide range of industries. This company scrapes the Internet for everything prospective employees may have said or done online in the past seven years. Then it assembles a dossier with examples of professional honors and charitable work, along with negative information that meets specific criteria: online evidence of racist remarks; references to drugs; sexually explicit photos, text messages or videos; flagrant displays of weapons or bombs and clearly identifiable violent activity. Their goal is to conduct pre-employment screenings that would help companies meet their obligation to conduct fair and consistent hiring practices while protecting the privacy of job candidates. Their reports remove references to a person's religion, race, marital status, disability and other information protected under federal employment laws, which companies are not supposed to ask about during interviews. Also, job candidates must first consent to the background check, and they are notified of any adverse information found. The searches are designed to reduce the risk that employers may confuse the job candidate with someone else or expose the company to information that is not legally allowable or relevant. The research comes from such major social platforms as Facebook, Twitter and MySpace, and comments on blogs and posts on smaller social sites, like Tumblr, the blogging site, as well as Yahoo user groups, e-commerce sites, bulletin boards and even Craigslist.

Info Registry   www.inforegistry.com
Accurate Background   www.accuratebackground.com
ADP   www.adp.com

Sterling Infosystems   www.sterlinginfosystems.com

One of the largest players in the criminal-background-check business. Its employees sift reams of court records, on behalf of clients ranging from Wal-Mart to Walt Disney, to suss out which job applicants or employees have a record of violent crime, drug dealing or other felonious behavior.

Sterling Talent Solutions   www.sterlingtalentsolutions.com/

A pre-employment background screening company that was founded in 1975 and based in New York, has 4,000 employees in 20 offices globally, including a large presence in Manhattan and in Greater Seattle.

Worldbox Business Intelligence   www.worldbox.net

An independent service, providing online company credit reports, company profiles, company ownership and management reports, legal status and history details as well as financial and other business information on over 50 million companies worldwide, covering all emerging and major markets.

My Background Check   http://mybackgroundcheck.preemploy.com/

Small businesses have the advantage of ordering enterprise quality background checks without the obligation of long term commitments and high contract minimums at affordable prices. They offer small '10' quantity packages with the searches designed for small businesses so users can order when they need them, and order based on their unique hiring schedule. Pre-employ packages must be purchased in bundles of 10. So, rather than paying for background checks one at a time, users have to pay for all 10 up- front. However, the checks don't have to be completed all at once, and they never expire.

Deverus, Inc.   **www.deverus.com**

This company stepping forward and addressing the issue of uptime standards head-on. They're investing significantly in a new, expanded infrastructure, including a second redundant, co-located data center in Dallas that company officials say will help them set new benchmarks for uptime, auditability, and disaster preparedness previously unheard of in the background check industry. Employers and background check companies run almost a million background checks per month using online solutions from deverus, which continuously strives to set new industry standards for system uptime, quality of service, and client support.

E-Renter   **www.e-renter.com**

A Consumer Reporting Agency. We have 24/7 online direct access to consumer and business credit files as well as many other databases for credit, criminal, eviction, driving records, property deed records, assessor records, etc. E-Renter services are used by: Individual landlords, Property management companies, Tenant screening companies Businesses who need employee screening, and Businesses extending credit to consumers

HireRight   **www.hireright.com**

Specializes in helping organizations of all sizes and locations efficiently implement, manage and control their screening programs.

Checkr   **www.checkr.com**

A leading software-based background screening company, serving more than 3000 organizations worldwide. Companies like Uber, Zenefits, and Warby Parker rely on Checkr to deliver background checks with an unparalleled combination of speed, accuracy, and compliance. Accredited by the National Association of Professional Background Screeners (NAPBS), Checkr is a privately held company headquartered in San Francisco, CA.

Resources:
www.businessnewsdaily.com/7638-best-background-check-services.html
www.fundera.com/blog/best-background-check-sites
www.hrotoday.com/uncategorized/4914/

5.2   Key Industry Statistics

1.   Research indicates that of the companies who conduct screening, 81 percent verify education, 79 percent check previous employment, 59 percent check references, 37 percent look into criminal records and 21 percent inspect motor vehicle records.

2.	According to Right Management, replacing a bad hire can cost a company as much as five times the employee's annual salary in recruitment, training, severance and lost productivity.
3.	According to the U.S. Chamber of Commerce, dishonest employees can cost a business up to two percent of its gross sales.
4.	More than 80 percent of U.S. businesses currently perform typical employer background checks, according to the Society of Human Resource Management.
5.	More than half of the resumes received by businesses may contain exaggerated or fraudulent information and/or significant omissions.
6.	Embezzlement costs commerce about $4 Billion dollars a year.
7.	Over 30% of all business failures are the result of negligent hiring practices.
8.	Of the negligent hiring cases that go to trial, 66% result in jury awards averaging more than $600,000.
9.	The Small Business Administration reports that for every dollar an employer invests in personnel screening, they save between five to sixteen dollars in reduced absenteeism, productivity, turnover, safety, insurance, and in employer liability.
10.	The Association of Certified Fraud Examiners estimates that occupational fraud and abuse costs organizations about $600 billion annually, or roughly 6% of gross revenues.
11.	On average, states are unable to account for 24% of registered sex offenders.
12.	According to the U.S. Postal Service, those who fail a pre-employment drug test are 77% more likely to be discharged from employment within 1 year.
13.	The FBI performed nearly 2.8 million background checks on people wanting to buy guns in December, a record month that capped a record year in 2018.
14.	 The most popular searches being performed are criminal searches (97%), identity checks (81%) and previous employment or reference checks (58%).
	Source:
	www.biia.com/employment-screening-critical-to-success-of-small-businesses
15.	The Department of Labor in the US calculates a bad hire can exceed 30% of an employee's annual wage, so someone hired by a small firm at $50,000 annually could end up costing them more than $15,000.

Resources:
https://www.hireright.com/resources/industry-fast-facts

5.3   Industry Trends

We will determine the trends that are impacting our consumers and indicate ways in which our customers' needs are changing and any relevant social, technical or other changes that will impact our target market. Keeping up with trends and reports will help management to carve a niche for our business, stay ahead of the competition and deliver products that our customers need and want.

1.	About 42% of Best-in-Class organizations cite that one of the top two ways their onboarding process will change in 2009 is automation.

2. Projected growth in technology adoption among Best-in-Class organizations will center mostly on tools that leverage data collected in the pre-hire phase in order to pre-populate new employee forms. The automation of forms and tasks management will provide immediate benefits in terms of time savings, data accuracy, and overall readiness.

3. Executive-level background checks are becoming increasingly more popular.

4. ScreeningWorks, a new Web-based tenant screening solution for independent rental owners (IROs) and managers from RentGrow Inc offers access to comprehensive and affordable background screening that improves their decision-making process for finding the most qualified tenants.

5. Industry insiders credit the 9/11 attacks and several high-profile court cases for the growing demand for screeners.

6. As a result of the recession and higher unemployment, it is likely that employers will need to scrutinize applications even more carefully, to be on the watch for fraudulent credentials, such as inflated or fictional employment history or educational degrees

7. The non-profit trade organization for the screening Industry, the National Association of Professional Background Screeners has announced the introduction of an accreditation program.

8. International background checks are becoming very accessible to employers.

9. There has been a seamless integration of Applicant Tracking Systems background screening systems.

10. There has been an increase in the number of class action lawsuits against screening firms, particularly when it comes to various notices required under the federal Fair Credit Reporting Act, and accuracy requirements in the federal law.

11. Increased requirements by federal and state governments for more background checks in sensitive industries, such as child care workers and health workers.

12. There has been a big increase in the number of Background Checks for people seeking gun permits

13. Lawmakers are seeking to require background checks on private gun sales, and purchases at firearms shows.

14. Lawmakers are seeking to require background checks for all public and private school teachers, employees and workers at licensed early education centers, with fingerprints to be matched against a federal database.

15. Employers have started scouring the web—social networking sites in particular—to check up on potential hires.

16. More companies are conducting free background checks using social media sites and personal online databases.
Resources:
http://www.digitaltrends.com/social-media/how-to-run-a-free-background-check/
Examples:
http://www.zabasearch.com/

17. The industry is trending towards one-stop shopping, offering pre-employment drug and alcohol testing as well as education verification, fingerprinting, credit and driving history reports, INS verification, and background checks for criminal

or terrorist activities.

18. With the growing economy and tight competition, larger firms showing a renewed emphasis on attempting to acquire market share by acquisitions.

19. This industry is attracting more technologists who have experience in working with 'big data' systems.

20. Over the last few years, regulators at federal, state, and municipal level have moved to pass and implement new laws and rules to govern background checks and to safeguard the privacy of individuals.

21. The need to guard against poor background checks and inaccurate data is pushing business and individuals away from conducting their internal background screening.

22. A growing number of businesses and individuals are looking to make the background screening a continual process and are engaging in periodic re-checks of already screened individuals to identify people who have committed offenses since the last screening process.

23. More companies are now opting to outsource the process of background screening to professionals or qualified vendors so as to transfer litigation risks and also for the purposes of complying with the FCRA current practices and regulations.
Source: www.gethppy.com/hrtrends/top-5-background-screening-trends

24. There has been an increasing number of FCRA class-action lawsuits against employers over alleged violations that could have easily been avoided by a careful review of disclosure and authorization forms and processes.
Sources:
www.shrm.org/resourcesandtools/hr-topics/talent-acquisition/pages/2016-
    employment-screening-trends.aspx
www.hiresafe.com/top-5-background-check-trends-2016-background-check-
    compliance/

Resources:
http://www.esrcheck.com/ESR-Top-Ten-Background-Check-Trends
https://www.paycor.com/resource-center/background-check-strategies-and-trends
https://easybackgrounds.com/five-background-screening-trends-that-will-impact-hiring-
    in-2018/

5.4   Industry Key Terms

We will use the following term definitions to help our company to understand and speak the language of our industry.

Adverse Action Letter
If a company denies a position of employment based on the supplied report from a background check company, this constitutes adverse action. In this case, the organization has an obligation to provide the applicant with a notification of the decision, a copy of the report, a copy of the applicant's consumer rights, and information on the supplier of the consumer report.

Background Checks
Can access a full range of data including: credit records, academic records, social security number, personal references, driving records, criminal records, workers' compensation.

Ban-the-box Laws
These policies are named as such because they mandate the removal of application questions that pertain to criminal history. These laws or ordinances can exist on city, county or state levels and usually stipulate when in the employment process you can run a background check. We will research the laws in our area to determine whether or not we are beholden to ban-the-box laws.

The Fair Credit Reporting Act (FCRA)
Under the FCRA, a business is required to have employees sign a disclosure form granting authorization to perform a background check. The FCRA is not just restricted to credit reports but includes all "consumer reports." Laws will vary from state to state in how and what information can be used during the pre-employment screening process. For instance, your state laws may prohibit using certain aspects of a criminal record during a background check. Your state may have different laws, such as California's Investigative Consumer Reporting Agencies Act. Consult with local regulators and legal counsel before going too deep into the criminal past of a new hire.
Resource:
https://www.adpselect.com/pdf/ADPFairCreditReportingActWhitePaper.pdf

The American With Disabilities Act (ADA)
The Equal Employment Opportunity Commission (EEOC) defines a disability as a person who: has a physical or mental impairment that substantially limits one or more major life activities; has a record of such an impairment; or is regarded as having such an impairment. Under ADA, employers are restricted in using medical or disability data in the hiring process. Simply put, you cannot ask during the interview or background check about a person's disabilities. The ADA covers businesses with 15 or more employees, including state and local governments.

Employment-at-Will
The employee may leave at any time and that the employer may terminate the employee at any time, whether for cause or not. Employment-at-will statements are designed to make sure that the business is not creating or implying that an employment contract will be created, should the applicant be hired.

Employee Onboarding
This is the process of introducing new employees to your company in an organized and effective manner.

Expungement
A legal process that involves an individual submitting a formal request to a judge asking to seal part or all his/her criminal record so cannot be viewed by the general public. If a

record is expunged and a background check is completed, it should not appear on the report because it is no longer a conviction.

Hard Inquiry

Provides more detailed information to the creditor and typically requires consent because it requires a social security number. When a person applies for credit or a loan, signing the loan application provides consent to the lender to pull a credit report, or perform a hard inquiry.

Negligent Hiring

A legal doctrine whereby an employer is responsible for the negligent or destructive actions of an employee when due diligence--such as conducting background checks-- would have revealed the employee's propensity to commit such actions.

Personally Identifiable Information (PII)

Includes information such as name, birth date, and Social Security number (SSN).

Pre-employment Screening

The process of using psychometric testing, background checks, and drug testing to determine the background and identity of hiring a new employee

Soft Inquiry

Generally, occurs when a prospective employer is conducting a background check. A soft inquiry also occurs when a creditor is pre-screening candidates for special offers. For example, all those pre-approved credit card applications that come in the mail are generated from soft inquiries. Soft inquiries can occur without consent or knowledge. If a person pulls their own credit report, this also shows as a soft inquiry.

Resources:

https://www.hireright.com/resources/screening-glossary

6.0 Strategy and Implementation Summary

Exclusivity within _____ (complex/community name) is a significant competitive edge. It gives _____ (company name) geographic and protected domain as the most convenient source of fine wines and spirits for over _____ (#) current residents.

Our sales strategy is based on serving our niche markets better than the competition and leveraging our competitive advantages. These advantages include superior attention to understanding and satisfying customer needs and wants, creating a one-stop HR solution, and packaged value pricing. The objectives of our marketing strategy will be to recruit new customers, retain existing customers, get good customers to spend more and return more frequently. Establishing a loyal customer base is very important because such core customers will not only generate the most lifetime sales, but also valuable referrals.

We will generate word-of-mouth buzz through direct-mail campaigns, exceeding customer expectations, developing a Web site, getting involved in community events with local businesses, and donating our services to local non-profit organizations in exchange for press release coverage. Our sales strategy will seek to convert potential and first-time customers into long-term relationships and referral agents. The combination of our competitive advantages, targeted marketing campaign and networking activities, will enable _____ (company name) to continue increasing our market share.

6.1.0   Promotion Strategy

Promotion strategies will be focused to the target market segment. Given the importance of word-of-mouth and referrals, we shall strive to efficiently service all our customers to gain their business regularly, which is the recipe for our long-term success. We shall focus on direct business marketing, publicity, educational seminars, and advertising as proposed. Our promotion strategy will focus on generating referrals from existing clients, demonstrating our community involvement, generating volume sales of basic services, encouraging trial of new services and upgrading customers to new membership status.

Our promotional strategies will also make use of the following tools:
- **Advertising**
  - Yearly anniversary parties to celebrate the success of each year.
  - Yellow Pages ads in the book and online.
  - Flyers promoting special promotion events.
  - Doorknob hangers, if not prohibited by neighborhood associations.
  - Banners to promote a themed promotional event.

- **Local Marketing / Public Relations**
  - Client raffle for gift certificates or discount coupons
  - Participation in local civic groups.
  - Press release coverage of our sponsoring of events at the local Chamber of Commerce.
  - Article submissions to magazines describing the benefits of background

checks.

    O Sales Brochure to convey our program specialties to prospective customers.

    0 Seminar presentations to local civic and business groups, explaining how to evaluate screening vendors.

- **Local Media**
  - o Direct Mail - We will send quarterly postcards and annual direct mailings to businesses within a ___ (50?) mile radius of our offices. It will contain an explanation of the benefits of our background check services.
  - o Radio Campaign - We will make "live on the air" presentations of our trial service coupons to the disk jockeys, hoping to get the promotions broadcasted to the listening audience. We will also make our HR expertise available for talk radio programs.
  - o Newspaper Campaign - Placing several ads in local community newspapers and business journals to launch our initial campaign. We will include a trial coupon.
  - o Website – We will collect email addresses for a monthly newsletter.
  - o Cable TV advertising on local community-based shows focused on business programming.

6.1.1   Grand Opening

Our Grand Opening celebration will be a very important promotion opportunity to create word-of-mouth advertising results. We will advertise the date of our grand opening in local newspapers and on local radio.

We will do the following things to make the open house a successful event:
1. Enlist local business support to contribute a large number of door prizes.
2. Use a sign-in sheet to create an email/mailing list.
3. Sponsor a _____ competition.
4. Schedule appearance by local celebrities.
5. Create a festive atmosphere with balloons, beverages and music.
6. Get the local radio station to broadcast live from the event and handout fun gifts.
7. Offer an application fee waiver.
8. Giveaway our logo imprinted T-shirts as a contest prize.
9. Allow potential customers to view your facility and ask questions.
10. Print promotional flyers and pay a few kids to distribute them locally.
11. Arrange for face painting, storytelling, clowns, and snacks for everyone.
12. Arrange for local politician to do the official opening ceremony so all the local newspapers came to take pictures and do a feature story.
13. Arrange that people can tour our facility on the open day in order to see our facilities, collect sales brochures and find out more about our services.
14. Allocate staff members to perform specific duties, handout business cards and sales brochures and instruct them to deal with any questions or queries.

16. Organize a drawing with everyone writing their name and phone numbers on the back of business cards and give a voucher as a prize to start a marketing list.
17. Hand out trial coupons.

6.1.2   Value Proposition

Our value proposition will summarize why a consumer should use our services. We will enable quick access to our broad line of quality and innovative services. Our value proposition will convince prospects that our services will add more value and better solve their need for a convenient, one-stop background check service.

We will use this value proposition statement to target customers who will benefit most from using our services. These are businesses that need to conduct pre-employment and ongoing background checks and landlords who need to pre-screen tenant applicants.

Our screening solution must meet the following strategic benchmarks to support our value proposition:
1. Leverage the latest and best screening technologies.
2. Capture a comprehensive range of information, some of which is difficult to access and integrate.
3. Deliver the information quickly to key internal decision-makers.
4. Be easy to read, understand and use by virtually any appropriately authorized manager in the organization.

Our value proposition will be concise and appeal to the customer's strongest decision-making drivers, which are one-stop convenience for all hiring processes, time response quickness, accuracy and reliability, delivered with unparalleled customer service support.

Recap of Our Value Proposition:
Trust – We are known as a trusted business partner with strong customer and vendor endorsements. We have earned a reputation for quality, integrity, and delivery of comprehensive background checks.
Quality – We offer _____ experience and extensive professional backgrounds in _____ at competitive rates.
Experience – Our ability to bring people with ___ (#) years of _____ experience with deep technical knowledge is at the core of our success.
True Vendor Partnerships – Our true vendor partnerships enable us to offer the resources of much larger organizations with greater flexibility.
Customer Satisfaction and Commitment to Success – Through partnering with our customers and delivering quality solutions, we have been able to achieve an impressive degree of repeat and referral business. Since _____ (year), more than _____% of our business activity is generated by existing customers. Our philosophy is that "our customer's satisfaction is our success." Our success will be measured in terms of our customer's satisfaction survey scores and testimonials.

6.1.3   Positioning Statement

We will create a positioning statement for our company that describes what distinguishes our business from the competition. We will keep it simple, memorable and snappy. We will test our positioning statement to make certain that it appeals to our target audience. We will continue to refine it until it speaks directly to our targeted customer wants, needs and aspirations. We will use our positioning statement in every written communication to customers. This will ensure that our message is consistent and comes across loud and clear. We will create quality image marketing materials that communicate our positioning.

Our positioning strategy will be the result of conducting in-depth consumer market research to find out what benefits customers want and how our background check services can meet those needs. Many service-oriented professions are leaning toward differentiating themselves on the basis of convenience. This is also what we intend to do. For instance, we plan to have extended, "people" hours via our online chat and discussion forums and to develop a platform that supports all HR hiring processes.

We will specialize in providing an industry leading, customizable, best-in-class set of background screening services that address business and consumer needs either being poorly met or not met at all by branded providers of mass-market background screening solutions.

We also plan to develop specialized services that will enable us to pursue a niche focus on specific interest-based programs, such as business background checks for investors and customers. These objectives will position us at the _____ (mid-level/high-end) of the market and will allow the company to realize a healthy profit margin in relation to its low-end, discount rivals and achieve long-term growth.

Market Positioning Recap
Price: The strategy is to offer competitive prices that are lower that the market leader yet set to indicate value and worth.
Quality: The background check quality will have to be very good as the finished service results will be showcased in highly visible situations.
Service: Highly individualized and customized service will be the key to success in this type of business. Personal attention to the customers will result in higher sales and word of mouth advertising.

6.1.4   Unique Selling Proposition (USP)

Our unique selling proposition will answer the question why a customer should choose to do business with our company versus any and every other option available to them in the marketplace. Our USP will be a description of a unique important benefit that our Background Check Service offers to customers, so that price is no longer the key to our sales.

Our USP will include the following:
Who our target audience is: _____
What we will do for them: _____
What qualities, skills, talents, traits do we possess that others do not: _____
What are the benefits we provide that no one else offers: _____
Why that is different from what others are offering: _____
Why that solution matters to our target audience: _____

6.1.5   Distribution Strategy

Customers can contact the _____ (company name) by telephone, fax, internet and by dropping in. Our nearest competitors are ____ (#) miles away in either direction. We will also stock request items for regular area residents.

Our customers will have the following access points:
1.   **Order by Phone**
       Customers can contact us 24 hours a day, 7days a week at _____.
       Our Customer Service Representatives will be available to assist customers
       Monday through Friday from ____ a.m. to ____ p.m. EST.
2.   **Order by Fax**
       Customers may fax their orders to _____ anytime.
       They must provide: Account number, Billing and shipping address, Purchase
       order number, if applicable, Name and telephone number, Product
       number/description, Unit of measure and quantity ordered and Applicable sales
       promotion source codes.
3.   **Order Online**
       Customers can order online at www._____.com.Once the account is
       activated, customers will be able to place orders, browse the catalog, check stock
       availability and pricing, check order status and view both order and transaction
       history.
4.   **In-person**
       All customers can be serviced in person at our facilities Monday through Friday
       from ____ a.m. to ____ p.m. EST.

We plan to pursue the following distribution channels: (select)

		Number	Reason Chosen	Sales Costs
1.	Our own retail outlets			
2.	Independent retail outlets			
3.	Chain store retail outlets			
4.	Wholesale outlets			
5.	Independent distributors			
6.	Independent commissioned sales reps			
7.	In-house sales reps			

8. Direct mail using own catalog or flyers _____

9. Catalog broker agreement _____

10. In-house telemarketing _____

11. Contracted telemarketing call center _____

12. Cybermarketing via own website _____

13. Online sales via amazon, eBay, etc. _____

14. TV and Cable Direct Marketing _____

6.1.6   Sales Rep Plan

We will use sales reps to pursue business from major corporations across the country.

1. In-house or Independent   _____

2. Salaried or Commissioned   _____

3. Salary or Commission Rate   _____

4. Salary Plus Commission Rate   _____

5. Special Performance Incentives   _____

6. Negotiating Parameters   Price Breaks/Added Services/
                                            _____

7. Performance Evaluation Criteria   No. of New Customers/Sales Volume/
                                            _____

8. Number of Reps   _____

9. Sales Territory Determinants   Geography/Demographics/
                                            _____

10. Sales Territories Covered   _____

11. Training Program Overview   _____

12. Training Program Cost   _____

13. Sales Kit Contents   _____

14. Primary Target Market   _____

15. Secondary Target Market   _____

Rep Name	Compensation Plan	Assigned Territory

6.2   Competitive Advantages

A **competitive advantage** is the thing that differentiates a business from its competitors. It is what separates our business from everyone else. It answers the questions: "Why do customers buy from us versus a competitor?", and "What do we offer customers that is unique?". We will make certain to include our key competitive advantages into our marketing materials. We will use the following competitive advantages to set us apart from our competitors. The distinctive competitive advantages which ___(company name) brings to the marketplace are as follows: (Note: Select only those you can support)

Our Primary Competitive Advantages:

1. Availability of background check reports using many different search parameters.
2. Provide multiple types of reports regarding criminal and personal background history, civil court records, sex offender status, business history documents and professional license verification.
3. Our reports will contain relevant, targeted information presented in an understandable, and easy-to-read format.
4. Easy ordering and accessing of reports without complex terms and restrictions.
5. Provide comprehensive information about what the reports include.
6. Provide the highest level of customer service when dealing with the sensitive records contained in background reports.
7. Provide only accurate and verified search results.
8. Customer support provided via a variety of contact methods, including telephone, Chat, and email support, and respond to questions quickly.
9. Provide other support options, including website help menu and FAQs pages.
10. Adherence to all relevant state and federal privacy and access laws.

Other Competitive Advantages:

1. Unrestricted access to all client search results.
2. Instant lookups and printable reports.
3. Over _____ (#) records at client fingertips.
4. Client can get data from public and private sources.
5. One Stop-Shop for all information needs.
6. Sophisticated cross-database searches enabled.
7. Expert assisted customer support.
8. Easy-to-use and User-friendly search process.
9. Use of the most recent technology to search databases nationwide.
10. Our Applicant Tracking System, Drug Testing, Career Center and Compliance tools will streamline the client's recruit-to-hire process.
11. Our company works with several legal firms as well as in-house legal experts to stay current on federal, state and local laws, regulations, or pending legislation ensuring consistent compliance.
12. The executive management team receives weekly updates to make certain all requested searches are handled according to company guidelines and county, state and federal regulations.
13. Our website has a section devoted to legislative updates and is an additional vehicle for keeping our clients updated on important issues affecting the screening process.
14. As a member of the National Association of Professional Background Screeners (NAPBS), we provide only Fair Credit Reporting Act (FCRA) compliant services.
15. All searches performed through our system are in full compliance with the FCRA as well as all other federal, state, local and international regulations.
16. We take pride in providing world-class customer service.
17. A live, knowledgeable customer service representative is always available to answer client questions.
18. We are dedicated to ensuring our clients remain 100% compliant with the Fair

Credit Reporting Act (FCRA).

19. We offer competitive pricing regardless of the client company's size or volume.

20. We will customize an employment screening program to fit both the client's budget and needs.

21. We constantly screen our researchers for accuracy and thoroughness.

22. Our strict attention to detail ensures the client will always have the most comprehensive data available to help with hiring decisions.

23. We are a one-stop source for any and all background check services available.

24. We care about our client applicant's Privacy Info and we are dedicated to securing and protecting the private information we deal with on a daily basis.

25. We utilize strict document and data protection policies to ensure that no private information can be accessed by unauthorized individuals.

26. We shred all personal documents once they have been processed and protect our online system utilizing the most secure technology available.

27. We absolutely never sell data to any third-party entity.

28. We are members of the Better Business Bureau, the National Association of Professional Background Screeners and ConcernedCRAs.com, a group of like-minded consumer reporting agencies dedicated to consumer protection.

29. By utilizing the latest technology and the most extensive and experienced research network available, we provide the fastest turnaround times in the industry.

30. Our average turnaround time for a Criminal Records search is __ (#) hours, with nearly all completed within two days.

31. We provide a secure, easy-to-use web-based system for submitting and receiving background checks.

32. Once a background check is completed the results are automatically e-mailed or faxed to your designated employees.

33. We provide our client's employees, free of charge, any initial or ongoing training required to maximize the effective use of our system.

34. We offer a 'Free Applicant Tracking System' to effortlessly capture and screen applicants from the client's website, online job posting.

35. We will offer discounts and other incentives for referrals.

36. We have the technological and professional staffing capabilities to provide our customers with the highest possible level of personalized service.

37. We have an ethnically diverse and multilingual staff, which is critical for a service-oriented business.

38. We have formed alliances that enable us to provide one-stop shopping or an array of services through a single access point.

6.2.1   Branding Strategy

Our branding strategy involves what we do to shape what the customer immediately thinks our business offers and stands for. The purpose of our branding strategy is to reduce customer perceived purchase risk and improve our profit margins by allowing use to charge a premium for our background check services.

We will invest $_____ every year in maintaining our brand name image, which will differentiate our background check business from other companies. The amount of money spent on creating and maintaining a brand name will not convey any specific information about our products, but it will convey, indirectly, that we are in this market for the long haul, that we have a reputation to protect, and that we will interact repeatedly with our customers. In this sense, the amount of money spent on maintaining our brand name will signal to consumers that we will provide products and services of consistent quality.

We will use the following ways to build trust and establish our personal brand:
1.   Build a consistently published blog and e-newsletter with informational content.
2.   Create comprehensive social media profiles.
3.   Contribute articles to related online publications.
4.   Earn career certifications
5.   Remain readily accessible.
6.   Find your voice and Use it to be relatable on the human level.
7.   Create a persona that combines who you are and who you want to be.
8.   Stick with the niche in which you can offer the greatest value.

Resources:
https://www.abetterlemonadestand.com/branding-guide/

Our key to marketing success will be to effectively manage the building of our brand platform in the marketplace, which will consist of the following elements:

Brand Vision - our envisioned future of the brand is to be the recognized source for background check solutions to manage the complications of employee screening.

Brand Attributes - Partners, problem solvers, responsive, integrity, privacy, comprehensive, reliable, flexible and easy to work with.

Brand Essence - the shared soul of the brand, the spark of which is present in every experience a customer has with our background checking services, will be "Integrity" and "Responsive" This will be the core of our organization, driving the type of people we hire and the type of behavior we expect.

Brand Image - the outside world's overall perception of our organization will be that we are the 'background checking' pros who are alleviating the complications of selecting the right screening method for the right occasion.

Brand Promise - our concise statement of what we do, why we do it, and why customers should do business with us will be, "To realize solid values and make informed hiring judgments with the help of our knowledgeable staff"

We will use the following methodologies to implement our branding strategy:
1.   Develop processes, systems and quality assurance procedures to assure the consistent adherence to our quality standards and mission statement objectives.
2.   Develop business processes to consistently deliver upon our value proposition.
3.   Develop training programs to assure the consistent professionalism and responsiveness of our employees.
4.   Develop marketing communications with consistent, reinforcing message content.

5. Incorporate testimonials into our marketing materials that support our promises.
6. Develop marketing communications with a consistent presentation style. (Logo design, company colors, slogan, labels, packaging, stationery, etc.)
7. Exceed our brand promises to achieve consistent customer loyalty.
8. Use surveys, focus groups and interviews to consistently monitor what our brand means to our customers.
9. Consistently match our brand values or performance benchmarks to our customer requirements.
10. Focus on the maintenance of a consistent number of key brand values that are tied to our company strengths.
11. Continuously research industry trends in our markets to stay relevant to customer needs and wants.
12. Attach a logo-imprinted product label and business card to all products, marketing communications and invoices.
13. Develop a memorable and meaningful tagline that captures the essence of our brand.
14. Prepare a one-page company overview and make it a key component of our sales presentation folder.
15. Hire and train employees to put the interests of customers first.
16. Develop a professional website that is updated with fresh content on a regular basis.
17. Use our blog to circulate content that establishes our niche expertise and opens a two-way dialogue with our customers.
18. Attractive and tasteful uniforms will also help our staff's morale. The branding will become complete with the addition of our corporate logo, or other trim or accessories which echo the style and theme of our establishment.
19. Create an effective slogan with the following attributes:
    a. Appeals to customers' emotions.
    b. Shows off how our service benefits customers by highlighting our customer service or care.
    c. Has 8 words or less and is memorable
    d. Can be grasped quickly by our audience.
    e. Reflects our business' personality and character.
    f. Shows sign of originality.
20. Create a Proof Book that contains before and after photos, testimonial letters, our mission statement, copies of industry certifications and our code of ethics.
21. Make effective use of trade show exhibitions and email newsletters to help brand our image.

The communications strategy we will use to build our brand platform will include the following items:

Website - featuring product line information, research, testimonials, cost benefit analysis, frequently asked questions, and policy information. This website will be used as a tool for both our sales team and our customers.

Presentations, brochures and mailers geared to the business manager, explaining the benefits of our services line as part of a comprehensive employee screening plan.

Presentations and brochures geared to the corporate decision maker explaining the benefits of our screening programs in terms of positive outcomes, reduced cost from complications, and reduced risk of lawsuits or negative survey events.

A presentation and recruiting brochure geared to prospective sales people that emphasizes the benefits of joining our organization.

Training materials that help every employee deliver our brand message in a consistent manner.

6.2.2   Brand Positioning Statement

We will use the following brand positioning statement to summarize what our brand means to our targeted market:

To _____ (target market) _____ (company name) is the brand of _____ (product/service frame of reference) that enables the customer to _____ (primary performance benefit) because _____ (company name) _____ (products/services) _____ (are made with/offer/provide) the best _____ (key attributes)

6.3   Business SWOT Analysis

Definition: SWOT Analysis is a powerful technique for understanding our Strengths and Weaknesses, and for looking at the Opportunities and Threats faced.

Strategy: We will use this SWOT Analysis to uncover exploitable opportunities and carve a sustainable niche in our market. And by understanding the weaknesses of our business, we can manage and eliminate threats that would otherwise catch us by surprise. By using the SWOT framework, we will be able to craft a strategy that distinguishes our business from our competitors, so that we can compete successfully in the market.

Strengths   (select)

What background check services are we best at providing?
What unique resources can we draw upon?

1.   Our location is in the heart of a commercial complex and is in close proximity to a popular _____ with ample parking facilities.
2.   Provide detailed screening results in record time so clients can make informed decisions faster.
3.   The nearest competition is __ miles away.
4.   Our office has been extensively renovated with many communications upgrades.
5.   Seasoned executive management professionals, sophisticated in business knowledge, experienced in the background check industry.
6.   Strong networking relationships with many different organizations,

including _____.

7. Excellent staff are experienced, highly trained and customer attentive.
8. Wide diversity of packaged service offerings.
9. High customer loyalty.
10. The proven ability to establish excellent personalized client service.
11. Strong relationships with database suppliers, that offer flexibility and respond to special customer requirements.
12. Good referral relationships.
13. Work one-on-one with companies in diverse industries to meet specific screening needs.
14. Client loyalty developed through a solid, trusting reputation with repeat clients.
15. Our business has a focused target market of ___ (mid-sized businesses?).
16. Sales staff with ____ technology credentials.
17. Consistently deliver accurate, FCRA compliant background checks.
18. Our methodologies reflect a strict adherence to industry recognized standards.
19. Our platforms integrate with leading applicant tracking system (ATS) technology.
20. Our self-service dashboard helps organizations to identify, view, analyze and understand how their background screening program is performing.
21. _____

Weaknesses

In what areas could we improve?
Where do we have fewer resources than others?
1. Lack of developmental capital to complete Phase I start-up.
2. New comer to the industry.
3. Lack of marketing experience.
4. The struggle to build brand equity.
5. A limited marketing budget to develop brand awareness.
6. Finding dependable and people-oriented staff.
7. We need to develop the information systems that will improve our productivity and operations management.
8. Don't know the needs and wants of local businesses.
9. The owner must deal with the industry experience learning curve.
10. Challenges caused by the cyclical nature of the business.
11. _____

Opportunities

What opportunities are there for new and/or improved services?
What trends could we take advantage of?
1. Increased concerns over security and privacy issues.
2. Could take market share away from existing competitors.
3. Greater need for mobile services by time starved consumers.
4. Growing market with a significant percentage of the target market still not

aware that _____ (company name) exists.

5. The ability to develop many long-term customer relationships.
6. Expanding the range of service packaged offerings.
7. Greater use of direct advertising to promote our services.
8. Establish referral relationships with local businesses serving the same target market segment.
9. Networking with non-profit organizations.
10. Landlords will need and expect a greater range of tenant checking services.
11. Increased public awareness of the importance of 'green' matters.
12. Strategic alliances offering sources for referrals and joint marketing activities to extend our reach.
13. _____ (supplier name) is offering co-op advertising.
14. A competitor has overextended itself financially and is facing bankruptcy.
15. _____

Threats

What trends or competitor actions could hurt us?
What threats do our weaknesses expose us to?

1. Another background screening company could move into this area.
2. Further declines in the economic forecast.
3. Inflation affecting operations for gas, labor, and other operating costs.
4. Keeping trained efficient staff and key personnel from moving on or starting their own business venture.
5. Imitation competition from similar indirect service providers.
6. Price differentiation is a significant competition factor.
7. The government could enact legislation that could affect information access and usage.
8. We need to do a better job of assessing the strengths and weaknesses of all our competitors.
9. Sales of inferior services by mass discounters.
10. _____

Recap:

We will use the following strengths to capitalize on recognized opportunities:

1. _____
2. _____

We will take the following actions to turn our weaknesses into strengths and prepare to defend against known threats.

1. _____
2. _____

6.4.0   Marketing Strategy

Our Marketing strategy will focus on the following:

1. Developing a reputation for a superior range of background checking services, competitive prices, and exceptional customer service.
2. Developing strong relationships with our database access providers to guarantee the best services obtainable.
3. Keeping the staff focused, satisfied and motivated in their roles, to help keep our productivity and customer service at the highest obtainable levels.
4. Maintaining the visibility of our business through regular advertising to our target business community.
5. Reaching out to potential wholesale clients, businesses and community organizations, with commissioned independent sales reps.
6. Doing activities that can stimulate additional business: sharing HR knowledge via seminars, publishing a newsletter, and offering customer service through our website
7. Extending our market penetration through outside commissioned sales reps and a website.

_____ (company name) intends to actively seek out and attract new customers, whose needs go beyond the need for quick simple access. Our online website will the primary focus of this program. This service will offer an interactive feature that will act as a database of our broad product selection and will primarily be focused on our custom HR services. The goals for this service will be for it to serve as a compilation of our service selection, in which a user will be able to categorize our entire range of services in several different ways and then be able to view packaged service descriptions and usage suggestions. The service is intended to make our clients more comfortable with our product lines. It will provide a way for our customers to survey the features and benefits of our services so that they may be able to make an informed purchase decision. This system seeks to create client demand through education.

In phase one of our marketing plan, we will gain exposure to our target markets through the use of selective trial discounts and grand opening promotional tactics. We will be taking a very aggressive marketing stance in the first year of business in hopes of gaining customer loyalty. In our subsequent years, we will focus less resources on advertising as a whole. But, we do plan to budget for advertising promotions on a continual and event specific basis.

Our marketing strategy is based on establishing _____ (company name) as the one-stop resource of choice for HR managers in need of a single recruiting and screening platform. We will start our business with our known personal referral contacts and then continue our campaign to develop recognition among other business groups. We will develop and maintain a database of our contacts in the field. We will work to maintain and exploit our existing relationships throughout the start-up process and then use our marketing tools to communicate with other potential referral sources.

The marketing strategy will create awareness, interest and appeal from our target markets. Its ultimate purpose is to encourage repeat purchases and get customers to refer professional contacts. To get referrals we will provide incentives and excellent service and build relationships with clients by caring about what the client needs and wants to accomplish.

We will use newsletter sign-up forms and surveys to collect customer email addresses and feed our client relationship management (CRM) software system. This system will automatically send out, on a predetermined schedule, follow-up materials, such as article reprints, seminar invitations, email messages, surveys and e-newsletters. We will offset some of our advertising costs by asking our suppliers and other local merchants to place ads in our newsletter.

Current Situation
We will study the current marketing situation on a weekly basis to analyze trends and identify sources of business growth. As onsite owners, we will be on hand daily to insure customer service. Our services include services of the highest quality and a prompt response to feedback from customers. Our extensive and detailed financial statements, produced monthly, will enable us to stay competitive and exploit presented opportunities.

Marketing Budget
Our marketing budget will be a flexible $_____ per quarter. The marketing budget can be allocated in any way that best suits the time of year.
Marketing budget per quarter:

Newspaper Ads	$_____	Radio advertisement	$_____
Web Page	$_____	Customer Contest	$_____
Direct Mail	$_____	Sales Brochure	$_____
Trade Shows	$_____	Seminars	$_____
Superpages	$_____	Google Adwords	$_____
Giveaways	$_____	Vehicle Signs	$_____
Business Cards	$_____	Flyers	$_____
Labels/Stickers	$_____	Videos/DVDs	$_____
Pro Bono Services	$_____	Newsletter	$_____
Email Campaigns	$_____	Sales Reps Comm.	$_____
Other	$_____		

Total: $_____

Our objective in setting a marketing budget has been to keep it between _____ (5?) and _____ (7?) percent of our estimated annual gross sales.

Marketing Mix
New customers will primarily come from word-of-mouth and our referral program. The overall market approach involves creating brand awareness through targeted advertising, public relations, co-marketing efforts with select alliance partners, direct mail, email campaigns (with constant contact.com), seminars and a website.

Video Marketing

We will link to our website a series of YouTube.com based video clips that talk about our range of background screening services and demonstrate our expertise with certain target market segments. We will create business marketing videos that are both entertaining and informational and improve our search engine rankings.

The video will include:

Client testimonials - We will let our best customers become our instant sales force because people will believe what others say about us more readily than what we say about ourselves.

Product Demonstrations - We will train and pre-sell our potential clients on our most popular products and services by talking about and showing them. Often, our potential clients don't know the full range and depth of our products and services because we haven't taken the adequate time to explain them.

Include Business Website Address on the screen.

Frequently Asked Questions - We will answer questions that we often get and anticipate objections we might get and give great reasons to convince potential clients that we are the best background screening provider.

Include a Call to Action - We have the experience and the know-how to support your HR hiring practices, so call us, right now, and let's get started.

Seminar - Include a portion of a seminar on how conduct thorough pre-employment background investigations.

Comment on industry trends and product news - We will appear more in-tune and knowledgeable in our market if we can talk about what's happening in our industry and marketplace.

Resources: www.businessvideomarketing.tv
                        www.hotpluto.com
                        www.hubspot.com/video-marketing-kit
                        www.youtube.com/user/mybusinessstory

Analytics Report
http://support.google.com/youtube/bin/static.py?hl=en&topic=1728599&guide=1
        714169&page=guide.cs

Note: Refer to Video Marketing Tips in rear marketing worksheets section.

Example:
www.youtube.com/user/AccurateBackgroundTV

Top 11 places where we will share our videos online:

YouTube   **www.youtube.com**

This very popular website allows you to log-in and leave comments and ratings on the videos. You can also save your favorite videos and allows you to tag posted videos. This makes it easier for your videos to come up in search engines.

Google Video   **http://video.google.com/**

A video hosting site. Google Video is not just focused on sharing videos online, but this is also a market place where you can buy the videos you find on this site using Google search engine.

Yahoo! Video   **http://video.yahoo.com/**

Uploading and sharing videos is possible with Yahoo Video!. You can find several types of videos on their site and you can also post comments and ratings for the videos.

Revver   http://www.revver.com/

This website lets you earn money through ads on your videos and you will have a 50/50 profit split with the website. Another great deal with Revver is that your fans who posted your videos on their site can also earn money.

Blip.tv   http://blip.tv/

Allows viewers to stream and download the videos posted on their website. You can also use Creative Commons licenses on your videos posted on the website. This allows you to decide if your videos should be attributed, restricted for commercial use and be used under specific terms.

Vimeo   http://www.vimeo.com/

This website is family safe and focuses on sharing private videos. The interface of the website is similar to some social networking sites that allow you to customize your profile page with photos from Flickr and embeddable player. This site allows users to socialize through their videos.

Metacafe   http://www.metacafe.com/

This video sharing site is community based. You can upload short-form videos and share it to the other users of the website. Metacafe has its own system called VideoRank that ranks videos according to the viewer reactions and features the most popular among the viewers.

ClipShack   http://www.clipshack.com/

Like most video sharing websites, you can post comments on the videos and even tag some as your favorite. You can also share the videos on other websites through the html code from ClipShack and even sending it through your email.

Veoh   http://www.veoh.com/

You can rent or sell your videos and keep the 70% of the sales price. You can upload a range of different video formats on Veoh and there is no limit on the size and length of the file. However, when your video is over 45 minutes it has to be downloaded before the viewer can watch it.

Jumpcut   http://download.cnet.com/JumpCut/3000-18515_4-10546353.html

Jumpcut allows its users to upload videos using their mobile phones. You will have to attach the video captured from your mobile phone to an email. It has its own movie making wizard that helps you familiarize with the interface of the site.

DailyMotion   www.dailymotion.com

As one of the leading sites for sharing videos, Dailymotion attracts over 114 million unique monthly visitors (source: comScore, May 2018) 1.2 billion videos views worldwide (source: internal). Offers the best content from users, independent content creators and premium partners. Using the most advanced technology for both users and content creators, provides high-quality and HD video in a fast, easy-to-use online service that also automatically filters infringing material as notified by content owners.

Offering 32 localized versions, their mission is to provide the best possible entertainment experience for users and the best marketing opportunities for advertisers, while respecting content protection.

Business Cards

Our business card will include our company logo, complete contact information, name and title, association logos, slogan or markets serviced, licenses and certifications. The center of our bi-fold card will contain a listing of the benefits of the services we offer. We will give out multiple business cards to friends, business associates, and to each customer, upon the completion of the service. We will also distribute business cards in the following ways:

1. Attached to invoices, surveys, flyers and door hangers.
2. Included in customer sales presentation folders.
3. We will leave a stack of business cards in a Lucite holder with the local Chamber of Commerce and any other businesses offering free counter placement.

We will use fold-over cards because they will enable us to list all of our services and complete contact instructions on the inside of the card.

We will place the following referral discount message on the back of our business cards:
- Our business is very dependent upon referrals. If you have associates who could benefit from our quality services, please write your name at the bottom of this card and give it to them. When your contact presents this card upon their first visit, he or she will be entitled to 10% off discount. And, on your next invoice, you will also get a 10% discount as a thank you for your referral.
Resource:
www.vistaprint.com

Direct Mail Package
To build name recognition and to announce the opening of our background check service, we will create a mail package consisting of a tri-fold brochure containing a discount coupon to welcome our new customers. We plan to make a mailing to local subscribers of Business Journals. From those identified local customers, we shall ask them to complete a survey and describe their perception of our business, and any specific services they would like to see added. Those customers returning completed surveys would receive a premium (giveaway) gift.

Trade Shows
We will exhibit at as many local trade shows per year as possible. These include trade association shows, business spot-lights with our local Chamber of Commerce, and more. The objective is to get our company name and service out to as many businesses as possible. When exhibiting at a trade show, we will put our best foot forward and represent ourselves as professionals. We will be open, enthusiastic, informative and courteous. We will exhibit our services with sales brochures, logo-imprinted giveaways, and a computer to run our video presentation through. We will use a 'free drawing' for a gift basket prize and a sign-in sheet to collect names and email addresses. We will also develop a questionnaire or survey that helps us to assemble an ideal customer profile and qualify the leads we receive. We will train our booth attendants to answer all type of questions and to handle objections. We will also seek to present educational seminars at the show to gain increased publicity, and name and expertise recognition. Most

importantly, we will develop and implement a follow-up program to stay-in-touch with prospects.

We will regularly attend the annual trade shows for the National Association of Professional Background Screeners (NAPBS) and the Background Investigator's Pre-Employment Screeners Conference.

_____ (company name) will be appearing at the following tradeshows and events:
National Retail Federation (NRF) 2010 Loss Prevention Conference & Expo
   Georgia World Congress Center, Atlanta, GA
SHRM Talent & Staffing Management Conference & Exposition
   Gaylord Hotel. Washington, D.C.
SHRM 2019 Annual Conference & Exposition
   Georgia World Congress Center, Atlanta, Ga.
Taleo World 2019
HR Technology Conference & Exposition
   McCormick Place, West Wing, Chicago, Ill.
Staffing World 2018
   Venetian Resort Hotel and Casino., Las Vegas, Nev.
Resources: www.tsnn.com   www.expocentral.com
      www.acshomeshow.com/ www.EventsInAmerica.com
      www.Biztradeshows.com

Networking
Networking will be a key to success because referrals and alliances formed can help to improve our professional image and keep our business growing. We will strive to build long-term mutually beneficial relationships with our networking contacts and join the following types of organizations:
1.   We will form a LeTip Chapter to exchange business leads.
2.   We will join the local BNI.com referral exchange group.
3.   We will join the Chamber of Commerce to further corporate relationships.
4.   We will join the Rotary Club, Lions Club, Kiwanis Club, Church Groups, etc.
5.   We will do volunteer work for American Heart Assoc. and Habitat for Humanity.
6.   We will become an affiliated member of the local board of Realtors and the Women's Council of Realtors.

Relationship Building Network   www.rbninfo.com/
RBN is one of the largest, most prolific business networking groups.

We will use our metropolitan _____ (city) Chamber of Commerce to target prospective business contacts. We will mail letters to each prospect describing our services. We will follow-up with phone calls.

Newsletter
We will develop a one-page newsletter to be handed out to attendees at seminars and other types of events. The monthly newsletter will be used to build our brand and update

clients on industry and legislative developments. The newsletter will be produced in-house and for the cost of paper and computer time. We will include the following types of information:

1.   Our involvement with charitable events.
2.   New Compliant Service Introductions
3.   Featured employee/client of the month.
4.   New industry technologies/Press Releases.
5.   Client endorsements/testimonials/referral program details.
6.   Classified ads from local sponsors and suppliers.
7.   Announcements / Upcoming events/ Coupons/Helpful Articles.
Resources: Microsoft Publisher
Example: http://www.corporatescreening.com/resources/cs-e-newsletter/

We will adhere to the following newsletter writing guidelines:
1.   We will provide content that is of real value to our subscribers.
2.   We will provide solutions to our subscriber's problems or questions.
3.   We will communicate regularly on a weekly basis.
4.   We will create HTML Messages look professional and allow us to track how many people click on our links and/or open our emails.
5.   We will not pitch our business opportunity in our Ezine very often.
6.   We will focus our marketing dollars on building our Ezine subscriber list.
7.   We will focus on relationship building and not the conveying of a sales message.
8.   We will vary our message format with videos, articles, checklists, quotes, pictures and charts.
9.   We will recommend occasionally affiliate products in some of our messages to help cover our marketing costs.
10.   We will consistently follow the above steps to build a database of qualified prospects and customers.
Resources:
www.constantcontact.com
www.mailchimp.com
http://lmssuccess.com/10-reasons-online-business-send-regular-newsletter-customers/
www.smallbusinessmiracles.com/how/newsletters/
www.fuelingnewbusiness.com/2010/06/01/combine-email-marketing-and-social-media-
        for-ad-agency-new-business/

Vehicle Signs

We will place magnetic and vinyl signs on our vehicles and include our company name, phone number, company slogan and website address, if possible. We will create a cost-effective moving billboard with high-quality, high-resolution vehicle wraps. We will wrap a portion of the vehicle or van to deliver excellent marketing exposure.
Resource: http://www.fastsigns.com/

Advertising Wearables

We will give all preferred club members an eye-catching T-shirt or sweatshirt with our company name and logo printed across the garment to wear about town. We will also give them away as a thank you for customer referral activities. We will ask all employees to wear our logo-imprinted shirts.

Sales Brochures

The sales brochure will enable us to make a solid first impression when pursing business from commercial accounts. Our sales brochure will include the following contents and become a key part of our sales presentation folder and direct mail package:

- Contact Information
- Business Description/Mission
- Customer Testimonials
- List of Services/Benefits
- Competitive Advantages
- Owner/Management Resumes
- Trial Coupon
- Business Hours

Examples:

https://www.backgroundprofiles.com/R-brochure.pdf
http://www.corragroup.com/PDF/Corra%20Screening%20Brochure.pdf

Sales Brochure Design

1. Speak in Terms of Our Prospects Wants and Interests.
2. Focus on all the Benefits, not Just Features.
3. Put the company logo and Unique Selling Proposition together to reinforce the fact that your company is different and better than the competition.
4. Include a special offer, such as a discount, a free report, a sample, or a free trial to increase the chances that the brochure will generate sales.

We will incorporate the following Brochure Design Guidelines:

1. Design the brochure to achieve a focused set of objectives (marketing of programs) with a target market segment (residential vs. commercial).
2. Tie the brochure design to our other marketing materials with colors, logo, fonts and formatting.
3. List capabilities and how they benefit clients.
4. Demonstrate what we do and how we do it differently.
5. Define the value proposition of our engineering installing services
6. Use a design template that reflects your market positioning strategy.
7. Identify your key message (unique selling proposition)
8. List our competitive advantages.
9. Express our understanding of client needs and wants.
10. Use easy to read (scan) headlines, subheadings, bullet points, pictures, etc.
11. Use a logo to create a visual branded identity.
12. The most common and accepted format for a brochure is a folded A3 (= 2 x A4), which gives 4 pages of information.
13. Use a quality of paper that reflects the image we want to project.
14. Consistently stick to the colors of our corporate style.
15. Consider that colors have associations, such as green colors are associated with the environment and enhance an environmental image.
16. Illustrations will be appropriate and of top quality and directly visualize the product assortment, product application and production facility.

17. The front page will contain the company name, logo, the main application of your product or service and positioning message or Unique Selling Proposition.
18. The back page will be used for testimonials or references, and contact details.

Coupons

We will use coupons with limited time expirations to get prospects to try our background check service programs. We will also accept the coupons of our competitors to help establish new client relationships. We will run ads directing people to our Web site for a $___ coupon certificate. This will help to draw in new clients and collect e-mail addresses for the distribution of a monthly newsletter.

Examples:
http://www.retailmenot.com/coupons/backgroundcheck
http://couponfollow.com/site/backgroundchecks.com
http://www.promopro.com/store/backgroundchecks.com
https://www.couponchief.com/backgroundchecks
http://www.couponsock.com/coupon-codes/background-check

We will use coupons selectively to accomplish the following:
1. To introduce a new product or service.
2. To attract loyal customers away from the competition
3. To prevent customer defection to a new competitor.
4. To help celebrate a special event.

Types of Coupons:
1. Courtesy Coupons   Rewards for repeat business
2. Cross-Marketing Coupons   Incentive to try other products/services.
3. Companion Coupon   Bring a friend incentive.

Websites like Groupon.com, LivingSocial, Eversave, and BuyWithMe sell discount vouchers for services ranging from custom _____ to background checking consultations. Best known is Chicago-based Groupon. To consumers, discount vouchers promise substantial savings — often 50% or more. To merchants, discount vouchers offer possible opportunities for price discrimination, exposure to new customers, online marketing, and "buzz." Vouchers are more likely to be profitable for merchants with low marginal costs, who can better accommodate a large discount and for patient merchants, who place higher value on consumers' possible future return visits.

Cross-Promotions

We will develop and maintain partnerships with local businesses and organizations that cater to the needs of our customers, such as law firms and HR management consultants, and conduct cross-promotional marketing campaigns. These cross-promotions will require the exchanging of customer mailing lists and endorsements.

Premium Giveaways

We will distribute logo-imprinted promotional products at events, also known as giveaway premiums, to foster top-of-mind awareness (www.promoideas.org). These items include business cards with magnetic backs, mugs with contact phone number, technical booklets and calendars that feature important celebration date reminders.

Local Newspaper Ads

We will use these ads to announce the opening of our store and get our name established. We will adhere to the rule that frequency and consistency of message are essential. We will include a list of our top brand name programs and specialty background checking services. We will include a coupon to track the response in zoned editions of 'Shopper' Papers, Theater Bills, and Community Newsletters and Newspapers. We will use the ad to announce any weekly or monthly price specials.

Our newspaper ads will utilize the following design tips:

1. We will start by getting a media kit from the publisher to analyze their demographic information as well as their reach and distribution.
2. Don't let the newspaper people have total control of our ad design, as we know how we want our company portrayed to the market.
3. Make sure to have 1st class graphics since this will be the only visual distinction we can provide the reader about our business.
4. Buy the biggest ad we can afford, with full-page ads being the best.
5. Go with color if affordable, because consumers pick color ads over black 82% of the time.
6. Ask the paper if they have specific days that more of our type of buyer reads their paper.
7. If we have a hit ad on our hands, we will make it into a circular or door-hanger to extend the life of the offer.
8. Don't change an ad because we are getting tired of looking at it.
9. We will start our headline by telling our story to pull the reader into the ad.
10. We will use "Act Now" to convey a sense of urgency to the reader.
11. We will use our headline to tell the reader what to do.
12. The headline is a great place to announce a free offer.
13. We will write our headline as if we were speaking to one person and make it personal.
14. We will use our headline to either relay a benefit or intrigue the reader into wanting more information.
15. Use coupons giving a dollar amount off, not a percentage, as people hate doing the math.

Local Publications

We will place low-cost classified ads in neighborhood publications to advertise our background screening services. We will also submit public relations and informative articles to improve our visibility and establish our expertise and trustworthiness. These publications include the following:

1. Neighborhood/Association Newsletters
2. Local Business Journals
3. Local Chamber of Commerce Newsletter
4. Realtor Magazines

Resources:

Hometown News   www.hometownnews.com
Pennysaver   www.pennysaverusa.com

Publication Type	Ad Size	Timing	Circulation	Section	Fee

Business Journal Display Ads

We will consider placing display ads in business journals read by professionals and possibly rent a list of their local subscribers for a planned direct mailing. The mailing will describe our employee background checking service programs. We will use empirical data to prove how our targeted public relations programs can actually save companies money, and help their workforce to be more productive.

Resource: The Business Journals http://www.bizjournals.com/

The premier media solutions platform for companies strategically targeting business decision makers. Delivers a total business audience of over 10 million people via their 42 websites, 62 publications and over 700 annual industry leading events. Their media products provide comprehensive coverage of business news from a local, regional and national perspective.

Publication Type	Ad Size	Timing	Circulation	Section	Fee

Article Submissions

We will pitch articles to Realtor magazines, local newspapers, business magazines and internet articles directories to help establish our specialized expertise and improve our visibility. Hyperlinks will be placed within written articles and can be clicked on to take the customer to another webpage within our website or to a totally different website. These clickable links or hyperlinks will be keywords or relevant words that have meaning to our background checking business. In fact, we will create a position whose primary function is to link our business with opportunities to be published in local publications.

We will write articles that serve to educate businesses about the necessity of background checks as well as how small- to mid-sized HR departments can protect themselves against negligent hiring litigation.

We will write a 1,000-word piece on a topic that reflects our background check consulting expertise and submit it for publication in the Sunday opinion section of our local newspaper and the *New York Times*. We will also submit articles or post to blogs or email newsletters that were created around a background checking or screening theme. We will do extensive research to find the blogger or other "thought leaders" out there who have a sway over discussion in our specific field of background checking and their own audience. We will reach out to these influential bloggers, because they will provide a very powerful way to promote our background check company. Their audience may be smaller, but it will be much more concentrated and passionate about the subject of background checks and will thus take action in much higher numbers. Our objective will be to locate a single-author blog with a large audience that is highly focused, and the author favors or endorses our approach to background checks. We will then seek to build a long-term, mutually beneficial relationship with the author. We will attempt to make friends with him or her and show them that our methodology is sound and relevant to their audience, so that they will confidently and actively promote our methods and principles to their followers. In fact, we will take the following approach:

1.   We will focus on a relevant idea to the background check theme of the blog and endeavor to add value to the selected blog over time.
2.   We will leave some thoughtful comments on their blog, highlighting certain helpful ideas from our background checking consulting approach.
3.   We will forward interesting articles with a different perspective on the blogger's position or focus, to add content value from the blogger's perspective.
4.   We will pose questions in our cover letter like; "do you think maybe this might be interesting to your audience?"

Sample Blog Content: www.backgroundcheck.org/background-check-guide/

Publishing requires an understanding of the following publisher needs:

1.   Review of good work.   2.   Editor story needs.
3.   Article submission process rules   4.   Quality photo portfolio
5.   Exclusivity requirements.   6.   Target market interests

Our Article Submission Package will include the following:

1.   Well-written materials   2.   Good references
3.   High-quality Photographs   4.   Well-organized outline.

Examples of General Publishing Opportunities:

1.   Document a new solution to old problem   2.   Publish a research study
3.   Negligent hiring prevention advice   4.   Present a different viewpoint
5.   Introduce a local angle on a hot topic.   6.   Reveal new screening trend.
7.   Share HR specialty niche expertise.   8.   Share hiring benefits

Examples of Specific Article Titles:

1.   "How to Evaluate and Compare Screening Vendors"
2.   "Using Due Diligence to Prevent Negligent Hiring"
3.   "How Deep Can You Probe Job Candidates?"
4.   "The Lawful Use of Credit Reports"
5.   "Background Screening: The Risks and Solutions"
6.   "How Well Do You Really Know Your Employees?"

7. The Advantages of Employee Background Checks
8. What Is a Legit Background Check?
9. What Does a Background Check Verify?
10. How to Design an Employee Background Check Policy.
11. 9 TIPS FOR SELECTING A PRE-EMPLOYMENT BACKGROUND SCREENING COMPANY
   Ex: www.evancarmichael.com/Human-Resources/5885/9-Tips-for-Selecting-a-PreEmployment-Background-Screening-Company.html
12. "How to Choose a Background Checking Service Company"
   Ex: www.businessnewsdaily.com/7636-choosing-a-background-check-service.html
13. "The Importance of Establishing a Company Screening Policy"
   Ex: www.intellicorp.net/marketing/uploadedFiles/Background%20Check%20Basics%20Whitepaper%20-%205.5.13.pdf
14. "The Pros and Cons of Background Checks"
   Ex: http://www.amof.info/why-background.htm
15. "Five Steps for a Successful Screening Program in Financial Services"
   Ex: www.employeescreen.com/iqblog/compliance/5-steps-to-a-successful-background-check-in-financial-services/
16. "How to Use Criminal Background Checks and Not Get Sued"
   Ex: http://smallbiztrends.com/2013/09/criminal-background-checks-not-get-sued.html
17. "What Cannot Be in a Background Check Report?"
   Ex: www.privacyrights.org/employment-background-checks-jobseekers-guide
18. "Just How Important are Pre-employment Background Checks?"
   Ex: www.texasfraudsolutions.com/2018/02/03/importance-of-pre-employment-background-checks-for-your-business/

19. "Why You Should Background Check Your Business Partner"
   Ex: www.youngupstarts.com/2013/09/04/why-you-should-background-check-your-business-partner/

20. "The Dos and Don'ts of Conducting Background Checks"
   Ex: www.sba.gov/blogs/dos-and-donts-conducting-background-checks

21. "Seven Ways in Which Employment Screening Can Help Your Business to Succeed"
   Ex: www.jobdig.com/articles/2443/7_Ways_in_Which_Employment_Screening_Can_Improve_Your_Company's_Success.html

22. "How to Use an HR Strategy to Gain a Competitive Advantage"
   Ex: www.cleverism.com/hr-strategy-competitive-advantage/

Write Articles with a Closing Author Resource Box or Byline
1. Author Name with credential titles.　2. Explanation of area of expertise.
3. Mention of a special offer.　4. A specific call to action

5.	A Call to Action Motivator	6.	All possible contact information
7.	Helpful Links	8.	Link to our Company Website.

Article Objectives:

Article Topic	Target Audience	Target Date

Article Tracking Form

SubjectPublication	Target Audience	Business Development	Resources Needed	Target Date

Possible Magazines and Newspapers to submit articles include:

1.	The Wall Street Journal	2.	HR Management Magazine
3.	Entrepreneur Magazine	4.	HRO Today
5.	Workforce Management	6.	HR Magazine
7.	SHRM Online	8.	Human Resource Executive Mag.
9.	PIMagazine.com	10.	Pursuit Magazine

Resources:
Writer's Market	www.writersmarket.com
Directory of Trade Magazines	www.techexpo.com/tech_mag.html

Internet article directories include:

http://ezinearticles.com/	http://www.mommyshelpercommunity.com
http://www.wahm-articles.com	http://www.ladypens.com/
http://www.articlecity.com	http://www.amazines.com
http://www.articledashboard.com	http://www.submityourarticle.com/articles
http://www.webarticles.com	http://www.articlecube.com
http://www.article-buzz.com	http://www.free-articles-zone.com
www.articletogo.com	http://www.content-articles.com
http://article-niche.com	http://superpublisher.com
www.internethomebusinessarticles.com	http://www.site-reference.com
http://www.articlenexus.com	www.articlebin.com
http://www.articlefinders.com	www.articlesfactory.com
http://www.articlewarehouse.com	www.buzzle.com
http://www.easyarticles.com	www.isnare.com
http://ideamarketers.com/	//groups.yahoo.com/group/article_announce
http://clearviewpublications.com/	www.ebusiness-articles.com
http://www.goarticles.com/	www.authorconnection.com/
http://www.webmasterslibrary.com/	www.businesstoolchest.com
http://www.connectionteam.com	www.digital-women.com/submitarticle.htm
http://www.MarketingArticleLibrary.com	www.searchwarp.com
http://www.dime-co.com	www.articleshaven.com
http://www.allwomencentral.com	www.marketing-seek.com
http://www.reprintarticles.com	www.articles411.com

http://www.articlestreet.com   www.articleshelf.com
http://www.articlepeak.com   www.articlesbase.com
http://www.simplysearch4it.com   www.articlealley.com
http://www.zongoo.com   www.selfgrowth.com

Speaking Engagements

We will use speaking engagements as an opportunity to expose our areas of expertise to prospective clients. By speaking at conferences and forums put together by professional and industry trade groups, we will increase our firm's visibility, and consequently, its prospects for attracting new business. Public speaking will give us a special status and make it easier for our speakers to meet prospects. Attendees expect speakers to reach out to the audience, which gives speakers respect and credibility. We will identify speaking opportunities that will let us reach our targeted audience of mid-sized business owners who belong to the local Chamber of Commerce. We will designate a person who is responsible for developing relationships with event and industry associations, submitting proposals and, most importantly, staying in touch with contacts. We will tailor our proposals to the event organizers' preferences.

Proposed Speech Topics:
1.   The Benefits of Pre-Employment Background Investigations
2.   The Benefits and Risks of Using Social Networking Sites by Hiring Managers
3.   The Top 10 Things HR Professionals Look for in Screening Firms
4.   How to Reduce Exposure to Workplace Violence and Theft.
5.   How to Uncover Education and Reference Fraud on Resumes
6.   The Importance of Post-Hire Screens

Speaking Proposal Package:
1.   Topic/Agenda   2.   Target Audience
3.   Speaker Biography   4.   List of prior speaking engagements
5.   Previous engagement evaluations

Speech Tracking Form

Group/Class	Subject/ Topic	Business Development Potential	Resources Needed	Target Date

We will use the following techniques to leverage the business development impact of our speaking engagements:
1.   Send out press releases to local papers announcing the upcoming speech. We will get great free publicity by sending the topic and highlights of the talk to the newspaper.
2.   Produce a flyer with our picture on it and distribute it to our network.
3.   Send publicity materials to our prospects inviting them to attend our presentation.
4.   Whenever possible, get a list of attendees before the event. Contact them and

introduce yourself before the talk to build rapport with your audience. Arrive early and don't leave immediately after your presentation.

5.   Always give out handouts and a business card. Include marketing materials and something of value to the recipient, so that it will be retained and not just tossed away. You might include tips or secrets you share in your talk.

6.   Give out an evaluation form to all participants. This form should request names and contact information. Offer a free consultation if it's appropriate. Follow up within 72 hours with any members of the audience who could become ideal clients.

7.   Have a place on the form where participants can list other groups that might need speakers, along with the name of the program chairperson or other contact person.

8.   Offer a door prize as incentive for handing in the evaluation. When you have collected all of the evaluations, you can select a winner of the prize.

9.   Meet with audience members, answer their questions and listen to their concerns. Stay after your talk and mingle with the audience. Answer any questions that come up and offer follow-up conversations for additional support.

10.   Request a free ad in the group's newsletter in exchange for your speech.

11.   Send a thank-you note to the person who invited you to speak. Include copies of some of the evaluations to show how useful it was.

Speaking Engagement Package

1.   Video or DVD of prior presentation.   2.   Session Description
3.   Learning Objectives   4.   Takeaway Message
5.   Speaking experience   6.   Letters of recommendation
7.   General Biography   8.   Introduction Biography

Resource:
www.toastmasters.com

Online Classified Ad Placement Opportunities

The following free classified ad sites will enable our background check business to thoroughly describe the benefits of our using our screening services:

1.   **Craigslist.org**   2.   Ebay Classifieds
3.   Classifieds.myspace.com   4.   KIJIJI.com
5.   //Lycos.oodle.com   6.   Webclassifieds.us
7.   USFreeAds.com   8.   www.oodle.com
9.   Backpage.com   10.   stumblehere.com
11.   Classifiedads.com   12.   gumtree.com
13.   Inetgiant.com   14.   www.sell.com
15.   Freeadvertisingforum.com   16.   Classifiedsforfree.com
17.   www.olx.com   18.   www.isell.com
19.   Base.google.com   20.   www.epage.com
21.   Chooseyouritem.com   22.   www.adpost.com
23.   Adjingo.com   24.   Kugli.com

Sample Classified Ad:
Searching for the ability to cost-effectively and reliably screen pre-employment job

applicants? We have been serving the _____ area since _____ (year). We have the most complete selection of job applicant and tenant screening tools.

_____ is a website that provides an affordable, flat-rate background check service for anyone in the United States. All the information in our database is 100% legal and can be searched with convenient ease. In under 1 minute you can have the facts relating to people's public records. This includes, but is not limited to the following: Arrest Records, Jail Records, Sentencing Files, Parolees, Sex Offenders, Mugshots, Missing People, Court Records, Bankruptcy Records, Census Records, Cellphone Traces, Death Records, Marital Records, Criminal Records, and Inmate Records.

Why Use Our Service?
A background check is a great way to find out information about individuals before hiring them for a job or renting space to them. Some sites will charge you per background check, making it a costly endeavor. Our site offers an affordable yearly rate as low as $___ a year. For this price, you will get Unlimited Public Record Searches In Every State.

Give us a call at _____ or visit us at _____ (Website) to sample our services or view our seminar schedule or to arrange a free, no-obligation consultation.

Two-Step Direct Response Classified Advertising
We will use 'two-step direct response advertising' to motivate readers to take a step or action that signals that we have their permission to begin marketing to them in step two. Our objective is to build a trusting relationship with our prospects by offering a free unbiased, educational report in exchange for permission to continue the marketing process. This method of advertising has the following benefits:
1.   Shorter sales cycle.   2.   Eliminates need for cold calling.
3.   Establishes expert reputation.   4.   Better qualifies prospects
5.   Process is very trackable.   6.   Able to run smaller ads.

Sample Two Step Lead Generating Classified Ad:
FREE Report Reveals "The Benefits of Pre-Employment Background Checks"
Or….. "How to Compare and Evaluate Background Screening Service Providers".
Call 24 hour recorded message and leave your name and address.
Your report will be sent out immediately.
Note: The respondent has shown they have an interest in our service specialty.
We will also include a section in the report on our range of HR services and our complete contact information, along with a time limited trial discount coupon.

Post ads on Craigslist every three days:
Post an ad about your business on the website www.craigslist.com , under the appropriate section in the city or town where you live. Ads are placed chronologically and when too many ads are above yours, you get fewer calls. You will get the best results if you delete and repost your ad every three days.

Yellow Page Ads

Research indicates that the use of the traditional Yellow Page Book is declining, but that new residents or people who don't have many personal acquaintances will look to the Yellow Pages to establish a list of potential businesses to call upon. Even a small 2" x 2" boxed ad can create awareness and attract the desired target client, above and beyond the ability of a simple listing. We will use the following design concepts:

1. We will use a headline to sell people on what is unique about our service.
2. We will include a service guarantee to improve our credibility.
3. We will include a coupon offer and a tracking code to monitor the response rate and decide whether to increase or decrease our ad size in subsequent years.
4. We will choose an ad size equal to that of our competitors and evaluate the response rate for future insertion commitments.
5. We will include our hours of operation, motto or slogan and logo.
6. We will include our key competitive advantages.
7. We will list under the same categories as our competitors.
8. We will use some bold lettering to make our ad standout.
9. We will utilize yellow books that also offer an online advertising dimension.

Resources:
www.superpages.com
www.yellowpages.com
Examples:
http://www.yellowpages.com/miami-fl/criminal-background-check
http://www.yellowpages.com/akron-oh/criminal-background-check

Ad Information:

Book Title: _____	Coverage Area: _____
Yearly Fee: $_____	Ad Size: _____ page
Renewal date: _____	Contact: _____

Cable Television Advertising

Cable television will offer us more ability to target certain market niches or demographics with specialty programming. We will use our marketing research survey to determine which cable TV channels our customers are watching. It is expected that many watch the Bloomberg and Fox Business Channels and the Golf Channel. Our plan is to choose the audience we want, and to hit them often enough to entice them to take action. We will also take advantage of the fact that we will be able to pick the specific areas we want our commercial to air. Ad pricing will be dependent upon the number of households the network reaches, the ratings the particular show has earned, contract length and the supply and demand for a particular network.

Resource:
Spot Runner   www.spotrunner.com
Television Advertising   http://televisionadvertising.com/faq.htm

Ad Information:

Length of ad "spot": ___ seconds   Development costs: $____ (onetime fee)

Length of campaign: __ (#) mos.   Runs per month: Three times per day

Cost per month.: $_____   Total campaign cost: $_____.

Radio Advertising

We will use non-event based radio advertising. This style of campaign is best suited for non-retail businesses, such as our Background Checking Company. We will utilize a much smaller schedule of ads on a consistent long-range basis (48 to 52 weeks a year) with the objective of continuously maintaining top-of-mind-awareness. This will mean maintaining a sufficient level of awareness to be either the number one or number two choice when a triggering-event, such as an employee hiring, moves the business manager into the market for background checking services and forces "a consumer choice" about which company in the consumer's perception might help them the most. This consistent approach will utilize only one ad each week day (260 days per year) and allow our company to cost-effectively keep our message in front of consumers once every week day. The ad copy for this non-event campaign, called a positioning message, will not be time-sensitive. It will define and differentiate our business' "unique market position" and will be repeated for a year.

Note: On the average, listeners spend over 3.5 hours per day with radio.

Radio will give us the ability to target our audience, based on radio formats, such as news-talk, classic rock and the oldies. Radio will also be a good way to get repetition into our message, as listeners tend to be loyal to stations and parts of the day.

1. We will use radio advertising to direct prospects to our Web site, advertise a limited time promotion or call for an informational brochure.
2. We will try to barter our services for radio ad spots.
3. We will use a limited-time offer to entice first-time customers to use our background checking services.
4. We will explore the use of on-air community bulletin boards to play our public announcements about community sponsored events.
5. We will also make the radio station aware of our expertise in the background screening field and our availability for interviews.
6. Our choice of stations will be driven by the market research information we collect via our surveys.
7. We will capitalize on the fact that many stations now stream their programming on the internet and reach additional local and even national audiences, and if online listeners like what they hear in our streaming radio spot, they can click over to our website.
8. Our radio ads will use humor, sounds, compelling music or unusual voices to grab attention.
9. Our spots will tell stories or present situations our target audience can relate to.
10. We will make our call to action, a website address or vanity phone number, easy to remember and tie it in with our company name or message.
11. We will approach radio stations about buying their unsold advertising space for deep discounts. (Commonly known at radio stations' as "Run of Station")

On radio, this might mean very early in the morning or late at night. We will talk to our advertising representatives and see what discounts they can offer when one of those empty spaces comes open.

Resources: Radio Advertising Bureau   www.RAB.com
               Radio Locator   www.radio-locator.com
               Radio Directory   www.radiodirectory.com

Ad Information:

Length of ad "spot": ___ seconds   Development costs: $____ (onetime fee)
Length of campaign: __ (#) mos.   Runs per month: Three times per day
Cost per month.: $_____   Total campaign cost: $_____.

Resources:

www.lfmaudio.com/best-practises-for-creating-radio-ads-your-listeners-will-respond-to/

Script Resources:

https://voicebunny.com/blog/5-tips-make-radio-ads-grab-attention-sell/

www.voices.com/documents/secure/voices.com-commercial-scripts-for-radio-and-
        television-ads.pdf

http://smallbusiness.chron.com/say-30second-radio-advertising-spot-10065.html

https://voicebunny.com/blog/5-tips-make-radio-ads-grab-attention-sell/

Press Release Overview:

We will use market research surveys to determine the media outlets that our demographic customers read and then target them with press releases. We will draft a cover letter for our media kit that explains that we would like to have the newspaper print a story about the start-up of our new local business or a milestone that we have accomplished. And, because news releases may be delivered by feeds or on news services and various websites, we will create links from our news releases to content on our website. These links which will point to more information or a special offer, will drive our clients into the sales process. They will also increase search engine ranking on our site. We will follow-up each faxed package to the media outlet with a phone call to the business section editor.

Media Kit

We will compile a media kit with the following items:
1.   A pitch letter introducing our background checking and relevant newsworthiness for their readership/viewership.
2.   A press release with helpful newsworthy story facts.
3.   Biographical fact sheet or sketches of key personnel.
4.   Listing of product and service features and benefits to customers.
5.   Photos and digital logo graphics
6.   Copies of media coverage already received.
7.   FAQ
8.   Customer testimonials

9. Sales brochure
10. Media contact information
11. URL links to these online documents instead of email attachments.
12. Our blog URL address.

Press Releases

We will use well-written press releases to not only catch a reader's attention, but also to clearly and concisely communicate our business' mission, goals and capabilities.

The following represents a partial list of some of the reasons we will issue a free press release on a regular basis:

1. Announce Grand Opening Event and the availability of services.
2. Planned Open House Event
3 Addition of new product releases or service introduction.
4. Support for a Non-profit Cause or other local event, such as a Child Register Drive.
5. Presentation of a free seminar or workshop on screening techniques.
6. Report Survey Results
7. Publication of an article or book on industry compliance trends.
8. Receiving an Association Award.
9. Additional training/certification/licensing received.

Examples:
http://screeningintelligence.com/press-release/

We will use the following techniques to get our press releases into print:

1. Find the right contact editor at a publication, that is, the editor who specializes in business or lifestyle issues.
2. Understand the target publication's format, flavor and style and learn to think like its readers to better tailor our pitch.
3. Ask up front if the journalist is on deadline.
4. Request a copy of the editorial calendar--a listing of targeted articles or subjects broken down by month or issue date, to determine the issue best suited for the content of our news release or article.
5. Make certain the press release appeals to a large audience by reading a couple of back issues of the publication we are targeting to familiarize ourselves with its various sections and departments.
6. Customize the PR story to meet the magazine's particular style.
7. Avoid creating releases that look like advertising or self-promotion.
8. Make certain the release contains all the pertinent and accurate information the journalist will need to write the article and accurately answer the questions "who, what, when, why and where".
9. Include a contact name and telephone number for the reporter to call for more information.

PR Distribution Checklist

We will send copies of our press releases to the following entities:

1. Send it to clients to show accomplishments.

2.   Send to prospects to help prospects better know who you are and what you do.
3.   Send it to vendors to strengthen the relationship and to influence referrals.
4.   Send it to strategic partners to strengthen and enhance the commitment and support to our firm.
5.   Send it to employees to keep them in the loop.
6.   Send it to Employees' contacts to increase the firm's visibility exponentially.
7.   Send it to elected-officials who often provide direction for their constituents.
8.   Send it to trade associations for maximum exposure.
9.   Put copies in the lobby and waiting areas.
10. Put it on our Web site, to enable visitors to find out who we are and what our firm is doing, with the appropriate links to more detailed information.
11. Register the Web page with search engines to increase search engine optimization.
12. Put it in our press kit to provide members of the media background information about our firm.
13. Include it in our newsletter to enable easy access to details about company activities.
14. Include it in our brochure to provide information that compels the reader to contact our firm when in need of legal counsel.
15. Hand it out at trade shows and job fairs to share news with attendees and establish credibility.

Media List

Journalist	Interests	Organization	Contact Info

Distribution:

www.1888PressRelease.com	www.ecomwire.com
www.prweb.com	www.WiredPRnews.com
www.PR.com	www.eReleases.com
www.24-7PressRelease.com	www.NewsWireToday.com
www.PRnewswire.com	www.onlinePRnews.com
www.PRLog.org	**www.onlinepressreleases.com**
www.businesswire.com	www.marketwire.com
www.primezone.com	www.primewswire.com
www.xpresspress.com/	www.ereleases.com/index.html
www.Mediapost.com	
www.falkowinc.com/inc/proactive_report.html	

Journalist Lists: www.mastheads.org   www.easymedialist.com
                     www.helpareporter.com

Media Directories

Bacon's –	www.bacons.com/	AScribe –	www.ascribe.org/
Newspapers –	www.newspapers.com/	Gebbie Press –	www.gebbieinc.com/

Support Services

PR Web -	http://www.prweb.com
Yahoo News –	http://news.yahoo.com/

Google News –   http://news.google.com/
Resource:
http://www.ehow.com/how_2043935_write-press-release.html
https://blog.hubspot.com/marketing/press-release-template-ht

Media Resource Expert

We will send email and mail to local media outlets, like our local TV news stations, Local Newspapers, and News Radio Stations, to advise them that we are a readily available resource for background check related new stories. We will include our areas of specialty, and how we can contribute to media stories about _____ and home tasting and cocktail parties in general. We will also indicate our willingness to share our knowledge on how the public can prevent from being scammed by unethical _____. We will always be on the look-out for opportunities to interview with local and national reporters. We will sign up for the following services that notify companies of reporters looking for interviews:

Reporter Connection   http://reporterconnection.com/
ProfNet Connection   http://www.profnetconnect.com/
Muck Rack   https://muckrack.com/benefits
News Wise   www.newswise.com/
Pitch Rate   http://pitchrate.com/
Experts   www.experts.com
News Basis   http://newsbasis.com/

Help A Reporter Out   www.helpareporter.com/
HARO is an online platform that provides journalists with a robust database of sources for upcoming stories. It also provides business owners and marketers with opportunities to serve as sources and secure valuable media coverage.

Resources:
http://www.thebuzzfactoree.com/journalists-seeking-sources/
http://ijnet.org/en/blog/5-ways-find-sources-online

Sample Letter Template:
http://locksmithprofits.com/locksmith-guest-expert-marketing/

Direct Mail Campaign

A direct mail package consisting of a tri-fold brochure, letter of introduction, and reply card will be sent to a list of new businesses in _____ County. This list can be obtained from International Business Lists, Inc. (Chicago, IL) and is compiled from Secretary of State incorporation registrations, business license applications, announcements from newspaper clippings, and tax records. The letter will introduce _____ (company name), and describe our competitive advantages. The package will also include a promotional offer—the opportunity to sample our background check services. Approximately ten days after the mailing, a telephone follow-up will be conducted to make sure the brochure was received, whether the client has any questions, or would like to schedule an appointment.

Our direct mail program will feature the following key components:
1.   A call to action.
2.   Test marketing using a limited 100-piece mailing.
3.   A defined set of target markets.
4.   A follow up phone call.
5.   A personalized cover letter.
7.   A special trial offer with an expiration date.

Resource:

www.directmailquotes.com/rfq/quote1.cfm?affiliate=14

Postcards
1.   We will use a monthly, personalized, newsletter styled postcard, that includes pre-employment screening suggestions, to stay-in-touch with business customers.
2.   Postcards will offer cheaper mailing rates, staying power and attention-grabbing graphics, but require repetition, like most other advertising methods.
3.   We will develop an in-house list of potential clients for routine communications from open house events, seminar registrations, direct response ads, etc.
4.   We will use postcards to encourage users to visit our website and take advantage of a special offer.
5.   We will grab attention and communicate a single-focus message in just a few words.
6.   The visual elements of our postcard (color, picture, symbol) will be strong to help get attention and be directly supportive of the message.
7.   We will facilitate a call to immediate action by prominently displaying our phone number and website address.
8.   We will include a clear deadline, expiration date, limited quantity, or consequence of inaction that is connected to the offer to communicate immediacy and increase response.

Resource:

www.Postcardmania.com

Flyers
1.   We will seek permission to post flyers on the bulletin boards in local businesses, community centers, and local colleges.
2.   We will also insert flyers into our direct mailings.
3.   We will use our flyers as part of a handout package at seminar events.
4.   The flyers will feature a discount coupon and testimonials.
5.   The flyers will contain a listing of our service category benefits.

Referral Program
We understand the importance of setting up a formal referral network through contacts with the following characteristics:
1.   We will give a premium reward based simply on people giving referral names on the registration form or customer satisfaction survey.

2. Send an endorsed testimonial letter from a loyal customer to the referred prospect.
3. Include a separate referral form as a direct response device.
4. Provide a space on the response form for leaving positive comments that can be used to build a testimonial letter, that will be sent to each referral.
5. We will clearly state our incentive rewards, and terms and conditions.
6. We will distribute a newsletter to stay in touch with our clients and include articles about our referral program success stories.
7. We will encourage our staff at weekly meetings to seek referrals from their personal and business contacts.

Examples:
https://www.findoutthetruth.com/affiliate_program.htm

Methods:
1. Always have ready a 30-second elevator speech that describes what you do and who you do it for.
2. Use a newsletter to keep our name in front of referrals sources.
3. Repeatedly demonstrate to referral sources that we are also thinking about their practice or business.
4. Regularly send referrals sources articles on unique yet important topics that might affect their businesses.
5. Use Microsoft Outlook to flag our contacts to remind us it is time to give them some form of personal attention.
6. Ask referral sources for referrals.
7. Get more work from a referral source by sending them work.
8. Immediately thank a referral source, even for the mere act of giving his name to a third party for consideration.
9. Remember referral sources with generous gift baskets and gift certificates.
10. Schedule regular lunches with former school classmates and new contacts.

We will offer an additional donation of $ _____ to any organization whose member use a referral coupon to become a client. The coupon will be paid for and printed in the organization's newsletter.

Referral Tracking Form

Referral Source Name	Presently Referring Yes/No	No. of Clients Referred	Anticipated Revenue	Actions to be Taken	Target Date

Sample Referral Program
We want to show our appreciation to established customers and business network partners for their kind referrals to our business. _____ (company name) wants to reward our valued and loyal customers who support our _____ Programs by implementing a new

referral program. Ask any of our team members for referral cards to share with your business associates to begin saving towards your next _____ (product/service) purchase. We will credit your account $___ (?) for each new customer you refer to us as well as give them 10% off their first visit. When they come for their first visit, they should present the card upon arrival. We will automatically set you up a referral account.

Resources:
https://www.thebalance.com/how-to-get-testimonials-and-referrals-1794616

We will use software tools, such as those offered by providers like Extole, DirectTrack, and ReferralCandy, to create customized referral programs.

Resources:
http://brightsmack.com/marketing-strategies/37-referral-ideas-to-grow-your-business/
http://www.nisacards.com/Business-Referral-Marketing-Cards.aspx
https://www.referralsaasquatch.com/resources/
https://www.referralcandy.com/blog/47-referral-programs/
www.consultingsuccess.com/10-referral-strategies-to-grow-your-consulting-business

Resources:
Referral Program Software Packages
> www.invitebox.com
> www.referralsaasquatch.com/
> www.referralcandy.com/
> www.getambassador.com/

Statistics that support referral programs include:
92% of consumers trust peer recommendations, 40% trust advertising in search results, 36% trust online video ads, 36% trust sponsored ads on social networking sites and 33% trust online banner ads.

The average value of a referred customer is at least 16% higher than that of a non-referred customer with similar demographics and time of acquisition.

Examples:
www.extole.com/blog/an-epic-list-of-75-besties-referral-programs-for-2018/

Example:
Pass the word around to your business partners, friends, churches, and volunteer groups that CIA provides background screening solutions to match their needs! You will receive a $25 American Express gift card for each qualified referral. Once you have three or more referrals in a calendar year, you are qualified for our annual 'grand prize' drawing ($500 American Express gift card).Click here and use this PDF document to share with those who may need our services.
Source:
www.ciaresearch.com/system/website.nsf/WebForm?OpenForm&FORM=Referral

The Referral Details are as Follows:

1. You will receive a $__ (?) credit for every customer that you refer for _____ (products/services). Credit will be applied to your referral account on their initial visit.

2. We will keep track of your accumulated reward dollars and at any time we can let you know the amount you have available for use in your reward account.

3. Each time you visit ____ (company name), you can use your referral dollars to pay up to 50% of your total charge that day

4. Referral dollars are not applicable towards the purchase of _____ products.

5. All referral rewards are for _____ services and cannot be used towards _____ services.

Referral Coupon Template

Company Name: _____

Address: _____

Phone: _____ Website: _____

Print and present this coupon with your first order and the existing customer who referred you will receive a credit for $_____ towards _____.

Current customer	**Referred customer**
Name: _____	Name: _____
Address: _____	Address: _____
Phone: _____	Phone: _____
Email: _____	Email: _____
Date referred: _____	

Office use only

Credit memo number:_____

Credit issued date: _____   Credit applied by: _____

Invite-A-Friend

We will setup an aggressive invite-a-friend referral program. We will encourage new members or newsletter subscribers, during their initial registration process, to upload and send an invitation to multiple contacts in their email address books. We will encourage them by providing an added incentive, such as a free _____.

Seminars

Seminars present the following marketing and bonding opportunities:

1. Signage and branding as a presenting sponsor.

2. Opportunity to provide logo imprinted handouts.

3. Media exposure through advertising and public relations.

4. The opportunity for one-on-one interaction with a targeted group of consumers to demonstrate an understanding of their needs and our matching expert solutions.

5. Use of sign-in sheet to collect names and email addresses for database build.

6. Present opportunity to sell products, such as workbooks.

Possible seminar funding sources:
1.   Small registration fee to cover the cost of hand-outs and refreshments.
2.   Get sponsorship funding from partner/networking organizations.
3.   Sponsorship classified ads in the program guide or handouts.

We will establish our expertise and trustworthiness by offering free seminars on the following topics:
1.   How to Locate and Evaluate Background Check Companies
2.   How to Plan a Successful Hiring Program
3.   How to Lower Your Employee Hiring Risk Profile

Seminar target groups include the following:

1.	Corporations	2.	Country Clubs
3.	Stockbrokers	4.	Property Managers
5.	Private Individuals	6.	Realtors
7.	Attorneys	8.	Store Customers
9.	Insurance Brokers		

Seminar marketing approaches include:
1.   Posting to website and enabling online registrations.
2.   Email blast to in-house database using www.constantcontact.com
3.   Include seminar schedule in newsletter and flyer.
4.   Classified ads using craigslist.org

Seminar Objectives:

Seminar Topic	Target Audience	Handout	Target Date

Customer Reward / Loyalty Program

As a means of building business by word-of-mouth, customers will be encouraged and rewarded as repeat customers. This will be accomplished by offering a discounted _____ to those customers who sign-up for our frequent buyer card and purchase $____ of products and services within a ____ (#) month period.

Frequent Buyer Program Types:

1.	Punch Cards	Receive something for free after? Purchases.
2.	Dollar-for-point Systems	Accrue points toward a free product.
3.	Percentage of Purchase	Accrue points toward future purchases.

Resources:
http://www.refinery29.com/best-store-loyalty-programs
https://thrivehive.com/customer-retention-and-loyalty-programs/
http://blog.fivestars.com/5-companies-loyalty-programs/
www.americanexpress.com/us/small-business/openforum/articles/10-cool-mobile-apps-
        that-increase-customer-loyalty/

https://squareup.com/loyalty
www.consumerreports.org/cro/news/2013/10/retailer-loyalty-rewards-
        programs/index.htm

Sample: Loyalty Program
_____ (company name) LOYALTY PROGRAM
ACCRUE YOUR POINTS WITH THE FOLLOWING:
        Sign-up Bonus receive 1,000 points
        Pre-book your next visit receive 1,000 points
        Refer a Friend receive 2,500 points
        Retail Purchase receive 1 point/dollar spent
        Service Purchase receive 1 point/dollar spent
REDEEMING POINT VALUE 100 POINTS = $1
Ex: For a $100 purchase, you will redeem 10,000 points

E-mail Marketing

We will use the following email marketing tips to build our mailing list database, improve communications, boost customer loyalty and attract new and repeat business.
1.   Define our objectives as the most effective email strategies are those that offer value to our subscribers: either in the form of educational content or promotions. To drive sales, a promotional campaign is the best format. To create brand recognition and reinforce our expertise in our industry we will use educational newsletters.
2.   A quality, permission-based email list will be a vital component of our email marketing campaign. We will ask customers and prospects for permission to add them to our list at every touch-point or use a sign-in sheet.
3.   We will listen to our customers by using easy-to-use online surveys to ask specific questions about customers' preferences, interests and satisfaction.
4.   We will send only relevant and targeted communications.
5.   We will reinforce our brand to ensure recognition of our brand by using a recognizable name in the "from" line of our emails and including our company name, logo and a consistent design and color scheme in every email.

Resources:
https://www.thebalance.com/growing-and-nurturing-your-email-list-1794610
https://cbtnews.com/8-tips-drive-successful-email-marketing-campaign/
https://www.inman.com/2017/06/05/4-tips-for-effective-email-marketing/
https://due.com/blog/ways-take-good-care-email-list/

Every ____ (five?) to _____ (six?) weeks, we will send graphically-rich, permission-based, personalized, email marketing messages to our list of customers who registered on our website, or at a trade show or seminar. The emails will alert customers in a ____ (50?)-mile radius to promotions as well as other local events sponsored by our company. This service will be provided by either ExactTarget.com or ConstantContact.com. The email will announce a special seminar event and contain a short sales letter. The message will invite recipients to click on a link to our website to checkout more information about the event, then print out the page and bring it with them to the event. The software offered by these two companies will automatically personalize each email with the customer's name. The software also provides detailed click-through behavior reports that will enable us to evaluate the success of each message. The software will also allow us to dramatically scale back its direct mail efforts and associated costs. Our company will send a promotional e-mail about an event that the customer indicated was important to them in their registration application. Each identified market segment will get notified of new services, and business availabilities based on past buying patterns and what they've clicked on in our previous e-newsletters or indicated on their surveys. The objective is to tap the right customer's need at the right time, with a targeted subject line and targeted content. Our general e-newsletter may appeal to most customers, but targeted mailings that reach out to our various audience segments will build even deeper relationships and drive higher sales.

Resources:

www.constantcontact.com/pricing/email-marketing.jsp

www.deverus.com/resources/articles/item/66-5-ways-to-market-your-background-check-
     company

http://www.verticalresponse.com/blog/10-retail-marketing-ideas-to-boost-sales/

Google Reviews

We will use our email marketing campaign to ask people for reviews. We will ask people what they thought of our background check business or party planning services and encourage them to write a Google Review if they were impressed. We will incorporate a call to action (CTA) on our email auto signature with a link to our Google My Review page.

Source:

https://superb.digital/how-to-ask-your-clients-for-google-reviews/

Resources:

https://support.google.com/business/answer/3474122?hl=en

https://support.google.com/maps/answer/6230175?co=GENIE.Platform
     %3DDesktop&hl=en

www.patientgain.com/how-to-get-positive-google-reviews

Example:

We will tell our customers to:

1.   Go to https://www.google.com/maps
2.   Type in your business name, select the listing
3.   There's a "card" (sidebar) on the left-hand side. At the bottom, they can click 'Be the First to Write a Review' or 'Write a Review' if you already have one review.

Source:

https://www.reviewjump.com/blog/how-do-i-get-google-reviews/

Voice Broadcasting

A web-based voice broadcast system will provide a powerful platform to generate thousands of calls to clients and customers or create customizable messages to be delivered to specific individuals. Voice broadcasting and voice mail broadcast will allow our company to instantly send interactive phone calls with ease while managing the entire proccss right from the Web. We will instantly send alerts, notifications, reminders, GOTV - messages, and interactive surveys with ease right from the Web. The free VoiceShot account will guide us through the process of recording and storing our messages, managing our call lists, scheduling delivery as well as viewing and downloading real-time call and caller key press results. The voice broadcasting interface will guide us through the entire process with a Campaign Checklist as well as tips from the Campaign Expert. Other advanced features include recipient targeting, call monitoring, scheduling, controlling the rate of call delivery and customized text to speech (TTS).

Resource:

http://www.voiceshot.com/public/outboundcalls.asp

Facebook.com

We will use Facebook to move our businesses forward and stay connected to our customers in this fast-paced world. Content will be the key to staying in touch with our customers and keeping them informed. The content will be a rich mix of information, before and after photos, interactive questions, current trends and events, industry facts, education, promotions and specials, humor and fun. We will use the following step system to get customers from Facebook.com:

1. We will open a free Facebook account at Facebook.com.
2. We will begin by adding Facebook friends. The fastest way to do this is to allow Facebook to import our email addresses and send an invite out to all our patients.
3. We will post a video to get our customers involved with our Facebook page. We will post a video called "How to Reduce Workplace Violence and Theft through Pre-employment Screening." The video will be first uploaded to YouTube.com and then simply be linked to our Facebook page. Video will be a great way to get people active and involved with our Facebook page.
4. We will send an email to our customers base that encourages them to check out the new video and to post their feedback about it on our Facebook page. Then we will provide a link, driving customers to our Facebook page.
5. We will respond quickly to feedback, engage in the dialogue and add links to our response that direct the author to a structured mini-survey.
6. We will optimize our Facebook profile with our business keyword to make it an invaluable marketing tool and become the "go-to" expert in our industry
7. On a monthly basis, we will send out a message to all Facebook fans with a special offer, as Fan pages are the best way to interact with customers and potential customers on Facebook,
8. We will use Facebook as a tool for sharing success stories and relate the ways in which we have helped our customers.

9. We will use Facebook Connect to integrate our Facebook efforts with our regular website to share our Facebook Page activity. This will also give us statistics about our website visitors and add social interaction to our site.

Resource:
http://www.facebook.com/advertising/
http://www.socialmediaexaminer.com/how-to-set-up-a-facebook-page-for-business/
http://smallbizsurvival.com/2009/11/6-big-facebook-tips-for-small-business.html

Facebook Profiles represent individual users and are held under a person's name. Each profile should only be controlled by that person. Each user has a wall, information tab, likes, interests, photos, videos and each individual can create events.

Facebook Groups are pretty similar to Fan Pages but are usually created for a group of people with a similar interest and they are wanting to keep their discussions private. The members are not usually looking to find out more about a business - they want to discuss a certain topic.

Facebook Fan Pages are the most viral of your three options. When someone becomes a fan of your page or comments on one of your posts, photos or videos, that is spread to all of their personal friends. This can be a great way to get your information out to lots of people...and quickly! In addition, one of the most valuable features of a business page is that you can send "updates" about new products and content to fans and your home building brand becomes more visible.

Facebook Live lets people, public figures and Pages share live video with their followers and friends on Facebook.
Source:
https://live.fb.com/about/
Resource:
http://smartphones.wonderhowto.com/news/facebook-is-going-all-live-video-streaming-your-phone-0170132/

Facebook Business Page
Resources:
https://www.facebook.com/business/learn/set-up-facebook-page
https://www.pcworld.com/article/240258/how_to_make_a_facebook_page_for_your_small_business.html
https://blog.hubspot.com/blog/tabid/6307/bid/5492/how-to-create-a-facebook-business-page-in-5-simple-steps-with-video.aspx

Small Business Promotions
This group allows members to post about their products and services and is a public group designated as a Buy and Sell Facebook group.
Source: https://www.facebook.com/groups/smallbusinesspronotions/
Resource:

https://www.facebook.com/business/a/local-business-promotion-ads
https://www.facebook.com/business/learn/facebook-create-ad-local-awareness
www.socialmediaexaminer.com/how-to-use-facebook-local-awareness-ads-to-target-customers/

Facebook Ad Builder
https://waymark.com/signup/db869ac4-7202-4e3b-93c3-80acc5988df9/?partner=fitsmallbusiness

Facebook Lead Ads   **www.facebook.com/business/a/lead-ads**
A type of sponsored ad that appears in your audience's timeline just like other Facebook ads. However, the goal with lead ads is literally to capture the lead's info without them leaving Facebook. These ads don't link to a website landing page, creating an additional step.

Facebook Local Reach Ads
www.facebook.com/business/learn/facebook-create-ad-reach-ads
www.facebook.com/business/help/906073466193087?ref=fbb_reach

Best social media marketing practices:
1.   Assign daily responsibility for Facebook to a single person on your staff with an affinity for dialoguing.
2.   Set expectations for how often they should post new content and how quickly they should respond to comments – usually within a couple hours.
3.   Follow and like your followers when they seem to have a genuine interest in your area of health and wellness expertise.
4.   Post on the walls of not only your own Facebook site, but also on your most active, influential posters with the largest networks.
5.   Periodically post a request for your followers to "like" your page.
6.   Monitor Facebook posts to your wall and respond every two hours throughout your business day.

We will use Facebook in the following ways to market our background checking service:
1.   Promote our blog posts on our Facebook page
2.   Post a video of our service people in action.
3.   Make time-sensitive offers during slow periods
4.   Create a special landing page for coupons or promotional giveaways
5.   Create a Welcome tab to display a video message from our owner.
      Resource: Pagemodo.
6.   Support a local charity by posting a link to their website.
7.   Thank our customers while promoting their businesses at the same time.
8.   Describe milestone accomplishments and thank customers for their role.
9.   Give thanks to corporate accounts.
10.   Ask customers to contribute stories about _____ occurrences.
11.   Use the built-in Facebook polling application to solicit feedback.

12. Use the Facebook reviews page to feature positive comments from customers, and to respond to negative reviews.
13. Introduce customers to our staff with resume and video profiles.
14. Create a photo gallery of unusual _____ (requests/jobs?) to showcase our expertise.

We will also explore location-based platforms like the following:

- FourSquare
- Facebook Places
- GoWalla
- Google Latitude

As a background checking service also serving a local community, we will appreciate the potential for hyper-local platforms like these. Location-based applications are increasingly attracting young, urban influencers with disposable income, which is precisely the audience we are trying to attract. People connect to geo-location apps primarily to "get informed" about local happenings.

Examples:
www.facebook.com/pages/Accurate-Background/187734613134
https://www.facebook.com/nationsearch/

Foursquare.com

A web and mobile application that allows registered users to post their location at a venue ("check-in") and connect with friends. Check-in requires active user selection and points are awarded at check-in. Users can choose to have their check-ins posted on their accounts on Twitter, Facebook, or both. In version 1.3 of their iPhone application, foursquare enabled push-notification of friend updates, which they call "Pings". Users can also earn badges by checking in at locations with certain tags, for check-in frequency, or for other patterns such as time of check-in.
Resource:
https://foursquare.com/business/

Instagram

Instagram.com is an online photo-sharing, video-sharing and social networking service that enables its users to take pictures and videos, apply digital filters to them, and share them on a variety of social networking services, such as
Facebook, Twitter, Tumblr and Flickr. A distinctive feature is that it confines photos to a square shape, similar to Kodak Instamatic and Polaroid images, in contrast to the 16:9 aspect ratio now typically used by mobile device cameras. Users are also able to record and share short videos lasting for up to 15 seconds.

Resources:
http://www.wordstream.com/blog/ws/2015/01/06/instagram-marketing

We will use Instagram in the following ways to help amplify the story of our brand, get people to engage with our content when not at our store, and get people to visit our store or site:

1.   Let our customers and fans know about specific product availability.
2.   Tie into trends, events or holidays to drive awareness.
3.   Let people know we are open and our service range is spectacular.
4.   Run a monthly contest and pick the winning hash-tagged photograph to activate our customer base and increase our exposure.
5.   Encourage the posting and collection of happy onsite or offsite customer photos.

Examples:
https://www.instagram.com/socialcatfish/

Note: Commonly found in tweets, a hashtag is a word or connected phrase (no spaces) that begins with a hash symbol (#). They're so popular that other social media platforms including Facebook, Instagram and Google+ now support them. Using a hashtag turns a word or phrase into a clickable link that displays a feed (list) of other posts with that same hashtag. For example, if you click on #_____ in a tweet, or enter #_____ in the search box, you'll see a list of tweets all about _____.

Snapchat

This is a photo messaging app for iPhone and Android mobile devices. Users can take a picture or video and add text, drawings, and a variety of filters. They set a designated time limit, 1-10 seconds, and send to selected contacts from their list. Users can also set a "story" – a Snap that pins to their profile and is viewable for 24 hours after posting. Snapchat photos display for a maximum of 10 seconds (for 24 hours, in the case of a snap story) before becoming permanently inaccessible. The user may choose to save their snaps, but this will only save it to their local device. If the receiver uses the screenshot function on their phone, or chooses to replay a snap, the sender is notified. The point of Snapchat is to be fun and quirky, enticing and engaging your contacts with visual snippets of whatever you are doing. Teen and millennial users enjoy using Snapchat where they would traditionally send a text message. In many cases it's easier and more stimulating to send a quick clip of the property you are viewing, for example, than it would be to send a text description.

Snapchat is not useful as a lead generating tool, but it is exceptionally useful for client engagement and retention. When we meet with a client and exchange mobile contact information, we will ask if they use Snapchat and if we can add them to keep them updated on the property hunt. The beauty of the Snap is that is draws the client into the environment and makes them want to see more. We will use this limitation to our advantage and make our client feel compelled to request and attend more property showings. Snapchat is also a phenomenal tool to engage with existing clients. It will make buyers feel connected to the sales agent and the property searching process, which is conducive to converting sales and retaining these clients in the future. While the primary user demographic is in the millennial age range, the app is popular with many adults as well. Incorporating Snapchat into our client communication strategy will aid our ability to close deals swiftly and form long term client relationships.

Resources:
https://blog.hootsuite.com/smart-ways-to-use-snapchat-for-business/

http://smallbiztrends.com/2014/10/how-businesses-can-use-snapchat.html
http://nymag.com/selectall/2018/04/the-snapchat-101-the-best-coolest-smartest-weirdest-accounts.html
https://sites.google.com/site/backgroundcheckcompanies06/-how-to-find-people-on-snapchat-background-check-records-free-web

MySpace Advertising

MySpace.com offers a self-service, graphical "display" advertising platform that will enable our company to target our marketing message to our audience by demographic characteristics. With the new MySpace service, we will be able to upload our own ads or make them quickly with an online tool and set a budget of $25 to $10,000 for the campaigns. We can choose to target a specific gender, age group and geographic area. We will then pay MySpace each time someone clicks on our ad. Ads can link to other MySpace pages, or external websites. MyAds will let us target our ads to specific groups of people using the public data on MySpace users' profiles, blogs and comments. MySpace will enable our company to target potential customers with similar interests to our existing customer base, as revealed via our marketing research surveys. Also, the bulletin function on MySpace will allow us to update customers on company milestone achievements and coming events. We will also post a short video to our home page and encourage the sharing of the video with other MySpace users.
Examples:
https://myspace.com/instantcriminalchecks

LinkedIn.com

LinkedIn groups will be a fantastic source of information and a great source of leads for our background checking service business. LinkedIn ranks high in search engines and will provide a great platform for sending event updates to business associates. To optimize our LinkedIn profile, we will select one core keyword. We will use it frequently, without sacrificing consumer experience, to get our profile to skyrocket in the search engines. Linkedin provides options that will allow our detailed profile to be indexed by search engines, like Google. We will make use of these options, so our business will achieve greater visibility on the Web. We will use widgets to integrate other tools, such as importing your blog entries or Twitter stream into your profile and go market research and gain knowledge with Polls. We will answer questions to show our expertise and ask questions in Questions and Answers to get a feel for what customers and prospects want or think. We will publish our LinkedIn URL on all our marketing collateral, including business cards, email signature, newsletters, and web site. We will grow our network by joining industry and alumni groups related to our business. We will update our status examples of recent work and link our status updates with our other social media accounts. We will start and manage a group or fan page for our product, brand or business. We will share useful articles that will be of interest to customers, and request LinkedIn recommendations from customers willing to provide testimonials. We will post our presentations on our profile using a presentation application. We will ask our first-level contacts for introductions to their contacts and interact with LinkedIn on a regular basis to reach those who may not see us on other social media sites. We will link to articles posted elsewhere, with a summary of why it's valuable to add to our credibility and list our newsletter subscription information and archives. We will post discounts and package deals. We will buy a LinkedIn direct ad that our target market will see. We will find vendors and contractors through connections.

Examples:

www.linkedin.com/company/one-source-the-background-check-company

Podcasting

Podcasting is a way of publishing audio broadcasts via the internet through MP3 files, which users can listen to using PCs and i-Pods. Our podcasts will provide both information and advertising. Our podcasts will allow us to pull in a lot of customers. Our monthly podcasts will be heard by ___ (#) eventual subscribers. Podcasts can now be downloaded for mobile devices, such as an iPod. Podcasts will give our company a new way to provide information and an additional way to advertise. Podcasting will give our business another connection point with customers. We will use this medium to communicate on important issues, what is going on with a planned event, and other things of interest to our HR customers. The programs will last about 10 minutes and can be downloaded for free on iTunes. The purpose is not to be a mass medium. It is directed at a niche market with an above-average educational background and very special interests. It will provide a very direct and a reasonably inexpensive way of reaching our targeted audience with relevant information about our background screening services.

Resources: www.apple.com/itunes/download/.
                www.cbc.ca/podcasting/gettingstarted.html

Examples:

www.hireright.com/blog/2018/09/podcast-top-background-screening-trends-in-2018-2/

Blogging

We will use our blog to keep customers and prospects informed about products, events and services that relate to our background screening business. Our blog will show readers that we are a good source of expert information that they can count on. With our blog, we can quickly update our customers anytime our company releases a new product, the holding of a contest or are placing member services on special pricing. We will use our blog to share customer testimonials and meaningful product usage stories. Our visitors will be able to subscribe to our RSS feeds and be instantly updated without any spam filters interfering. We will also use the blog to solicit product usage recommendations and future service addition suggestions. Additionally, blogs are free and allow for constant ease of updating.

Our blog will give our company the following benefits:
1.   A cost-effective marketing tool.
2.   An expanded network.
3.   A promotional platform for new services.
4.   An introduction to people with similar interests.
5.   Builds credibility and expertise recognition.

We will use our blog for the following purposes:
1. To share customer testimonials, experiences and meaningful success stories.
2. Update our clients anytime our background checking company releases a new service.
3. Supply advice on party planning options.
4. Discuss research findings.
5. To publish helpful content.
6, To welcome feedback in multiple formats.
7. Link together other social networking sites, including Twitter.
8. To improve Google rankings.
9. Make use of automatic RSS feeds.

We will adhere to the following blog writing guidelines:
1. We will blog at least 2 or 3 times per week to maintain interest.
2. We will integrate our blog into the design of our website.
3. We will use our blog to convey useful information and not our advertisements.
4. We will make the content easy to understand.
5. We will focus our content on the needs of our targeted audience.

Our blog will feature the following on a regular basis:
1. Useful articles and assessment coupons.
2. Give away of a helpful free report in exchange for email addresses
3. Helpful information for our professional referral sources, as well as clients, and online and offline community members.
5. Use of a few social media outposts to educate, inform, engage and drive people back to our blog for more information and our free report.

To get visitors to our blog to take the next action step and contact our firm we will do the following:
1. Put a contact form on the upper-left hand corner of our blog, right below the header.
2. Put our complete contact information in the header itself.
3. Add a page to our blog and title it, "Become My Client.", giving the reader somewhere to go for the next sign-up steps.
4. At the end of each blog post, we will clearly tell the reader what to do next; such as subscribe to our RSS feed, or to sign up for our newsletter mailing list.

Subscribe to the ESR News Blog
The ESR News Blog provides up to date information about the employment background check industry to employers, HR professionals, security, recruiters, and consumers. ESR News covers a variety of topics including Ban the Box, credit reports, criminal records, data privacy, Equal Employment Opportunity Commission (EEOC), E-Verify, Fair Credit Reporting Act (FCRA), international screening, jobs reports, lawsuits involving screening, social media background checks, and workplace violence. To

subscribe to the ESR News Blog, please fill out the following required fields (*) and press SUBMIT.
Source: www.esrcheck.com/wordpress/2015/12/23/background-check-industry-will-
continue-to-both-expand-and-consolidate-simultaneously-in-2016/

Example:
The SafeScreener.com blog is a valuable information source for human resource professionals and those seeking employment alike. We provide employment screening to hundreds of corporations and organizations throughout the United States. In doing so, we have an ongoing duty to stay abreast of changing trends as well as state and federal legislation. Here we bring you straightforward information on the how's, why's, do's and dont's, of applicant background checks.
Source:
http://safescreener.blogspot.com/2014/09/small-business-background-checks-are.html

Resources:
www.blogger.com
www.blogspot.com
www.wordpress.com

Examples:
www.hireright.com/blog/
https://www.nationsearch.com/blog

Twitter

We will use 'Twitter.com' as a way to produce new business from existing clients and generate prospective clients online. Twitter is a free social networking and micro-blogging service that allows its users to send and read other users' updates (otherwise known as tweets), which are text-based posts of up to 140 characters in length. Updates are displayed on the user's profile page and delivered to other users who have signed up to receive them. The sender can restrict delivery to those in his or her circle of friends, with delivery to everyone being the default. Users can receive updates via the Twitter website, SMS text messaging, RSS feeds, or email. We will use our Twitter account to respond directly to questions, distribute news, solve problems, post updates, and offer special discounts on background screening services.

We will provide the following instructions to register as a 'Follower' of _____ (company name) on Twitter:
1. In your Twitter account, click on 'Find People' in the top right navigation bar, which will redirect to a new page.
2. Click on 'Find on Twitter' which will open a search box that says: 'Who are you looking for?'
3. Type '_____ (company name) / _____ (owner name)' and click 'search'. This will bring up the results page.
4. Click the blue '_____' name to read the bio or select the 'Follow' button.

Resources:
https://twitter.com/hashtag/backgroundcheck?lang=en
Examples:
http://twitter.com/#!/court_records

Testimonial Marketing

We will either always ask for testimonials immediately after a completed project or contact our clients once a quarter for them. We will also have something prepared that we would like the client to say that is specific to a service we offer, or anything relevant to advertising claims that we have put together. For the convenience of the client we will assemble a testimonial letter that they can either modify or just sign off on. Additionally, testimonials can also be in the form of audio or video and put on our website or mailed to potential clients in the form of a DVD or Audio CD. A picture with a testimonial is also excellent. We will put testimonials directly on a magazine ad, slick sheet, brochure, or website, or assemble a complete page of testimonials for our sales presentation folder.

Examples:
https://www.trudiligence.com/testimonials

We will collect customer testimonials in the following ways:
1. Our website – A page dedicated to testimonials (written and/or video).
2. Social media accounts – Facebook fan pages offer a review tab, which makes it easy to receive and display customer testimonials.
3. Google+ also offers a similar feature with Google+ Local.
4. Local search directories – Ask customers to post more reviews on Yelp and Yahoo Local.
5. Customer Satisfaction Survey Forms

We will pose the following questions to our customers to help them frame their testimonials:
1. What was the obstacle that would have prevented you from buying this product?
2. "What was your main concern about buying this product?"
3. What did you find as a result of buying this product?
4. What specific feature did you like most about this product?
5. What would be three other benefits about this product?
6. Would you recommend this product? If so, why?
7. Is there anything you'd like to add?

Resource:
https://smallbiztrends.com/2016/06/use-customer-testimonials.html

Business Logo

Our logo will graphically represent who we are and what we do, and it will serve to help brand our image. It will also convey a sense of uniqueness and professionalism. The logo will represent our company image and the message we are trying to convey. Our business logo will reflect the philosophy and objective of the Background Check Services business. Our logo will incorporate the following design guidelines:

1. It will relate to our industry, our name, a defining characteristic of our company or a competitive advantage we offer.
2. It will be a simple logo that can be recognized faster.
3. It will contain strong lines and letters which show up better than thin ones.
4. It will feature something unexpected or unique without being overdrawn.
5. It will work well in black and white (one-color printing).
6. It will be scalable and look pleasing in both small and large sizes.
7. It will be artistically balanced and make effective use of color, line density and shape.
8. It will be unique when compared to competitors.
9. It will use original, professionally rendered artwork.
10. It can be replicated across any media mix without losing quality.
11. It appeals to our target audience.
12. It will be easily recognizable from a distance if utilized in outdoor advertising.

Examples:
www.designcontest.com/logo-design/logo-design-for-a-start-up-drug-testing-and-background-check-company/
www.google.com/search?q=background+check+company+design+logo&tbm=isch&tbo=u&source=univ&sa=X&ved=0ahUKEwiDsvmW5dXbAhXKx1kKHfugALAQ7AkIbA&biw=1920&bih=966

Resources: www.freelogoservices.com/ www.hatchwise.com
     www.logosnap.com   www.99designs.com
     www.fiverr.com   www.freelancer.com
     www.upwork.com

Logo Design Guide:
www.bestfreewebresources.com/logo-design-professional-guide
www.creativebloq.com/graphic-design/pro-guide-logo-design-21221

Fundraisers

Community outreach programs involving charitable fundraising and showing a strong interest in the local school system will serve to elevate our status in the community as a "good corporate citizen" while simultaneously increasing traffic. We will execute a successful fundraising program for our background check service and build goodwill in the community, by adhering to the following guidelines:

1. Keep It Local
   When looking for a worthy cause, we will make sure it is local so the whole neighborhood will support it.
2. Plan It

We will make sure that we are organized and outline everything we want to accomplish before planning the fundraiser.

3.   Contact Local Media

We will contact the suburban newspapers to do stories on the event and send out press releases to the local TV and radio stations.

4.   Contact Area Businesses

We will contact other businesses and have them put up posters in their stores and pass out flyers to promote the event.

5.   Get Recipient Support

We will make sure the recipients of the fundraiser are really willing to participate and get out in the neighborhood to invite everyone into our store for the event, plus help pass out flyers and getting other businesses to put up the posters.

6.   Give Out Bounce Backs

We will give a "bounce-back" coupon that allows for both a discount and an additional donation in exchange for customer next purchase. (It will have an expiration date of two weeks to give a sense of urgency.)

7.   Be Ready with plenty of product and labor on hand for the event.

Fundraiser Action Plan Checklist:
1.   Choose a good local cause for your fundraiser.
2.   Calculate donations as a percentage for normal sales.
3.   Require the group to promote and support the event.
4.   Contact local media to get exposure before and after the event.
5.   Ask area businesses to put up flyers and donate printing of materials.
6.   Use a bounce-back coupon to get new customers back.
7.   Be prepared with sufficient labor and product.

Resource:
www.thefundraisingauthority.com/fundraising-basics/fundraising-event/

Online Directory Listings

The following directory listings use proprietary technology to match customers with industry professionals in their geographical area. The local search capabilities for specific niche markets offer an invaluable tool for the customer. These directories help member businesses connect with purchase-ready buyers, convert leads to sales, and maximize the value of customer relationships. Their online and offline communities provide a quick and easy low or no-cost solution for customers to find a transcription specialist quickly. We intend to sign-up with all no cost directories and evaluate the ones that charge a fee.

National Association of Professional Background Screeners   www.napbs.com
E-Verifile   www.e-verifile.com/admin/ncdc_jurisdiction_info.html
Background Check Directory   www.backgroundcheckdirectory.com/
Best Services   www.businessnewsdaily.com/7638-best-background-check-services.html

Other General Directories Include:

Listings.local.yahoo.com	Switchboard Super Pages
YellowPages.com	MerchantCircle.com
Bing.com/businessportal	Local.com
Yelp.com	BrownBook.com
InfoUSA.com	iBegin.com
Localeze.com	Bestoftheweb.com
YellowBot.com	HotFrog.com
InsiderPages.com	MatchPoint.com
CitySearch.com	YellowUSA.com
Profiles.google.com/me	Manta.com
Jigsaw.com	LinkedIn.com
Whitepages.com	PowerProfiles.com
Judysbook.com	Company.com

Get Listed	http://getlisted.org/enhanced-business-listings.aspx
Universal Business Listing	https://www.ubl.org/index.aspx
	www.UniversalBusinessListing.org

Universal Business Listing (UBL) is a local search industry service dedicated to acting as a central collection and distribution point for business information online. UBL provides business owners and their marketing representatives with a one-stop location for broad distribution of complete, accurate, and detailed listing information.

Google Maps

We will first make certain that our business is listed in Google Maps. We will do a search for our business in Google Maps. If we don't see our business listed, then we will add our business to Google Maps. Even if our business is listed in Google Maps, we will create a Local Business Center account and take control of our listing, by adding more relevant information. Consumers generally go to Google Maps for two reasons: Driving Directions and to Find a Business.
Resource:
http://maps.google.com/

Bing Maps   www.bingplaces.com/
Makes it easy for customers to find our business.

Apple Maps

A web mapping service developed by Apple Inc. It is the default map system of iOS, macOS, and watchOS. It provides directions and estimated times of arrival for automobile, pedestrian, and public transportation navigation.
Resources:
 http://www.stallcupgroup.com/2012/09/19/three-ways-to-make-your-pawn-business-
        more-profitable-and-sellable/
http://www.apple.com/ios/maps/

https://en.wikipedia.org/wiki/Apple_Maps

Google Places

Google Places helps people make more informed decisions about where to go for Background Check Services. Place Pages connect people to information from the best sources across the web, displaying photos, reviews and essential facts, as well as real-time updates and offers from business owners. We will make sure that our Google Places listing is up to date to increase our online visibility. Google Places is linked to our Google Maps listing and will help to get on the first page of Google search page results when people search for a Background Check Services in our area.
Resource:
www.google/com/places

Yelp.com

We will use Yelp.com to help people find our local business. Visitors to Yelp write local reviews, over 85% of them rating a business 3 stars or higher In addition to reviews, visitors can use Yelp to find events, special offers, lists and to talk with other Yelpers. As business owners, we will setup a free account to post offers, photos and message our customers. We will also buy ads on Yelp, which will be clearly labeled "Sponsored Results". We will also use the Weekly Yelp, which is available in 42 city editions to bring news about the latest business openings and other happenings.
Examples:
www.yelp.com/biz/identico-hallandale-beach
Resources:
https://biz.yelp.com/advertise

Proactive Management of Online Reviews
Resource:
http://www.fiveyellow.com/

Manta.com

Manta is the largest free source of information on small companies, with profiles of more than 64 million businesses and organizations. Business owners and sales professionals use Manta's vast database and custom search capabilities to quickly find companies, easily connect with prospective customers and promote their own services. Manta.com, founded in 2005, is based in Columbus, Ohio.
Examples:
http://www.manta.com/c/mmdgm44/accurate-background-inc

Pay-Per-Click Advertising

Google AdWords, Yahoo! Search Marketing, and Microsoft adCenter are the three largest network operators, and all three operate under a bid-based model. Cost per click (CPC) varies depending on the search engine and the level of competition for a particular keyword. Google AdWords are small text ads that appear next to the search results on

Google. In addition, these ads appear on many partner web sites, including NYTimes.com (The New York Times), Business.com, Weather.com, About.com, and many more. Google's text advertisements are short, consisting of one title line and two content text lines. Image ads can be one of several different Interactive Advertising Bureau (IAB) standard sizes. Through Google AdWords, we plan to buy placements (ads) for specific search terms through this "Pay-Per-Click" advertising program. This PPC advertising campaign will allow our ad to appear when someone searches for a keyword related to our business, organization, or subject matter. More importantly, we will only pay when a potential customer clicks on our ad to visit our website. For instance, since we operate a Background Check Services in ___ (city), _____ (state), we will target people using search terms such as "Background Check Services, investigations, criminal checks, employment checks, in ____ (city), ____ (state)". With an effective PPC campaign our ads will only be displayed when a user searches for one of these keywords. In short, PPC advertising will be the most cost-effective and measurable form of advertising for our Background Check Services.
Resources:
http://adwords.google.com/support/aw/?hl=en
www.wordtracker.com   Google External Keyword Tool
http://www.google.com/support/analytics/.
http://www.wordstream.com/local-online-marketing
https://www.wordstream.com/keywords
https://adwords.google.com/KeywordPlanner

Yahoo Local Listings

We will create our own local listing on Yahoo. To create our free listing, we will use our web browser and navigate to http://local.yahoo.com. We will first register for free with Yahoo and create a member ID and password to list our business. Once we have accessed http://local.yahoo.com, we will scroll down to the bottom and click on "Add/Edit a Business" to get onto the Yahoo Search Marketing Local Listings page. In the lower right of the screen we will see "Local Basic Listings FREE". We will click on the Get Started button and log in again with our new Yahoo ID and password. The form for our local business listing will now be displayed. When filling it out, we will be sure to include our full web address (http://www.companyname.com). We will include a description of our Background Check services in the description section, but avoid hype or blatant advertising, to get the listing to pass Yahoo's editorial review. We will also be sure to select the appropriate business category and sub categories.
Examples:
https://local.yahoo.com/info-15778301-selectioncom-cincinnati

Sales Reps/Account Executives

_____ (company name) will use independent commissioned sales reps to penetrate markets outside of _____ (city/state). Management will work to keep in constant communication with the sales reps to ensure that their service is professional and timely. Independent sales representatives will provide the best mode for distribution to maintain pricing controls and higher margins. Independent sales reps are not full-time employees thus benefits are not necessary. Independent sales reps receive a flat commission based on gross sales. Our sales reps are set at a commission rate of ___ (15?) % of gross sales. The average sales rep can service up to ___ (#) accounts with the average location generating around $____ per year. We expect to have ___(#) independent sales reps covering ___ (#) states in place to sell the company's product. In addition to field calls, sales reps will represent the product line at all regional tradeshows, with the marketing director attending all national tradeshows.

Advertorials

An advertorial is an advertisement written in the form of an objective article and presented in a printed publication—usually designed to look like a legitimate and independent news story. We will use quotes as testimonials to back up certain claims throughout our copy and break-up copy with subheadings to make the material more reader-friendly. We will include the "call to action" and contact information with a 24/7 voicemail number and a discount coupon. The advertorial will have a short intro about a client's experience with our Background Check Services and include quotes, facts, and statistics. We will present helpful information about the importance of background screening.

Affiliate Marketing

We will create an affiliate marketing program to broaden our reach. We will first devise a commission structure, so affiliates have a reason to promote our business. We will give them ___ (10) % of whatever sales they generate. We will go after event planner bloggers or webmasters who get a lot of web traffic for our keywords. These companies would then promote our products/services, and they would earn commissions for the sales they generated. We will work with the following services to handle the technical aspects of our program.

ConnectCommerce	www.connectcommerce.com/
Commission Junction	www.cj.com
ShareASale	www.shareasale.com/
Share Results	
LinkShare	www.linkshare.com
Clickbank	www.clickbank.com
Affiliate Scout	http://affiliatescout.com/
Affiliate Seeking	www.affiliateseeking.com/
Clix Galore	www.clixgalore.com/

HotFrog.com

HotFrog is a fast-growing free online business directory listing over 6.6 million US businesses. HotFrog now has local versions in 34 countries worldwide.
Anyone can list their business in HotFrog for free, along with contact details, and products and services. Listing in HotFrog directs sales leads and enquiries to your business. Businesses are encouraged to add any latest news and information about their products and services to their listing. HotFrog is indexed by Google and other search

engines, meaning that customers can find your HotFrog listing when they use Google, Yahoo! or other search engines.
Resource:
http://www.hotfrog.com/AddYourBusiness.aspx

Local.com
Local.com owns and operates a leading local search site and network in the United States. Its mission is to be the leader at enabling local businesses and consumers to find each other and connect. To do so, the company uses patented and proprietary technologies to provide over 20 million consumers each month with relevant search results for local businesses, products and services on Local.com and more than 1,000 partner sites. Local.com powers more than 100,000 local websites. Tens of thousands of small business customers use Local.com products and services to reach consumers using a variety of subscription, performance and display advertising and website products.
Resource:
http://corporate.local.com/mk/get/advertising-opportunities

Autoresponder
An autoresponder is an online tool that will automatically manage our mailing list and send out emails to our customers at preset intervals. We will write a short article that is helpful to potential Background Check Services buyers. We will load this article into our autoresponder. We will let people know of the availability of our article by posting to newsgroups, forums, social networking sites etc. We will list our autoresponder email address at the end of the posting, so they can send a blank email to our autoresponder to receive our article and be added to our mailing list. We will then email them at the interval of our choosing with special offers. We will load the messages into our autoresponder and set a time interval for the messages to be mailed out.
Resource:
www.aweber.com

Database Marketing
Database marketing is a form of direct marketing using databases of customers or prospects to generate personalized communications in order to promote a product or service for marketing purposes. The method of communication can be any addressable medium, as in direct marketing. With database marketing tools, we will be able to implement customer nurturing, which is a tactic that attempts to communicate with each customer or prospect at the right time, using the right information to meet that customer's need to progress through the process of identifying a problem, learning options available to resolve it, selecting the right solution, and making the purchasing decision. We will use our databases to learn more about customers, select target markets for specific campaigns, through customer segmentation, compare customers' value to the company, and provide more specialized offerings for customers based on their transaction histories, demographic profile and surveyed needs and wants. This database will give us the capability to automate regular promotional mailings, to semi-automate the telephone

outreach process, and to prioritize prospects as to interests, timing, and other notable delineators. The objective is to arrange for first meetings, which are meant to be informal introductions, and valuable fact-finding and needs-assessment events.

We will use sign-in sheets, coupons, surveys and newsletter subscriptions to collect the following information from our clients:

1. Name
2. Telephone Number
3. Email Address
4. Home Address
5. Interest Area
6. Relevant Dates

We will utilize the following types of contact management software to generate leads and stay in touch with customers to produce repeat business and referrals:

1. Act   www.act.com
2. Front Range Solutions   www.frontrange.com
3. The Turning Point   www.turningpoint.com
4. Acxiom   www.acxiom.com/products_and_services/

We will utilize contact management software, such as ACT and Goldmine, to track the following:

1. Dates for follow-ups.
2. Documentation of prospect concerns, objections or comments.
3. Referral source.
4. Marketing Materials sent.
5. Log of contact dates and methods of contact.
6. Ultimate disposition.

Cause Marketing

Cause marketing or cause-related marketing refers to a type of marketing involving the cooperative efforts of a "for profit" business and a non-profit organization for mutual benefit. The possible benefits of cause marketing for business include positive public relations, improved customer relations, and additional marketing opportunities.
Cause marketing sponsorship by American businesses is rising at a dramatic rate, because customers, employees and stakeholders prefer to be associated with a company that is considered socially responsible. Our business objective will be to generate highly cost-effective public relations and media coverage for the launch of a marketing campaign focused on _____ (type of cause), with the help of the _____ (non-profit organization name) organization.
Resources:
www.causemarketingforum.com/
www.cancer.org/AboutUs/HowWeHelpYou/acs-cause-marketing

Courtesy Advertising

We will engage in courtesy advertising, which refers to a company or corporation "buying" an advertisement in a nonprofit dinner program, event brochure, and the like.

Our company will gain visibility this way while the nonprofit organization may treat the advertisement revenue as a donation. We will specifically advertise in the following non-profit programs, newsletters, bulletins and event brochures: _____

Meet-up Group
We will form a meet-up group to encourage people to participate in our workshop programs. We will also attend meetings sponsored by entrepreneurs and schools.
Resources:
www.meetup.com/create/
www.meetup.com/help/customer/portal/articles/615391-update-my-meetup-group-
    profile/

Marketing Associations/Groups
We will set up a marketing association comprised of complementary businesses. We will market our Background Check Services as a member of a group of complementary companies. Our marketing group will include a HR Consulting firm, an event planner, and a property management service. Any business that provides event services will be a likely candidate for being a member of our marketing group. The group will joint advertise, distribute joint promotional materials, exchange mailing lists, and develop a group website. The obvious benefit is that we will increase our marketing effectiveness by extending our reach.

BBB Accreditation
We will apply for BBB Accreditation to improve our perceived trustworthiness. BBB determines that a company meets BBB accreditation standards, which include a commitment to make a good faith effort to resolve any consumer complaints. BBB Accredited Businesses pay a fee for accreditation review/monitoring and for support of BBB services to the public. BBB accreditation does not mean that the business' products or services have been evaluated or endorsed by BBB, or that BBB has made a determination as to the business' product quality or competency in performing services.
Examples:
www.bbb.org/cleveland/business-reviews/screening-background-and-
    employment/absolute-background-check-in-fairview-park-oh-92001620/

Billboards
We will use billboard advertising to create brand awareness and strong name recognition. We will design Billboards that are eye-catching and informative and use easy to read fonts like Verdana. We will include our business name, location, a graphic, standout border and no more than eight words. In designing the billboard, we will consider the fact that the eye typically moves from the upper left corner to the lower right corner of a billboard. We will use colors that can be viewed by color blind people, such as yellow, black and blue, and pictures to contrast with the sky and other surroundings. We will keep the layout uncluttered and the message simple and include a direct call to action.

Depending on the billboards size and location, the cost will range from $1,000 to $5,000 per month. We will try to negotiate a discount on a long-term contract.

Example: What Do You Really Know About Your Future Mother-in-Law?

Resources:

Outdoor Advertising Association of America   www.oaaa.org
EMC Outdoor, Inc.   www.emcoutdoor.com

Sponsor Events

The sponsoring of events, such as golf tournaments, will allow our company to engage in what is known as experiential marketing, which is the idea that the best way to deepen the emotional bond between a company and its customers is by creating a memorable and interactive experience. We will ask for the opportunity to prominently display our company signage and the set-up of a booth from which to handout sample products and sales literature. We will also seek to capitalize on networking, speech giving and workshop presenting opportunities

Patch.com

A community-specific news and information platform dedicated to providing comprehensive and trusted local coverage for individual towns and communities. Patch makes it easy to: Keep up with news and events, Look at photos and videos from around town, Learn about local businesses, Participate in discussions and Submit announcements, photos, and reviews.

Mobile iPhone Apps

We will use new distribution tools like the iPhone App Store to give us unprecedented direct access to consumers, without the need to necessarily buy actual mobile *ads* to reach people. Thanks to Apple's iPhone and the App Store, we will be able to make cool mobile apps that may generate as much goodwill and purchase intent as a banner ad. We will research Mobile Application Development, which is the process by which application software is developed for small low-power handheld devices, such as personal digital assistants, enterprise digital assistants or mobile phones. These applications are either pre-installed on phones during manufacture, or downloaded by customers from various mobile software distribution platforms. iPhone apps make good marketing tools. The bottom line is iPhones and smartphones sales are continually growing, and people are going to their phones for information. Apps will definitely be a lead generation tool because it gives potential clients easy access to our contact and business information and the ability to call for more information while they are still "hot". Our apps will contain: directory of staffers, publications on relevant issues, office location, videos, etc.

We will especially focus on the development of apps that can accomplish the following:

1. **Mobile Reservations:** Customers can use this app to access mobile reservations linked directly to your in-house calendar. They can browse open slots and book appointments easily, while on the go.

2. **Appointment Reminders:** You can send current customers reminders of regular or special appointments through your mobile app to increase your yearly revenue per customer.

3. **Style Libraries**

   Offer a style library in your app to help customers to pick out a _____ style. Using a simple photo gallery, you can collect photos of various styles, and have customers browse and select specific _____.

4. **Customer Photos**

   Your app can also have a feature that lets customers take photos and email them to you. This is great for creating a database of customer photos for testimonial purposes, advertising, or just easy reference.

5. **Special Offers**

   Push notifications allow you to drive activity on special promotions, deals, events, and offers. If you ever need to generate revenue during a down time, push notifications allow you to generate interest easily and proactively.

6. **Loyalty Programs**

   A mobile app allows you to offer a mobile loyalty program (buy ten ___, get one free, etc.). You won't need to print up cards or track anything manually – it's all done simply through users' mobile devices.

7. **Referrals**

   A mobile app can make referrals easy. With a single click, a user can post to a social media account on Facebook or Twitter about their experience with your business. This allows you to earn new business organically through the networks of existing customers.

8. **Product Sales**

   We can sell ____ products through our mobile app. Customers can browse products, submit orders, and make payments easily, helping you open up a new revenue stream.

Resources: http://www.apple.com/iphone/apps-for-iphone/
                        http://iphoneapplicationlist.com/apps/business/
Software Development: http://www.mutualmobile.com/
                        http://www.avenuesocial.com/mob-app.php#
                        http://www.biznessapps.com/

Examples:
www.intomobile.com/2009/12/23/background-check-app-for-iphone-does-exactly-what-you-think-it-does/
Resource:
http://www.appolicious.com/pages/services

Transit Ads

According to the Metropolitan Transportation Authority, MTA subways, buses and railroads provide billions of trips each year to residents. Marketing our background checking service in subway cars and on the walls of subway stations will be a great way to advertise our business to a large, captive audience.

Restroom billboard advertising (Bathroom Advertising)

We will target a captive audience by placing restroom billboard advertising in select high-traffic venues with targeted demographics. A simple, framed ad on the inside of a bathroom stall door or above a urinal gets at least a minute of viewing, according to several studies. The stall door ads are a good choice for venues with shorter waiting times, such as small businesses, while large wall posters are well-suited to airports or movie theatres where people are more likely to be standing in line near the entrance or exit. Many new restroom based ad agencies that's specialize in restroom advertisement have also come about, such as; Zoom Media, BillBoardZ , Flush Media , Jonny Advertising, Insite Advertising, Inc, Wall AG USA, ADpower, NextMedia, and Alive Promo (American Restroom Association, 9/24/2009).

Resources:

http://www.indooradvertising.org/
http://www.stallmall.com/
http://www.zoommedia.com/

Tumblr.com

Tumblr will allow us to effortlessly share anything. We will be able to post text, photos, quotes, links, music, and videos, from our browser, phone, desktop, email, or wherever we happen to be. We will be able to customize everything, from colors, to our theme's HTML.

Examples:

http://screeningintelligence.tumblr.com/

thumbtack.com

A directory for finding and booking trustworthy local services, which is free to consumers.

Resource:

www.thumbtack.com/postservice

Examples:

http://venturebeat.com/2012/01/09/thumbtack-funding-4m/

Citysearch.com

Citysearch.com is a local guide for living bigger, better and smarter in the selected city. Covering more than 75,000 locations nationwide, Citysearch.com combines in-the-know editorial recommendations, candid user comments and expert advice from local businesses. Citysearch.com keeps users connected to the most popular and undiscovered places wherever they are.

Examples:

http://national.citysearch.com/profile/667443080/greensboro_nc/apex_background_check _inc_.html

Publish e-Book

Ebooks are electronic books which can be downloaded from any website or FTP site on the Internet. Ebooks are made using special software and can include a wide variety of media such as HTML, graphics, Flash animation and video. We will publish an e-book to establish our background checking expertise and reach people who are searching for ebooks on how to make better use our products and/or services. Included in our ebook will be links back to our website, product or affiliate program. Because users will have permanent access to it, they will use our ebook again and again, constantly seeing a link or banner which directs them to our site. The real power behind ebook marketing will be the viral aspect of it and the free traffic it helps to build for our website. ebook directories include:

www.e-booksdirectory.com/
www.ebookfreeway.com/p-ebook-directory-list.html
www.quantumseolabs.com/blog/seolinkbuilding/top-5-free-ebook-directories-subscribers/

Resource: www.free-ebooks.net/

Examples:
"Background Checks for Dummies"
www.hireright.com/blog/background-checks/new-ebook-background-checks-for-dummies#sthash.qNnNvgwm.dpbs

Sterling Talent Solutions
www.sterlingtalentsolutions.com/resources/expert-articles-and-ebooks/
Regularly publishes expert articles and eBooks by industry experts on emerging trends and issues impacting the search for top talent.

e-books are available from the following sites:

Amazon.com	Createspace.com
Lulu.com	Kobobooks.com
BarnesandNoble.com	Scribd.com
AuthorHouse.com	

Resource:
www.smartpassiveincome.com/ebooks-the-smart-way/

Business Card Exchanges
We will join our Chamber of Commerce or local retail merchants' association and volunteer to host a mixer or business card exchange. We will take the opportunity to invite social and business groups to our offices to enjoy wine tastings, and market to local businesses. We will also build our email database by collecting the business cards of all attendees.

Hubpages.com
HubPages has easy-to-use publishing tools, a vibrant author community and underlying revenue-maximizing infrastructure. Hubbers (HubPages authors) earn money by publishing their Hubs (content-rich Internet pages) on topics they know and love and earn recognition among fellow Hubbers through the community-wide HubScore ranking system. The HubPages ecosystem provides a search-friendly infrastructure which drives traffic to Hubs from search engines such as Google and Yahoo and enables Hubbers to earn revenue from industry-standard advertising vehicles such as Google AdSense and

the eBay and Amazon Affiliates program. All of this is provided free to Hubbers in an open online community.
Resource:
http://hubpages.crabbysbeach.com/blogs/
http://hubpages.com/learningcenter/contents
Examples:
http://tenantbackground.hubpages.com/hub/credit-background-check-before-hiring

Pinterest.com

The goal of this website is to connect everyone in the world through the 'things' they find interesting. They think that a favorite book, toy, or recipe can reveal a common link between two people. With millions of new pins added every week, Pinterest is connecting people all over the world based on shared tastes and interests. What's special about Pinterest is that the boards are all visual, which is a very important marketing plus. When users enter a URL, they select a picture from the site to pin to their board. People spend hours pinning their own content, and then finding content on other people's boards to "re-pin" to their own boards. We will use Pinterest for remote personal shopping appointments. When we have a customer with specific needs, we will create a board just for them with items we sell that would meet their needs, along with links to other tips and content. We will invite our customer to check out the board on Pinterest and let them know we created it just for them.

Examples:
http://pinterest.com/backgroundcheck/

Pinterest usage recommendation include:
1. Conduct market research by showing photos of potential service bundles or test launches, asking the customer base for feedback.
2. Personalize the brand by showcasing style and what makes the brand different, highlighting new and exciting things through the use of imagery.
3. Add links from Pinterest photos to the company webstore, putting price banners on each photo and providing a link where users can buy the services directly.
4. Share high-quality pictures or images and put links back to our blog/website.
5. We will create a video and add a Call to Action in the description or use annotations, such as check my YouTube article, for the viewers to Pin videos or follow our Pins on Pinterest.
6. Encourage followers' engagement with a call to action, because 'likes', background check questions, comments and 'repins' will help our pins get more authority and   visibility.
7. Optimize descriptions with keywords that people might be looking for when searching Pinterest, as we can add as many hashtags as we want.
8. Be consistent by pinning regularly.
9. Let people know we are on Pinterest by adding "Pin it" and "follow" buttons to our blog and/or website.

Resources:

www.copyblogger.com/pinterest-marketing/
www.shopify.com/infographics/pinterest
www.pinterest.com/entmagazine/retail-business/
www.pinterest.com/brettcarneiro/ecommerce/
www.pinterest.com/denniswortham/infographics-retail-online-shopping/
www.cio.com/article/3018852/e-commerce/how-to-use-pinterest-to-grow-your-business.html

Topix.com

Topix is the world's largest community news website. Users can read, talk about and edit the news on over 360,000 of our news pages. Topix is also a place for users to post their own news stories, as well as comment about stories they have seen on the Topix site. Each story and every Topix page comes with the ability to add your voice to the conversation.

Examples:
www.topix.com/forum/city/eagle-pass-tx/TJQ6DRH26KKJPP7G6/best-background-check-companies
www.topix.com/forum/student-societies/alpha-kappa-alpha/TRNA0V8JMPIRKB10A/p2

Survey Marketing

We will conduct a door-to-door survey in our targeted commercial area to illicit opinions to our proposed business. This will provide valuable feedback, lead to prospective clients and serve to introduce our background checking service business, before we begin actual operations.

'Green' Marketing

We will target environmentally friendly customers to introduce new customers to our business and help spread the word about going "green". We will use the following 'green' marketing strategies to form an emotional bond with our customers:

1. We will use clearly labeled 'Recycled Paper' and Sustainable Packaging, such as receipts and storage containers.
2. We will use "green", non-toxic cleaning supplies.
3. We will install 'green' lighting and heating systems to be more eco-friendly.
4. We will use web-based Electronic Mail and Social Media instead of using paper advertisements.
5. We will find local suppliers to minimize the carbon footprint that it takes for deliveries.
6. We will use products that are made with organic ingredients and supplies.
7. We will document our 'Green' Programs in our sales brochure and website.
8. We will be a Certified Energy Star Partner.
9. We will install new LED warehouse lighting exit signs, and emergency signs.
10. We will install motion detectors in low-traffic areas both inside and outside of warehouses.
11. We will implement new electricity regulators on HVAC units and compressors to lower energy consumption.

12. We will mount highly supervised and highly respected recycling campaigns.
13. We will start a program for waste product to be converted into sustainable energy sources.
14. We will start new company-wide document shredding programs.
15. We will use of water-based paints during the finishing process to reduce V.O.C.'s to virtually zero.
16. Use of solar panels for non-critical sections and facilities in the complex.
17. Use of only hybrid or electric vehicles.

Sticker Marketing

Low-cost sticker, label and decal marketing will provide a cost-effective way to convey information, build identity and promote our company in unique and influential ways. Stickers can be affixed to almost any surface, so they can go and stay affixed where other marketing materials can't; opening a world of avenues through which we can reach our target audience. Our stickers will be simple in design, and convey an impression quickly and clearly, with valuable information or coupon, printed optionally as part of its backcopy. Our stickers will handed-out at trade shows and special events, mailed as a postcard, packaged with product and/or included as part of a mailing package. We will insert the stickers inside our product or hand them out along with other marketing tools such as flyers or brochures. Research has found that the strongest stickers are usually less than 16 square inches, are printed on white vinyl, and are often die cut. Utilizing a strong design, in a versatile size, and with an eye-catching shape, that is, relevant to our business, will add to the perceived value of our promotional stickers.

We will adhere to the following sticker design tips:
1. We will strengthen our brand by placing our logo on the stickers and using company colors and font styles.
2. We will include our phone number, address, and/or website along with our logo to provide customers with a call to action.
3. We will write compelling copy that solicits an emotional reaction.
4. We will use die-cut stickers using unusual and business relevant shapes to help draw attention to our business.
5. We will consider that size matters and that will be determined by where they will be applied and the degree of desired visibility to be realized.
6. We will be aware of using color on our stickers as color can help create contrast in our design, which enables the directing of prospect eyes to images or actionable items on the stickers.
7. We will encourage customers to post our stickers near their phones, on yellow page book covers, on party invitations, on notepads, on book covers, on gift boxes and packaging, etc.
8. We will place our stickers on all the products we sell.

USPS Every Door Direct Mail Program

Every Door Direct Mail from the U.S. Postal Service® is designed to reach every home, every address, every time at a very affordable delivery rate. Every business and resident living in the _____ zip code will receive an over-sized post card and coupon announcing the _____ (company name) grand opening 7-days before the grand opening:

Price – USPS Marketing Mail™ Flats up to 3.3 oz
EDDM Retail® USPS Marketing Flats $0.177 per piece
EDDM BMEU USPS Marketing Mail at $0.156 per piece

Resource:
https://www.usps.com/business/every-door-direct-mail.htm
https://eddm.usps.com/eddm/customer/routeSearch.action

ZoomInfo.com
Their vision is to be the sole provider of constantly verified information about companies and their employees, making our data indispensible — available anytime, anywhere and anyplace the customer needs it. Creates just-verified, detailed profiles of 65 million businesspeople and six million businesses. Makes data available through powerful tools for lead generation, prospecting and recruiting.

Zipslocal.com
Provides one of the most comprehensive ZIP Code-based local search services, allowing visitors to access information through our online business directories that cover all ZIP Codes in the United States. Interactive local yellow pages show listings and display relevant advertising through the medium of the Internet, making it easy for everyone to find local business information.

Data.com/connect/index.jsp
A dynamic community with connections to millions of B2B decision makers. It's the fastest way to reach the right people, and never waste time hunting down the wrong person again.
Resource:
http://community.jigsaw.com/t5/How-to-Use-Jigsaw/bd-p/jigsawresourcecenter

BusinessVibes   www.businessvibes.com/about-businessvibes
A growing B2B networking platform for global trade professionals. BusinessVibes uses a social networking model for businesses to find and connect with international partner companies. With a network of over 5000+ trade associations, 20 million companies and 25,000+ business events across 100+ major industries and 175 countries, BusinessVibes is a decisive source to companies looking for international business partners, be they clients, suppliers, JV partners, or any other type of business contact.

Yext.com
Enables companies to manage their digital presence in online maps, directories and apps. Over 400,000 businesses make millions of monthly updates across 85+ exclusive global partners, making Yext the global market leader. Digital presence is a fundamental need for all 50 million businesses in the world, and Yext's mission is perfect location information in every hand. Yext is based in the heart of New York City with 350

employees and was named to Forbes Most Promising Companies lists for 2014 and 2018, as well as the Fortune Best Places to Work 2014 list.

Google+

We will pay specific attention to Google+, which is already playing a more important role in Google's organic ranking algorithm. We will create a business page on Google+ to achieve improved local search visibility. Google+ will also be the best way to get access to Google Authorship, which will play a huge role in SEO.
Resources:
https://plus.google.com/pages/create
http://www.google.com/+/brands/
https://www.google.com/appserve/fb/forms/plusweekly/
https://plus.google.com/+GoogleBusiness/posts
http://marketingland.com/beyond-social-benefits-google-business-73460
Examples:
https://plus.google.com/+hireright/posts
https://plus.google.com/+Nationsearch

Inbound Marketing

Inbound marketing is about pulling people in by sharing relevant background check information, creating useful content, and generally being helpful. It involves writing everything from buyer's guides to blogs and newsletters that deliver useful content. The objective will be to nurture customers through the buying process with unbiased educational materials that turn consumers into informed buyers.
Resource:
www.Hubspot.com

Google My Business Profile   www.google.com/business/befound.html

We will have a complete and active Google My Business profile to give our background check company a tremendous advantage over the competition, and help potential customers easily find our firm and provide relevant information about our business. This is a free listing that connects to Google Maps. It's the primary way that Google knows where our service area is located, so we can come up for local searches. We will optimize our descriptions with keywords and try to get customer reviews to increase our ranking.

Google My Business will let us:
- Manage business listing info for search, maps and Google+
- Upload photos and/or a virtual tour of our business
- Share content and interacting with followers on Google+
- See reviews from across the web and responding to Google+ reviews
- Integrate with AdWords Express to create and track campaigns
- Access Insights reports, the new social analytics tool for Google+
- See information about our integrated YouTube and Analytics accounts
- Resource:

- https://www.wordstream.com/blog/ws/2014/06/12/google-my-business

Sampling Program

We will give each sample with a mini-survey to enable customers to rate the product or service and supply constructive feedback. This will also be a way to collect contact information for our database. We will also present sample reports on our website to show the comprehensiveness of our profiles and reports.

Examples:

www.goodhire.com/sample-full-background-check

https://www.datacheckinc.com/sample.php

Reddit.com

An online community where users vote on stories. The hottest stories rise to the top, while the cooler stories sink. Comments can be posted on every story, including stories about startup background check companies.

Examples:

https://www.reddit.com/r/legaladvice/comments/3845g0/what_is_the_best_way_to_run_an_extensive/

6.4.1   Strategic Alliances

We will focus our efforts on building strategic relationships within the community that we serve. We will form strategic alliances to accomplish the following objectives:
1.   To share marketing expenses.
2.   To realize bulk buying power on wholesale purchases.
3.   To engage in barter arrangements.
4.   To collaborate with industry experts.
5.   To set-up mutual referral relationships.

_____ (company name) will seek out opportunities to establish viable strategic alliances, such as co-marketing with HR management consulting firms. We will develop strategic alliances with the following service providers by conducting introductory 'cold calls' to their offices and making them aware of our capabilities by distributing our brochures and business cards:
1.   Corporate Offices   2.   Law Firms
3.   HR Consulting Firms   4.   Landlord Associations
5.   LexisNexis   6.   Colleges/Universities
7.   FBI Criminal Information Center   8.   Credit Bureaus
9.   Courthouses

We will assemble and present a sales presentation package that includes sales brochures, business cards, and a DVD presentation of basic party planning tips, and client testimonials. We will include coupons that offer a discount or other type of introductory deal. We will ask to set-up a take-one display for our sales brochures at the business registration counter.

We will promptly give the referring business any one or combination of the following agreed upon reward options:
1.   Referral fees
2.   Free services
3.   Mutual referral exchanges

We will monitor referral sources to evaluate the mutual benefits of the alliance and make certain to clearly define and document our referral incentives prior to initiating our referral exchange program.

Resources:
http://corp.talentwise.com/About/Partners

6.4.2   Monitoring Marketing Results

To monitor how well _____ (company name) is doing, we will measure how well the advertising campaign is working by taking customer surveys. What we would like to know is how they heard of us and how they like and dislike about our services. In order to get responses to the surveys, we will be give discounts as thank you rewards.

Response Tracking Methods
Coupons: ad-specific coupons that easily enable tracking
Landing Pages: unique web landing pages for each advertisement
800 Numbers: unique 1-800-# per advertisement
Email Service Provider: Instantly track email views, opens, and clicks
Address inclusion of dept # or suite #.

Our financial statements will offer excellent data to track all phases of sales. These are available for review on a daily basis. _____ (company name) will benchmark our objectives for sales promotion and advertising in order to evaluate our return on invested marketing dollars and determine where to concentrate our limited advertising dollars to realize the best return. We will also strive to stay within our marketing budget.

Key Marketing Metrics
We will use the following two marketing metrics to evaluate the cost-effectiveness of our marketing campaign:
1. The cost to acquire a new customer: The average dollar amount invested to get one new client. Example: If we invest $3,000 on marketing in a single month and end the month with 10 new customers, our cost of acquisition is $300 per new customer.
2. The lifetime value of the average active customer. The average dollar value of an average customer over the life of their business with you. To calculate this metric for a given period of time, we will take the total amount of revenue our business generated during the time period and divide it by the total number of customers we had from the beginning of the time period.
3. We will track the following set of statistics on a weekly basis to keep informed of the progress of our business:
   A. Number of total referrals.
   B. Percentage increase of total referrals (over baseline).
   C. Number of new referral sources.
   D. Number of new customers/month.
   E. Number of Leads

Key Marketing Metrics Table
We've listed some key metrics in the following table. We will need to keep a close eye on these, to see if we meet our own forecasted expectations. If our numbers are off in too many categories, we may, after proper analysis, have to make substantial changes to our marketing efforts.

Key Marketing Metrics	2018	2019	2020
Revenue			
Leads			
Leads Converted			
Avg. Transaction per Customer			
Avg. Dollars per Customer			
Number of Referrals			

Number of PR Appearances
Number of Testimonials
Number of New Club Members
Number of Returns
Number of BBB Complaints
Number of Completed Surveys
 Number of Blog readers
Number of Twitter followers
Number of Facebook Fans

Metric Definitions

1.   Leads: Individuals who step into the store to consider a purchase.
2.   Leads Converted: Percent of individuals who actually make a purchase.
3.   Average Transactions Per Customer: Number of purchases per customer per month. Expected to rise significantly as customers return for more and more _____ items per month
4.   Average $ Per Customer: Average dollar amount of each transaction. Expected to rise along with average transactions.
5.   Referrals: Includes customer and business referrals
6.   PR Appearances: Online or print mentions of the business that are not paid advertising. Expected to be high upon opening, then drop off and rise again until achieving a steady level.
7.   Testimonials: Will be sought from the best and most loyal customers. Our objective is ___ (#) per month) and they will be added to the website. Some will be sought as video testimonials.
8.   New Loyalty Club Members: This number will rise significantly as more customers see the value in repeated visits and the benefits of club membership.
9.   Number of Returns/BBB Complaints: Our goal is zero.
10.   Number of Completed Surveys: We will provide incentives for customers to complete customer satisfaction surveys.

6.4.3   Word-of-Mouth Marketing

We plan to make use of the following techniques to promote word-of-mouth advertising:
1.   Repetitive Image Advertising
2.   Provide exceptional customer service.
3.   Make effective use of loss leaders.
2.   Schedule in-store activities, such as demonstrations or special events.
3.   Make trial easy with a coupon or introductory discount.
4.   Initiate web and magazine article submissions
5.   Utilize a sampling program
6.   Add a forward email feature to our website.
7.   Share relevant and believable testimonial letters

8.   Publish staff bios.
9.   Make product/service upgrade announcements
10. Hold contests or sweepstakes
12. Have involvement with community events.
13. Pay suggestion box rewards
14. Distribute a monthly newsletter
15. Share easy-to-understand information (via an article or seminar).
16. Make personalized marketing communications.
17. Structure our referral program.
18. Sharing of Community Commonalities
19. Invitations to join our community of shared interests.
20. Publish Uncensored Customer Reviews
21. Enable Information Exchange Forums
22. Provide meaningful comparisons with competitors.
23. Clearly state our user benefits.
24. Make and honor ironclad guarantees
25. Provide superior post-sale support
26. Provide support in the pre-sale decision making process.
27. Host Free Informational Seminars or Workshops
28. Get involved with local business organizations.
29. Issue Press Release coverage of charitable involvements.
30. Hold traveling company demonstrations/exhibitions/competitions.

6.4.4   Customer Satisfaction Survey

We will design a customer satisfaction survey to measure the "satisfaction quotient" of our Background Check customers. By providing a detailed snapshot of our current customer base, we will be able to generate more repeat and referral business and enhance the profitability of our background check company.

Our Customer Satisfaction Survey will include the following basics:
1.   How do our customers rate our background checking business?
2.   How do our customers rate our competition?
3.   How well do our customers rate the value of our products or services?
4.   What new customer needs and trends are emerging?
5.   How loyal are our customers?
6.   What can be done to improve customer loyalty and repeat business?
7.   How strongly do our customers recommend our business?
8.   What is the best way to market our business?
9.   What new value-added services would best differentiate our business from that of our competitors?
10. How can we encourage more referral business?
11. How can our pricing strategy be improved?
11. How can our pricing strategy be improved?
12. Why did our best customers first come to our website and why they continue to

come back.

Our customer satisfaction survey will help to answer these questions and more. From the need for continual new products and services to improved customer service, our satisfaction surveys will allow our business to quickly identify problematic and underperforming areas, while enhancing our overall customer satisfaction.

Resources:
https://www.survata.com/
https://www.google.com/insights/consumersurveys/use_cases
www.surveymonkey.com
http://www.smetoolkit.org/smetoolkit/en/content/en/6708/Customer-Satisfaction-Survey-
    Template-
http://smallbusiness.chron.com/common-questions-customer-service-survey-1121.html
http://smallbiztrends.com/2014/11/tailoring-survey-questions-for-your-industry.html
http://www.amplituderesearch.com/customer-satisfaction-surveys.shtml

Examples:
https://bib.com/index.cfm/company/customer-satisfaction
www.uscis.gov/sites/default/files/USCIS/Verification/E-Verify/E-Verify_Native_
    Documents/UCSIC_E-VerifyCustomerSatisfactionSurveyFinalReport2012.pdf

6.4.5   Marketing Training Program

Our Marketing Training Program will include both an initial orientation and training, as well as ongoing continuing education classes. Initial orientation will be run by the owner until an HR manager is hired. For one week, half of each day will be spent in training, and the other half shadowing the operations manager.

Training will include:
    Learning the entire selection of background checking services.
    Understanding our Mission Statement, Value Proposition, Position Statement and
        Unique Selling Proposition.
    Appreciating our competitive advantages.
    Understanding our core message and branding approach.
    Learning our store's policies; returns processing, complaint handling, etc.
    Learning our customer services standards of practice.
    Learning our customer and business referral programs.
    Learning our Membership Club procedures, rules and benefits.
    Becoming familiar with our company website, and online ordering options.
    Service procedures specific to the employee's role.

    Ongoing workshops will be based on customer feedback and problem areas identified
        by mystery buyers, which will better train employees to educate customers. These

ongoing workshops will be held _____ (once?) a month for _____ (three?) hours.

6.5   Sales Strategy

The development of our sales strategy will start by developing a better understanding of our customer needs. To accomplish this task, we will pursue the following research methods:

1.   Join the associations that our target customers belong to.
2.   Contact the membership director and establish a relationship to understand their member's needs, challenges and concerns.
3.   Identify non-competitive suppliers who sell to our customer to learn their challenges and look for partnering solutions.
4.   Work directly with our customer and ask them what their needs are and if our business may offer a possible solution.

The Management of our background screening business will focus on daily sales revenue goals and explaining any variances. Best value services will be identified to assist customers with smart purchase selections. Online database access will be geared to the customer's convenience. The situation will be monitored to ensure that the company invests adequately in its own service delivery operations.

Sales feedback will be elicited to stimulate ideas, approaches, relate success stories, instruct in new techniques, share news, and implement improvements. Major accounts will be solicited through networking, cold call solicitations via sales agents, and opportunistic encounters at any time by management.

Our initial focus will be on making the basic screening services we offer of the highest possible quality. Only when those services are well-established, will we consider expanding our range of services offered.

We will become a one-stop HR resource center, and offer customized screening and applicant tracking programs. We will also be very active in the community, building a solid reputation with business and real estate professionals, and community leaders.

Our clients will be primarily obtained through word-of-mouth referrals, but we will also advertise introductory offers to introduce people to our preferred club membership program. The combination of the perception of higher report accuracy, exceptional purchase guidance, innovative targeted screening services and the recognition of superior value should turn referral leads into satisfied customers.

The company's sales strategy will be based on the following elements:
    Advertising in the Yellow Pages - two inch by three-inch ads describing our services will be placed in the local Yellow Pages.
    Placing classified advertisements in the regional editions of business journals.

Word of mouth referrals - generating sales leads in the local community through customer referrals.

Our basic sales strategy is to:
Develop a website for lead generation by _____ (date).
Provide exceptional customer service.
Accept payment by all major credit cards, cash, PayPal and check.
Survey our customers regarding products and services they would like to see added.
Sponsor charitable and other community events.
Provide tours of the facility so customers can learn how to be discriminating customers and build a trust bond with our operations.
Motivate employees with a pay-for-performance component to their straight salary compensation package, based on profits and customer satisfaction rates.
Build long-term customer relationships by putting the interests of customers first.
Establish mutually beneficial referral relationships with local businesses.

6.5.1 Customer Retention Strategy

We will use the following post-purchase techniques to improve customer retention, foster referrals and improve the profitability of our business:
1. Keep the offices sparkling clean and well-organized.
2. Use only well-trained sales associates and technicians.
3. Actively solicit customer feedback and promptly act upon their inputs.
4. Tell customers how much you appreciate their business.
5. Call regular customers by their first names.
6. Send thank you notes.
7. Offer free new product trial demos.
8. Change displays and sales presentations on a regular basis.
9. Practice good phone etiquette
10. Respond to complaints promptly.
11. Reward referrals.
12. Publish a monthly opt-in direct response newsletter with customized content, dependent on recipient stated information preferences.
13. Develop and publish a list of frequently asked questions.
14. Issue Preferred Customer Membership Cards.
15. Hold informational seminars and workshops.
16. Provide an emergency hotline number.
17. Publish code of ethics and our service guarantees.
18. Help customers to make accurate competitor comparisons.
19. Build a stay-in-touch (drip marketing) communications calendar.
20. Keep marketing communications focused on our competitive advantages.
21. Offer repeat user discounts and incentives.
22. Be supportive and encouraging, and not judgmental.
23. Measure customer retention and look at recurring revenue and customer surveys.
24. Build a community of shared interests by offering a website forum or discussion

group for professionals and patients to allow sharing of knowledge.

25.   Offer benefits above and beyond those of our competitors.

26.   Issue reminder emails and holiday gift cards.

We will also consider the following Customer Retention Programs:

Type of Program	Customer Rewards
Frequency Purchase Loyalty Program	Special Discounts
	Free Product or Services
'Best Customer' Program	Special Recognition/Treatment/Offers
Affinity Programs	Sharing of Common Interests
	Accumulate Credit Card Points
Customer Community Programs	Special Event Participation
Auto-Knowledge Building Programs	Purchase Recommendations based
	On Past Transaction History
Profile Building Programs	Recommendations Based on Stated
	Customer Profile Information.

6.5.2   Sales Forecast

Our sales projections are based on the following:

1.   Actual sales volumes of local competitors

2.   Interviews with competitor owners and managers

3.   Observations of sales and traffic flows at competitor sites.

4.   Government and industry trade statistics

5.   Local population demographics and projections.

6.   Discussions with suppliers.

7.   Ratio Trend Analysis of historical transaction data.

Our sales forecast is an estimated projection of expected sales over the next three years, based on our chosen marketing strategy, economic conditions, national threat assessments and assumed competitive environment.

Sales are expected to be below average during the first year, until a regular customer base has been established. It has been estimated that it takes the average background check business a minimum of two years to establish a significant customer base. After the customer base is built, sales will grow at an accelerated rate from word-of-mouth referrals and continued networking efforts. We expect sales to steadily increase as our marketing campaign, employee training programs and contact management system are executed. By using advertising, especially discounted introductory coupons, as a catalyst for this prolonged process, ____(company name) plans to attract more customers sooner. Throughout the first year, it is forecasted that sales will incrementally grow until profitability is reached toward the end of year ___(one?). Year two reflects a conservative growth rate of ____ (20?) percent. Year three reflects a growth rate of _____ (25?) percent. We expect to be open for business on ____ (date) and start with an initial enrollment of ____ (#) patients. With our unique product and service offerings, along with our thorough and aggressive marketing strategies, we believe that sales forecasts are actually on the conservative side.

Table: Sales Forecast

Sales	Annual Sales		
	2018	**2019**	**2020**
Employment Screening			
Tenant Screening			
Custom Screening Solutions			
Drug Testing			
Fingerprinting			
DMV Driving Records			
DOT Drug and Alcohol Verification			
Employment Credit Reports			
Tenant Credit Reports			
SSN Verification			
Employment Verification			
Professional Reference Checks			
License and Credential Verification			
Education Verification			
Skills and Behavioral Testing			
Criminal County Court Check			
Form I-9 and E-Verify			
Electronic Application Process			
Screening Consulting Services			
Volunteer Background Checks			
Business Background Checks			
Misc.			
Total Unit Sales			
Direct Cost of Sales:			
Employment Screening			
Tenant Screening			
Custom Screening Solutions			
Drug Testing			
Fingerprinting			
DMV Driving Records			
DOT Drug and Alcohol Verification			
Employment Credit Reports			
Tenant Credit Reports			
SSN Verification			
Employment Verification			
Professional Reference Checks			
License and Credential Verification			
Education Verification			
Skills and Behavioral Testing			

Criminal County Court Check
Form I-9 and E-Verify
Electronic Application Process
Screening Consulting Services
Volunteer Background Checks
Business Background Checks
Misc.
Subtotal Direct Cost of Sales

6.6 Merchandising Strategy

Merchandising is that part of our marketing strategy that is involved with promoting the sales of our software products, as by consideration of the most effective means of selecting, pricing, displaying, and advertising items for sale.

The décor of the merchandising, demo and showroom areas is extremely important to sales. Display units are primary, but lighting, furniture, wall surfaces, window treatments, carpeting, accessories and countertops will all play important supporting roles. We will monitor our sales figures and data to confirm that products in demand are well-stocked and slow-moving products are phased-out. We will improve telephone skills of employees to boost phone orders. We will attach our own additional business labels to all products to promote our complete line of background screening products and services.

6.7 Pricing Strategy

We will consider the following factors when developing our pricing strategy:
1. Type of background check
2. Jurisdictions in which the search must be conducted
3. Access fees been paid for the information
4. Competitors price
5. Information needed by the client
6. Duration

Pricing will be based on competitive parity guidelines. Prices will be consistent with those of our direct competitors, with the exception of very high-volume operations with powerful pricing leverage. Pricing will be monitored continuously against competitive sources who we can readily research. Our plan is to discount initially to build our customer base and then to discount based on volume and type of corporate client.

Services and Pricing

Criminal Background Checks

National Criminal Background Check	$19.95
National Criminal Background Check plus SSN Trace	add'l $5.00
SSN Trace	$7.00

Property Reports

Property Valuation	$9.99
Detailed Property Profile	$29.99
Property Legal and Vesting Report	$24.99
Property Document Image	$17.00

Credit Reports

Pre-employment credit report	$_____ (15.00)
Tenant screening credit report	$_____ (15.00)
Finance credit report	$_____ (12.00)

Note: All report results are instant and come straight from the credit bureau.

Executive Job Applicant Comprehensive Review	$_____ (2,000.00)

Driving Records (MVRs)

Instant driving records are available to corporate customers only.

All report results are instant and come straight from the Department of Motor Vehicles.

We are not interested in being the low-price leader, as our pricing strategy plays a major role in whether we will be able to create and maintain customers for a profit. Our revenue structure must support our cost structure, so the salaries we pay to our staff are balanced by the revenue we collect.

The average market pricing for criminal record screening services is between $10 to $50, depending on the exact type of checks involved. We will run an initial discount offer for the first few months to get our first customers and build a relationship with companies that regularly need such background screening services. Eventually, how to price employment background checks and credit history checks will depend on the competition and our service level, as big clients are always prepared to pay more for comprehensive and reliable employee background screening services.

Most national background checks search each state's online databases. These types of criminal background checks usually cost $25-$45.
Source:
https://blog.verifirst.com/blog/bid/305407/cost-of-a-background-check-how-much-
        should-you-pay

Other Pricing Examples:

	Price Range
Criminal Searches	$7 – 20

Credit History		$5 – 10	
Motor Vehicle Records		$3 – 10	
Verifications		$7 – 15	
Rental History		$4 – 10	
Drug Testing (Lab Conducted)		$25 – 50	

Bulk Pricing Schedule
Nationwide Basic Background Check
Regularly priced @ $14.95
25+ @ $13.95 each = $348.75   Save $25.00
50+ @ 12.95 each = $647.50
100+ @ $9.95 each = $995.00

Price List Comparison

Competitor Service	Our Price	Competitor Price	B/(W) Competitor

We will adopt the following pricing guidelines:
1. We must insure that our price plus service equation is perceived to be an exceptional value proposition.
2. We must refrain from competing on price, but always be price competitive.
3. We must develop value-added services, and bundle those with our products to create offerings that cannot be easily price compared.
4. We must focus attention on our competitive advantages.
5. Development of a pricing strategy based on our market positioning strategy, which is ____ (mass market value leadership/exceptional premium niche value?)
6. Our pricing policy objective, which is to _____ (increase profit margins/   achieve revenue maximization to increase market share/lower unit costs).
7. We will use marketplace intelligence and gain insights from competitor pricing.
8. We will solicit pricing feedback from customers using surveys and interviews.
9. We will utilize limited time pricing incentives to penetrate niche markets
10. We will conduct experiments at prices above and below the current price to determine the price elasticity of demand. (Inelastic demand or demand that does not decrease with a price increase, indicates that price increases may be feasible.)
11. We will keep our offerings and prices simple to understand and competitive, based on market intelligence.
12. We will consider a price for volume strategy on certain items and study the effects of price on volume and of volume on costs, as in a recession, trying to recover these costs through a price increase can be fatal.

Determining the costs of servicing business is the most important part of covering our expenses and earning profits. We will factor in the following pricing formula: Product Cost + Materials + Overhead + Labor + Profit + Tax = Price

Materials are those items consumed in the delivering of the service.

Overhead costs are the variable and fixed expenses that must be covered to stay in business. Variable costs are those expenses that fluctuate including vehicle expenses, rental expenses, utility bills and supplies. Fixed costs include the purchase of equipment, service ware, marketing and advertising, and insurance. After overhead costs are determined, the total overhead costs are divided among the total number of transactions forecasted for the year.

Labor costs include the costs of performing the services. Also included are Social Security taxes (FICA), vacation time, retirement and other benefits such as health or life insurance. To determine labor costs per hour, keep a time log. When placing a value on our time, we will consider the following: 1) skill and reputation; 2) wages paid by employers for similar skills and 3) where we live. Other pricing factors include image, inflation, supply and demand, and competition.

Profit is a desired percentage added to our total costs. We will need to determine the percentage of profit added to each service. It will be important to cover all our costs to stay in business. We will investigate available computer software programs to help us price our services and keep financial data for decision-making purposes. Close contact with customers will allow our company to react quickly to changes in demand.

We will develop a pricing strategy that will reinforce the perception of value to the customer and manage profitability, especially in the face of rising inflation. To ensure our success, we will use periodic competitor and customer research to continuously evaluate our pricing strategy. We intend to review our profit margins every six months.

6.8 Differentiation Strategies

We will use differentiation strategies to develop and market unique products for different customer segments. To differentiate ourselves from the competition, we will focus on the assets, creative ideas and competencies that we have that none of our competitors has. The goal of our differentiation strategies is to be able to charge a premium price for our unique products and services and/or to promote loyalty and assist in retaining our customers.

Background screening services are our specialty, but we also offer several e-recruiting options and value-added services to help manage the client's onboarding program collectively with our background screening services. Through our service portals, clients will be able to post jobs, screen candidates, pre-select candidate background screening, and verify right to work documentation.

To help protect our clients from possible lawsuits, we will do the following:
1. Make certain that we do not commit violations when conducting background checks.
2. Verify our results by crosschecking to ensure that our background check results are accurate.

3.   Advise on clients on compliance issues, by staying abreast of the latest legal requirements for different jurisdictions.
4.   Participate in the Background Screening Accreditation Program (BSAP), which is a rigorous process through which organizations have to undergo to receive NAPBS Accreditation.
5.   Instruct the client to first make a "clear and conspicuous" written disclosure to the prospective employee of the planned background check.
6.   If the employer takes the adverse action, it must provide a "pre-adverse action" notice to the affected person, which must include a copy of the consumer report and a statutory "Summary of Rights." Note: The purpose of this notice requirement is to permit the individual to discuss the report with the employer before the employer implements the adverse action.

Resources:

http://abovethelaw.com/2015/02/employers-running-background-checks-top-10-tips-to-avoid-joining-the-fair-credit-reporting-act-litigation-club/

Differentiation in our background check company will be achieved in the following types of ways, including:

                                                      Explanation
☐ Product features   _____
☐ Complementary services   _____
☐ Technology embodied in design _____
☐ Location   _____
☐ Service innovations   _____
☐ Superior service   _____
☐ Creative advertising   _____
☐ Better supplier relationships _____

Source:

http://scholarship.sha.cornell.edu/cgi/viewcontent.cgi?article=1295&context=articles

Differentiating will mean defining who our perfect target market is and then catering to their needs, wants and interests better than everyone else. It will be about using surveys to determine what's most important to our targeted market and giving it to them consistently. It will not be about being "everything to everybody"; but rather, "the absolute best to our chosen targeted group".

In developing our differentiation strategy will we use the following form to help define our differences:

1.   Targeted customer segments   _____
2.   Customer characteristics   _____
3.   Customer demographics   _____
4.   Customer behavior   _____
5.   Geographic focus   _____
6.   Ways of working   _____

7.   Service delivery approach   _____
8.   Customer problems/pain points   _____
9.   Complexity of customers' problems   _____
10.   Range of services   _____

We will use the following approaches to differentiate our products and services from those of our competitors to stand apart from standardised offerings:

1.   Superior quality
2.   Unusual or unique product features
3.   More responsive customer service
4.   Rapid product or service innovation
5.   Advanced technological features
6.   Engineering design or styling
7.   Additional product features
8.   An image of prestige or status

Specific Differentiators will include the following:

1.   Being a Specialist in one procedure
2.   Utilizing advanced/uncommon technology
3.   Possessing extensive experience
4.   Building an exceptional facility
5.   Consistently achieving superior results
6.   Having a caring and empathetic personality
7.   Giving customer s WOW experience, including a professional customer welcome package.
8.   Enabling convenience and 24/7 online accessibility
9.   Calling customers to express interest in their challenges.
10.   Keeping to the appointment schedule.
11.   Remembering customer names and details like they were family
12.   Assuring customer fears.
13.   Building a visible reputation and recognition around our community
14.   Acquiring special credentials or professional memberships
15.   Providing added value services, such as taxi service, longer hours, financing plans, and post-sale services.

Primary Differentiation Strategies:

1.   Due to the increase in two-income families, many service-oriented businesses are leaning toward differentiating themselves on the basis of convenience. We plan to have two shifts, an early morning shift and an evening shift in which the store will be fully functional from ___ (5) A.M. to ___ (12) A.M. or later on various days of the week.
2.   We will utilize software systems that will enable us to personalize each customer's buying experience, including easy access to customer transaction history, preference profile and information about all the products of interest to that client.
3.   Wide aisles and the open floor design will make it easier not only to navigate the many offerings, but to see them from afar, a feature that will speed up service for

customers looking to get in and out quickly.

4. We will offer a comfortable seating area for wine tasting events. (if permitted?)
5. We will add a range of financial services, including money transfers, check cashing and bill payments, to become a one-stop destination.
6. We will enable the online and fax ordering of our products and services.
7. We will install kiosks to connect customers with various vendors, including the ability to order movie and theater tickets, download ring tones, book hotel rooms and redeem credit card points.

Other differentiation strategies include the following:
1. Our system will also have built-in risk management features that handle the automatic sending of adverse action notification letters.
2. All of our background screening services can be easily combined to build one convenient solution that easily integrates into the client's existing hiring process.
3. We will utilize software systems that will enable us to personalize each customer's buying experience, including easy access to customer transaction history, preference profile and information about all the products of interest to that client.
4. We will develop a referral program that turns our clients into referral agents.
5. We will use regular client satisfaction surveys to collect feedback, improvement ideas, referrals and testimonials.
6. We will promote our "green" practices, such as establishing a recycling program, purchasing recycled-content office goods and responsibly handling wastes.
7. We will customize our offerings according to the language, cultural influences, customs, interests and preferences of our local market to create loyalty and increase sales.
8. We will develop the expertise to satisfy the needs of targeted market segments with customized and exceptional support services.

6.9 Milestones   (select)

The Milestones Chart is a timeline that will guide our company in developing and growing our business. It will list chronologically the various critical actions and events that must occur to bring our business to life. We will make certain to assign real, attainable dates to each planned action or event.

_____ (company name) has identified several specific milestones which will function as goals for the company. The milestones will provide a target for achievement as well as a mechanism for tracking progress. The dates were chosen based on realistic delivery times and necessary construction times. All critical path milestones will be completed within their allotted time frames to ensure the success of contingent milestones. The following table will provide a timeframe for each milestone.

Table: Milestones

Milestones	Start Date	End Date	Budget Responsibility
Business Plan Completion			
Secure Permits/Licenses			
Locate & Secure Space			
Obtain Insurance Coverage			
Secure Additional Financing			
Get Start-up Supplies Quotes			
Obtain County Certification			
Purchase Office Equipment			
Renovate Facilities			
Define Marketing Programs			
Install Equipment/Displays			
Technology Systems			
Set-up Accounting System			
Develop Office Policies			
Develop Procedures Manual			
Arrange Support Service Providers			
Finalize Media Plan			
Create Facebook Brand Page			
Open Twitter Account			
Coduct Blogger Outreach			
Develop Personnel Plan			
Develop Staff Training Programs			
Hire/Train Staff			
Implement Marketing Plan			
Get Website Live			
Conduct SEO Campaign			
Form Strategic Alliances			
Purchase Start-up Inventory/Supplies			
Press Release Announcements			
Advertise Grand Opening			
Kickoff Advertising Program			
Join Community Orgs./Network			
Conduct Satisfaction Surveys			
Evaluate/Revise Plan			
Devise Growth Strategy			
Measure Marketing Return on $$$			
Monitor Social Media Networks			
Respond positively to reviews			
Revenues Exceed $_____			
Reach Profitability			
Totals:			

7.0 Website Plan Summary

_____ (company name) is currently developing a website at the URL address www. (company name).com. We will primarily use the website to promote an understanding of the importance of performing accurate and reliable background checks by posting helpful articles and circulating information about coming events. Supplying the visitors to our websites with this information will make a huge difference in turning our website visitors into new customers.

The website will be developed to offer customers a product catalog for online orders. The overriding design philosophy of the site will be ease of use. We want to make the process of placing an order as easy and fast as possible thereby encouraging increased sales. We will incorporate special features such as a section that is specific to each customer, so the customer can easily make purchases of repeat items. Instead of going through the website every month and locating their monthly needs, the site will capture regularly ordered items for that specific customer, significantly speeding up the ordering process. This ease-of-use feature will help increase sales as customers become more and more familiar with the site and appreciate how easy it is to place an order.

We will also provide multiple incentives to sign-up for various benefits, such as our newsletters and promotional sale notices. This will help us to build an email database, which will supply our automated customer follow-up system. We will create a personalized drip marketing campaign to stay in touch with our customers and prospects.

We will develop our website to be a resource for web visitors who are seeking knowledge and information about laws concerning background checks, with a goal to service the knowledge needs of our customers and generate leads. Our home page will be designed to be a "welcome mat" that clearly presents our service offerings and provides links through which visitors can gain easy access to the information they seek. We will use our website to match the problems our customers face with the solutions we offer.

We will use the free tool, Google Analytics (http://www.google.com/analytics), to generate a history and measure our return on investment. Google Analytics is a free tool that can offer insight by allowing the user to monitor traffic to a single website. We will just add the Google Analytics code to our website and Google will give our firm a dashboard providing the number of unique visitors, repeat traffic, page views, etc. This will help to stop wasting our company's money on inefficient marketing. Using an analytic program will show exactly which leads are paying off, and which ones to do without. We will find out what's bringing our site the most traffic and how to improve upon that.

To improve the readability of our website, we will organize our website content in the following ways.

1.   Headlines
2.   Bullet points
3.   Callout text
4.   Top of page summaries

To improve search engine optimization, we will maximize the utilization of the following;

1.	Links	2.	Headers
3.	Bold text	4.	Bullets
5.	Keywords	6.	Meta tags

This website will serve the following purposes:

About Us	How We Work/Our Philosophy
Contact Us	Customer service contact info
Our Services	Menu
Sample Reports	Background/Criminal/Court Records
Register Here	Order Form
My Account	Member Log-in
Frequently Asked Questions	FAQs
Club Membership	Sign-up
Newsletter Sign-up	Join Mailing List
Newsletter Archives	Articles
Upcoming Events	Schedule
Customer Testimonials	Letters w/photos
Affiliate Program	Referral Program Details
Directions	Location directions.
Customer Satisfaction Survey	Feedback
Press Releases	Community Involvement
Strategic Alliance Partners	Links
Resources	Professional Associations
Our Blog	Center diary/Accept comments
Refer-a-Friend	Viral marketing
YouTube/Facebook Video Clips	Seminar Presentation/Testimonials
Satisfaction Guarantee	
Code of Ethics	
Forms and Downloads	Release Forms/Letters
Compliance	Relevant Laws
Terms of Service	
Privacy Policy	
Career Opportunities	

7.1   Website Marketing Strategy

Our online marketing strategy will employ the following distinct mechanisms:

1.   Search Engine Submission

This will be most useful to people who are unfamiliar with _____ (company name) but are looking for a local background check company. There will also be searches from customers who may know about us, but who are seeking additional information.

Search Engine Optimization (SEO)
SEO is a very important digital marketing strategy because search engines are the primary method of finding information for most internet users. SEO is simply the practice of improving and promoting a website in order to increase the number of visitors a site receives from search engines. Basic SEO techniques will range from the naming of webpages to the way that other websites link to our website. We will also need to get our business listed on as many relevant online directories as possible, such as Google, Yelp, Kudzu and Yahoo Local, write a blog that solicit comments and be active on social media sites.
We will also try to incorporate local terms potential clients would use, such as "_____ (city) background check company." This will make it more likely that local customers will find us close to the top of their search.
Resource;
https://www.semrush.com/
www.officerreports.com/blog/wp-content/uploads/2014/11/SEOmoz-The-
        Beginners-Guide-To-SEO-2012.pdf

2.   Website Address (URL) on Marketing Materials
      Our URL will be printed on all marketing communications, business cards, letterheads, faxes, and invoices and product labels. This will encourage a visit to our website for additional information

3.   Online Directories Listings
      We will list our website on relevant, free and paid online directories and website service locators.
      The good online directories possess the following features:
      Free or paid listings that do not expire and do not require monthly renewal.
      Ample space to get your advertising message across.
      Navigation buttons that are easy for visitors to use.
      Optimization for top placement in the search engines based on keywords that people typically use to find background check service providers.
      Direct links to your website, if available.
      An ongoing directory promotion campaign to maintain high traffic volumes to the directory site.

4. Strategic Business Partners
    We will use a Business Partners page to cross-link to prominent _____ (city) area software web sites as well as the city Web sites and local business sites. We will also cross-link with brand name service providers.

5.   YouTube Posting
      We will produce a video of testimonials from several of our satisfied clients and educate viewers as to the range of our services. Our research indicates that the YouTube video will also serve to significantly improve our ranking with the Google Search Engine.

6. Exchange of links with strategic marketing partners.
We will cross-link to non-profit businesses that accept our gift certificate donations as in-house run contest prize awards.

7. E-Newsletter
Use the newsletter sign-up as a reason to collect email addresses and limited profiles and use embedded links in the newsletter to return readers to website.

8. Create an account for our photos on flickr.com
Use the name of our site on flickr so we have the same keywords access.

9. Geo Target Pay Per Click (PPC) Campaign
Available through the Google Adwords program. Example keywords include background checks, employment screening, credit reports, education verification, tenant screening, driving records and _____ (city).

10. Post messages on Internet user groups and forums.
Get involved with background check and verification related discussion groups and forums and develop a descriptive signature paragraph.

11. Write up our own LinkedIn.com and Facebook.com bios.
Highlight our background and professional interests.

12. Facebook.com Brand-Building Applications:
As a Facebook member, we will create a specific Facebook page for our business through its "Facebook Pages" application. This page will be used to promote who we are and what we do. We will use this page to post alerts when we have new articles to distribute, news to announce, etc. Facebook members can then become fans of our page and receive these updates on their newsfeed as we post them. We will create our business page by going to the "Advertising" link on the bottom of our personal Facebook page. We will choose the "Pages" tab at the top of that page, and then choose "Create a Page." We will upload our logo, enter our company profile details, and establish our settings. Once completed, we will click the "publish your site" button to go live. We will also promote our Page everywhere we can. We will add a Facebook link to our website, our email signatures, and email newsletters. We will also add Facebook to the marketing mix by deploying pay-per-click ads through their advertising application. With Facebook advertising, we will target by specifying sex, age, relationship, location, education, as well as specific keywords. Once we specify our target criteria, the tool will tell us how many members in the network meet our target needs.

13. Blog to share our success stories and solicit comments
Blogging will be a great way for us to share information, expertise, and news, and

start a conversation with our customers, the media, suppliers, and any other target audiences. Blogging will be a great online marketing strategy because it keeps our content fresh, engages our audience to leave comments on specific posts, improves search engine rankings and attracts links. In the blog we will share fun drink recipes and party tips. We will also provide a link to our Facebook.com page.   Resource: www.blogger.com   www.blogspot.com

14.   Other Embedded Links
We will use social networking, article directory postings and press release web sites as promotional tools and to provide good inbound link opportunities.

15.   Issue Press Releases
We will create online press releases to share news about our new website. Resources: Sites that offer free press release services include: www.prweb.com www.1888pressrelease.com and www.pr.com/press-releases.

7.2   Development Requirements

A full development plan will be generated as documented in the milestones. Costs that _____ (company name) will expect to incur with development of its new website include:

Development Costs

User interface design	$_____ .
Site development and testing	$_____
Site Implementation	$. _____

Ongoing Costs

Website name registration	$_____ per year.
Site Hosting	$_____ or less per month.

Site design changes, updates and maintenance are considered part of Marketing.

The site will be developed by _____ (company name), a local start-up company. The user interface designer will use our existing graphic art to come up with the website logo and graphics. We have already secured hosting with a local provider, _____ (business name). Additionally, they will prepare a monthly statistical usage report to analyze and improve web usage and return on investment.

The plan is for the website to be live by ___(date). Basic website maintenance, including update and data entry will be handled by our staff. Site content, such as images and text will be maintained by _____ (owner name). In the future, we may need to contract with a technical resource to build the trackable article download and newsletter capabilities.

7.3   Sample Frequently Asked Questions

We will use the following guidelines when developing the frequently asked questions for the ecommerce section of the website:

1. Use a Table of Contents: Offer subject headers at the top of the FAQ page with a hyperlink to that related section further down on the page for quick access.
2. Group Questions in a Logical Way and group separate specific questions related to a subject together.
3. Be Precise with the Question: Don't use open-ended questions.
4. Avoid Too Many Questions: Publish only the popular questions and answers.
5. Answer the Question with a direct answer.
6. Link to Resources When Available: via hyperlinks so the customer can continue with self-service support.
7. Use Bullet Points to list step-by-step instructions.
8. Focus on Customer Support and Not Marketing.
9. Use Real and Relevant Frequently Asked Questions from actual customers.
10. Update Your FAQ Page as customers continue to communicate questions.

The following frequently asked questions will enable us to convey a lot of important information to our clients in a condensed format. We will post these questions and answers on our website and create a hardcopy version to be included in our sales presentation folder.

Why do a background check during pre-employment screening?
A background check is an opportunity to verify information provided by your candidate. It can also reveal information that was either mistakenly or intentionally omitted, such as residency in other regions where a criminal record might be located. Background checks also help confirm dates of attendance and degrees or certifications earned and can provide specific information about prior employment. The bottom line is that your applicant's history will be useful in predicting their future and a thorough background check helps you see both.

What can't be included in a background check?
There is some information that cannot be disclosed under any circumstances, including very sensitive personal information, such as financial and credit card data, passwords, medical records, driving records, insurance records, employment history, social security records and other non-public information. School records are confidential and cannot be released without the consent of the student. You cannot be discriminated against because you filed for bankruptcy, however, bankruptcies are a public record, so, it is easy for employers to obtain the information. Laws vary on checking criminal history. Some states don't allow questions about arrests or convictions beyond a certain point in the past. Others only allow consideration of criminal history for certain positions. Employers cannot request medical records and may not make hiring decisions based on an applicant's disability. They may only inquire about your ability to perform a certain job. The same holds true for Worker's Compensation. The military can disclose your name, rank, salary, assignments and awards without your consent. Driving records are not

confidential either and can be released without consent.

Can your data be used for Employee Checks?

_____ (company name) is not a consumer reporting agency as defined under the Fair Credit Reporting Act ("FCRA"), and the information in our databases has not been collected in whole or in part for the purpose of furnishing consumer reports, as defined in the FCRA. You may not use the Websites or Data to: (a) establish an individual's legibility for personal credit or insurance; (b) assess risks associated with existing consumer credit obligations; or (c) evaluate an individual for employment, promotion, reassignment or retention (including employment of household workers such a nannies, housekeepers, or contractors) or in conjunction with assessing the merits of entering into any other personal business transaction with another individual.

What do I do if my search resulted in outdated or wrong information?

_____ (company name) is a provider of information, gathered from publicly available data. We do not create, verify, or guarantee the accuracy of such data. We receive information from various sources, including Internet sites. We are not necessarily affiliated with or endorsed by these sources or compensated by them. All materials and information available through Our Services are provided "as is" and "as available", and without warranties of any kind, express or implied. We do not warrant that the information is always accurate, complete or current; that access to it will be available all the time, from every place, or that errors will be corrected. _____ (company name) disclaims any responsibility and any warranties for sales, purchases, financing or other types of transactions involving products and services on which Our Services provide information. Your use of Our Services is solely at your own risk.

How current is your data?

Our service allows you to conduct searches of various public records. Any data presented as a result of these searches is derived from records that are not in the control of ____ (company name) and may not always be accurate or complete. Please see the Warranties section in our Terms and Conditions page for more information. As such, we can neither control nor guarantee the accuracy or availability of public records.

In which U.S. states can I search criminal records?

Some states do not permit access to certain types of criminal records or restrict the types of information that may be retrieved by a criminal search. As a result, not all searches will return reports or records.

Do we provide SSN records or Credit Reports?

By law we are prohibited from releasing non-public information such as SSN Records or Credit Reports to non-licensed entities. Our SSN Search allows you to check the validity of the provided number.

How do I get the background check information?

Reports can be emailed directly to you, viewed online at _____, faxed to you or a combination of these.

Do you mail hard copies of my reports?

No, all search results are displayed electronically after which you can either print or download the reports. Your reports will be saved in your "Search History" for ___ days

Do we provide Birth Certificates?

_____ (company name) does not provide/send/issue Birth Certificates. Our Birth Records search may include the following information: Full Name, Birth City, Birth State and Full Date of Birth.

What does my _____ (company name) membership include?

After you make a purchase on our Website, you will gain access to our Member's area, which is a one stop source for all your information needs. The Member's area combines the power of over ___ (#) different searches, tools, and resources to help you in your investigation process. Our Member's area is conveniently divided into two types of searches, Direct and Unlimited. Your "Search Results Access" fee will grant you access to our Member's area and will also be your Direct search balance. You can use these funds to execute various Direct searches. The cost for each Direct search will be deducted from your Direct search balance. After the expenditure of your funds, your subsequent use of our products and services will be subject to our then current rates. You can also purchase an "Unlimited Search Pass" for an additional fee which will grant you access to our "Unlimited" section of the Member's area. Direct searches may include: Bankruptcy Records search, Birth Records search, Business Records search, Comprehensive Background search, Court Records Search, Criminal Records search, Death Index search, Email search, Federal Records search, Legal/Civil Judgments search, Marriage/Divorce search, People Search, Person Report, Property Records, Relatives search, Reverse Cell Phone search, Reverse Landline Phone search, Reverse IP search, Sex Offender Search, SSN Validation search, SSN Records search, Vessel/Watercraft Records search, and Warrant search.

How does your No Hit No Fee policy work?

For selected "Direct" searches we offer a No Hit No Fee policy which means that if your search produces no results we will not charge CIS account. Please note that the funds will be not credited back to your credit card or PayPal account. This is an internal credit.

How do I interpret the criminal search results?

Our Criminal Check report may yield an individual's criminal records or indicate a lack of relevant results for the specified search criteria. In order to use this service, customers pay a small search fee. While our Criminal Check report can yield useful information, please use extreme caution in interpreting the results of any criminal background search. A positive match does not guarantee the nature or even existence of an individual's criminal record. _____ (company name) is not responsible for explaining or analyzing Criminal Check results. For assistance in interpreting criminal records and other official documents, please contact a competent legal professional.

Is your service subscription based?

_____ (company name) does not support the practice of automated re-billing. Choosing to continue your business with us in the coming years is solely your decision, and we hope that you will choose us for all your investigative needs. If you wish to purchase additional searches you can do so inside the member's area. Every purchase is a separate transaction and requires you to re-submit your credit card information as we do not store any financial information.

How much does a Background Check cost?
Background Checks vary in cost depending on the number of searches included in the report. Most of our clients combine several searches, such as an Address History, County Criminal Search based on the address history and a Prior Employment Confirmation. By combining several searches into a single package, we can offer a better price. We also offer volume discounts to companies that order frequently, and these discounts are handled on a case-by-case basis.

What are my payment options?
Invoicing and payment can be made based on your customized background check program and can included company check, credit card, EFT, PayPal, or order-to-pay.

How long will it take to complete the background check?
Reports are complete in 48-72 hours. Address History Searches are returned instantly, Credit Reports are instant, some Statewide Criminal searches are instant, County Criminal searches are complete within 48 hours and the Education/Certification and Employment Confirmation are complete in 48-72 hours.

What type of information do you collect?
We collect personal information from you when you: (1) register on the site; (2) subscribe to one of our mailing lists; (3) contact us; and (4) order products and services. The information we collect includes your name, address, email address, and telephone number. We also store your searches for 60 days, after which time we delete them. If you make a purchase, our service provider, ClickBank, will collect your payment information, but does not share that information with us. Additionally, as part of the standard operation of the Site, we may collect certain non-personal information from you, including but not limited to your browser type, operating system, IP address and the domain name from which you accessed the Site. In addition, we may collect information about your browsing behavior, such as the date and time you visit the Site, the areas or pages of the Site that you visit, the amount of time you spend viewing the Site, the number of times you return to the Site, your search history and other click-stream data.

Do you notify anyone every time I conduct a search?
All your searches are confidential. No one is notified that you are searching for them.

What does the Comprehensive Background Report Include?
A Comprehensive Background search may include: Criminal Record Search, Civil Filings and Civil Actions, Misdemeanors and Felonies, Arrests and Warrants, Convictions and Incarcerations, Address History, Phone Numbers, Email Addresses, List

of Possible Associates, List of Neighbors, List of Relatives, Alias/Maiden Name Check, Property Ownership Search, Date of Birth, Area Sex Offender Check, Spouse/Roommates Locator
Neighborhood Statistics and Neighborhood Check.

What information do I need to run a background check on someone?
Our national criminal background check requires a first name and last name. The system will figure out common first name variations such as Tom, Thomas, Tommy, and so on. If you intend to use the report for employment screening, tenant screening, or any purpose related to the Fair Credit Reporting Act (FCRA), you must include a date of birth. We recommend using a social security number as well if you have it, but date of birth is the key piece of information. Most courts do not release social security numbers because of identity theft concerns.

Do I need a release form to do a background check? Do you have one we can use?
If you intend to use a criminal background check for employment purposes, the Fair Credit Reporting Act requires you to obtain written permission from the applicant in a clear and conspicuous manner. (There are some exceptions for the trucking industry.) If you do not have a form already available, click here for our release form. Our release form is in PDF format, which most computers already have.

Will the person I am doing the search on know that I have done it?
No, all searches on our website are anonymous to the extent permitted by law.

Is your website secure?
Yes. Our website is protected by SSL encryption and other methods. All web communications, including credit card numbers, are secure and encrypted.
If you need to e-mail us for any reason, please be aware that e-mail is not secure.

Resources:
www.businessnewsdaily.com/7636-choosing-a-background-check-service.html
www.nationsearch.com/frequently-asked-questions-ebook?hsCtaTracking=4cf30416-b2b7-477b-a179-c40dcaf0a0ad%7C77893032-fe3d-45ce-8402-a162d5af9739

7.4 Website Performance Summary

We will use web analysis tools to monitor web traffic, such as identifying the number of site visits. We will analyze customer transactions and take actions to minimize problems, such as incomplete sales and abandoned shopping carts. We will use the following table to track the performance of our website:

Category	2018		2019		2020	
	Fcst	Act	Fcst	Act	Fcst	Act
No. of Customers						
New Subscribers						

Unique Visitors _____

Total Page Views _____

Bounce Rate _____

Avg Time on Site _____

Page Views / Visit _____

No. of Products _____

Product Categories _____

Number of Incomplete Sales _____

Conversion Rate _____

Affiliate Sales _____

Customer Satisfaction Score _____

7.5 Website Retargeting/Remarketing

Research indicates that for most websites, only 2% of web traffic converts readers on the first visit. Retargeting will keep track of people who have visited our website and displays our ads to them as they browse online. This will bring back 98% of users who don't convert right away by keeping our brand at the top of their mind. Setting up a remarketing tracking code on our website will allow us to target past visitors who did not convert or take the desired action on our site. After people have been to our website and are familiar with our brand, we will market more aggressively to this 'warm traffic.'

Resource:
www.marketing360.com/remarketing-software-retargeting-ads/

8.0 Operations Plan

Operations include the business aspects of running our business, such as conducting quality assessment and improvement activities, auditing functions, cost-management analysis, and customer service. Our operations plan will present an overview of the flow of the daily activities of the business and the strategies that support them. It will focus on the following critical operating factors that will make the business a success:

1. We will enjoy the following advantages in the sourcing of our inventory:
    _____

2. We will utilize the following technological innovations in the customer relationship management (CRM) process:
    _____

3. We will make use of the following advantages in our distribution process:
    _____

4. We will develop the following in-house training program to improve worker productivity: _____

5. We will utilize the following system to better control inventory carrying costs.
    _____

6. We will implement the following quality control plan:
    _____

Quality Control Plan
Our Quality Control Plan will include a review process that checks all factors involved in our operations. The main objectives of our quality control plan will be to uncover defects and bottlenecks, and reporting to management level to make the decisions on the improvement of the whole production process. Our review process will include the following activities:
    Quality control checklist
    Finished service review
    Structured walkthroughs
    Statistical sampling
    Testing process

Operations Planning
We will use Microsoft Visio to develop visual maps, which will piece together the different activities in our organization and show how they contribute to the overall "value stream" of our business. We will rightfully treat operations as the lifeblood of our business. We will develop a combined sales and operations planning process where sales and operations managers will sit down every month to review sales, at the same time creating a forward-looking 12-month rolling plan to help guide the product development and manufacturing processes, which can become disconnected from sales. We will approach our operations planning using a three-step process that analyzes the company's current state, future state and the initiatives it will tackle next. For each initiative, such as launching a new product or service, the company will examine the related financials, talent and operational needs, as well as target customer profiles. Our management team

will map out the cost of development and then calculate forecasted return on investment and revenue predictions.

Our Process Overview

The following essential foundational steps will apply for all screenings:

We will receive a client order that consists of the applicant's completed and signed "Disclosure Regarding Background Investigation", referred to as the Consent Form.

The information disclosed on the FCRA compliant Consent Form (name, SSN and current address) will then be placed into the Credit Bureau database, which discloses where the individual has lived and worked, and directs what counties and states are to be searched.

The search will be conducted based upon the searches/search package our client has chosen, and the Search and Scope instructions provided.

We will contact and set-up accounts with the following agencies:
1.   Credit Bureaus (Experience, Equifax and TransUnion)
2.   State Police Department
3.   Department of Motor Vehicles (DMV)
4.   Local Courthouses
5.   Social Security Administration
6.   U.S. Department of Justice's National Sex Offender Registry
7.   Online County Property Tax Assessors
8.   Workers' Compensation Appeals Board (WCAB),
9.   National Archives and Records Administration web site: www.archives.gov/facilities/mo/st_louis/military_personnel_records.html
10.   FBI Criminal Information Center

We will contact each agency individually, present our business license, and ask to get set-up to order reports for our background check clients.

Pre-Employment Background Checks

The primary purpose of an employee background check is to verify the job applicant's identity. It is comparing the personal information the applicant provided—name, date of birth, addresses and Social Security number—with public and commercial records containing the same information. In most cases, the prospective employer will retain the services of a commercial public records aggregator, such as Merlin Information Services or TransUnion, to obtain a consumer report that may also include a credit history. In these situations, the federal Fair Credit Reporting Act (FCRA) requires the prospective employer to give written notice to the applicant and obtain his written consent to obtain his consumer report.

The following are types of information that employers often consult as part of a pre-employment check, and the laws governing their access and use in making hiring decisions:

1. Credit Reports

Under the Fair Credit Reporting Act (FCRA) employers must get an employee's written consent before seeking an employee's credit report. If you decide not to hire or promote someone based on information in the credit report, you must provide a copy of the report and let the applicant know of his or her right to challenge the report under the FCRA. Some states have more stringent rules limiting the use of credit reports.

2. Criminal Records

Employee background checks frequently include criminal records searches to determine if the applicant has committed any crime that will prohibit him from performing certain work. For example, a theft conviction disqualifies an applicant from a job involving handling money; a sex-related conviction disqualifies from a job requiring contact with children. In some states, a criminal history search is mandatory for certain employment, such as hiring a public-school employee in Minnesota. However, in some states there are limits placed on criminal record searches, such as in California, which prohibits reporting convictions more than seven years old. To what extent, a private employer may consider an applicant's criminal history in making hiring decisions varies from state to state. Because of this variation, we will consult with a lawyer or do further legal research on the law of our state before digging into an applicant's criminal past.

For FBI checks consult the following resources:

FBI Services for Businesses

The Federal Bureau of Investigation offers assistance to businesses in the areas of employee background investigation, antitrust investigation, trade secret and intellectual property protection, cyberspace patrol, economic espionage, and anti-terrorism.

FBI Criminal History Checks for Employment and Licensing

Advises employers to contact the agency requiring the background check or the appropriate state identification bureau (or state police) for the correct procedures to follow for obtaining an FBI fingerprint background check for employment or licensing purposes.

FBI Checks on Employees of Banks and Related Entities

Information on conducting criminal history background checks on employees of banking-related institutions.

3. Lie Detector Tests

The Employee Polygraph Protection Act prohibits most private employers from using lie detector tests, either for pre-employment screening or during the course of employment. The law includes a list of exceptions that apply to businesses that provide armored car services, alarm or guard services, or manufacture, distribute, or dispense pharmaceuticals. Even though there is no federal law specifically prohibiting you from using a written honesty test on job applicants, these tests frequently violate federal and state laws that protect against discrimination and violations of privacy. The tests are rarely reliable, so unless a business is one of the exceptions, most employers do not use lie detectors in the hiring process.

4. Medical Records

Under the Americans with Disabilities Act employers may inquire only about an applicant's ability to perform specific job duties and cannot request an employee's medical records. As long as the employee can do the job, with or without reasonable accommodation, an employer may not make a job decision (on hiring or promotion, for example) based on an employee's disability. Some states also have laws protecting the confidentiality of medical records.

5. Bankruptcy Filings

Bankruptcies are a matter of public record and may appear on an individual's credit report. The federal Bankruptcy Act prohibits employers from discriminating against applicants because they have filed for bankruptcy. These records are found through using a commercial public records aggregator, as well as directly from the court, using the Public Access to Court Electronic Records (PACER) database that the federal courts maintain. Thus, a prospective employer can use these records to assess an applicant's financial stability. The FCRA prohibits including bankruptcy filings more than 10 years old in an employee background check.

6. Military Service

Military service records may be released only under limited circumstances, and consent is generally required. The military may, however, disclose name, rank, salary, duty assignments, awards, and duty status without the member's consent.

7. Work and Education /School Records

Under the Family Educational Rights and Privacy Act and similar state laws, educational records (e.g., transcripts, recommendations, and financial information) are confidential, and will not be released by the school with a student's consent. Prospective employers routinely request personal information that includes the applicant's work and education history. Although the information is needed to assess an applicant's qualifications, the FCRA states that this information is confidential and subject to privacy protections. Thus, to comply with the FCRA, a prospective employer must obtain the applicant's written consent before seeking information related to work or education history.

8. Workers' Compensation Records

Workers' compensation appeals are part of the public record. Information from a workers' compensation appeal may be used in a hiring decision if the employer can show the applicant's injury might interfere with his ability perform required duties.

9. Lawsuits, Liens, Judgments

All counties maintain records of tax liens and judgments, and local courts maintain records of civil lawsuits, such as divorces, collections and harassment cases. These records are often searched as part of an employee background check and can give insight into how the applicant has conducted his personal affairs. The FCRA prohibits reporting these types of records in an employee background check if more than seven years old.

Business Background Checks

The most common place to start a business background check is the local Better Business Bureau, especially if it is a locally owned business. The Better Business Bureau can help you verify the company's address and company officers. As part of the business background check, they can also advise if there have been complaints against the company and if the issues were resolved or not. Another step in performing a business background check is typing a simple search in an internet search engine. It can reveal everything from their accomplishments to financial information. With the company's Federal Employer Identification Number (FEIN), it is possible to find out much more for a business background check. For instance, that number could be run through the Secretary of State website and reveal the company's officers, financial information and incorporation information. It will also indicate if the company had done business under another name. The Federal Employer Identification Number can also be run through Dun and Bradstreet's database to find out even more financial information.

Operations Management

We plan to write and maintain an Operations Manual and a Personnel Policies Handbook. The Operating Manual will be a comprehensive document outlining virtually every aspect of the business. The operating manual will include management and accounting procedures, hiring and personnel policies, and daily operations procedures, such as opening and closing the store, and how to _____. The manual will cover the following topics:

- Community Relations
- Media Relations
- Vendor Relations
- Competition Relations
- Environmental Concerns
- Intra Company Procedures
- Banking and Credit Cards
- Computer Procedures
- Quality Controls
- Open/Close Procedures
- Software Documentation
- Customer Relations
- Employee Relations
- Government Relations
- Equipment Maintenance Checklist
- Inventory Controls
- Accounting and Billing
- Financing
- Scheduling Procedures
- Safety Procedures
- Security Procedures

We will also develop a personnel manual. Its purpose is to set fair and equal guidelines in print for all to abide. It's the playbook detailing specific policies, as well as enforcement, thereby preventing any misinterpretation, miscommunication or ill feelings. This manual will reflect only the concerns that affect our personnel. A companion policy and procedure manual will cover everything else.

We will consolidate the number of suppliers we deal with to reduce the volume of paperwork and realize volume discounts. We also plan to develop a list of specific interview questions and a worksheet to evaluate, compare and pre-screen potential suppliers. We will also check vendor references and their rating with the Hoovers.com.

We will conduct a quality improvement plan, which consists of an ongoing process of improvement activities and includes periodic samplings of activities not initiated solely in response to an identified problem. Our plan will be evaluated annually and revised as necessary. Our client satisfaction survey goal is a ___ (98.0)% satisfaction rating.

Resources:

KMS Software Company   www.kmssoftware.com/
The pioneer of Online OnBoarding. Provides human capital management software that combines process automation and employee engagement technology to help strengthen the relationship between employers and employees around the world.

Bond International Software   www.bond-us.com/
Specializes in software and support for the global staffing industry. Their product 'Adapt' is the benchmark recruitment software that is used by more than 90% of the world's leading recruitment agencies.

Taleo Business Edition   www.taleo.com/LP/TBE-Refer/Intelius_PartnerRefer_pol.php
Provides a fully integrated, end-to-end recruitment solution built exclusively for small-to-midsize businesses. By leveraging this turn-key integration, clients can manage their background checks, skills testing, and drug screening programs from within the Taleo Business Edition applicant tracking system.

TazWorks, LLC   www.TazWorks.com
Developed the most powerful and efficient web-based background screening software in the industry. The eedesigned InstaScreen Premiere 2.0%u2122 showcases a very broad range of features to help make the background screening process simple and powerful.

Active Investigative Solutions LLC   www.physicalinspections.com
An accurate, timely and professional on-site inspection company.

Deverus, Inc.   www.deverus.com
A leading provider of web-based software and hosted support services for background screening companies, provides clients with superior technology, intuitive support, and a wide array of powerful business development tools.

9.0   Management Summary

The Management Plan will reveal who will be responsible for the various management functions to keep the business running efficiently. It will further demonstrate how that individual has the experience and/or training to accomplish each function. It will address who will do the planning function, the organizing function, the directing function, and the controlling function. We will also develop an employee retention plan because there are distinct cost advantages to retaining employees. It costs a lot to recruit and train a new employee, and in the early days, new employees are a lot less productive. We will need to make sure that our employees are satisfied in order to retain them and, in turn, create satisfied customers.

At the present time ___ (owner name) will run all operations for _____ (company name). _____ (His/Her) background in _____ (business management?) indicates an understanding of the importance of financial control systems. There is not expected to be any shortage of qualified staff from local labor pools in the market area.

_____ (owner name) will be the owner and operations manager of _____ (company name). His/her general duties will include the following:
1.   Oversee the daily operations
2.   Ordering inventory and supplies.
3.   Develop and implementing the marketing strategy
4.   Purchasing equipment.
5.   Arranging for the routine maintenance and upkeep of the facility.
6.   Hiring, training and supervision of new assistants.
7.   Scheduling and planning of seminars and other special events.
8.   Creating and pricing products and services.
9.   Managing the accounting/financial aspect of the business.
10.   Contract negotiation/vendor relations.

9.1   Owner Personal History

The owner has been working in the _____ industry for over ____ (#) years, gaining personal knowledge and experience in all phases of the industry. _____ (owner name) is the founder and operations manager of _____ (company name). The owner holds a degree from the University of _____ at _____ (city). .

Over the last _ (#) years, ___ (owner name) became quite proficient in a wide range of management activities and responsibilities, becoming an operations manager for ___ (former employer name) from __to _ (dates). There he/she was able to achieve _____. For ____ years he/she has managed a business similar to _____ (company name). _____ (His/her) duties included ____. Specifically, the owner brings _____ (#) years of experience as a ____ , as well as certification as a _____ from the _____ (National _____ Association). He/she is an experienced entrepreneur with ____ years of small business accounting, finance, marketing and management experience. Education includes college course work in business administration, banking and finance, investments, and commercial credit management. The owner will draw an annual salary of $____ from the business although most of this goes to repay loans to finance business start-up costs. These loans will be paid-in-full by _____ (month) of _____ (year).

9.2   Management Team Gaps

Despite the owner's and manager's experience in the _____ (?) industry, the company will also retain the consulting services of _____ (consultant company name). This company has over _____ (#) years of experience in the _____ industry and has successfully opened dozens of background check companies across the country. The Consultants will be primarily used for certification approval, market research, customer satisfaction surveys and to provide additional input in the evaluation of new business opportunities. The company also expects to retain the services of a local CPA to help the owner manage cash flow. Additionally, the business will make use of the following advisory board to provide support for strategic planning and human resource related issues.

The Board of Advisors will provide continuous mentoring support on business matters. Expertise gaps in legal, tax, marketing and personnel will be covered by the Board of Advisors. The owner will actively seek free business advice from SCORE, a national non-profit organization with a local office. This is a group of retired executives and business owners who donate their time to serve as business counselors to new business owners.

Advisory Resources Available to the Business Include:

	Name	Address	Phone
CPA/Accountant			
Attorney			
Insurance Broker			
Banker			
Business Consultant			
Wholesale Suppliers			
Trade Association			
Realtor			
SCORE.org			
Other			

9.2.1   Management Matrix

Name	Title	Credentials	Functions	Responsibilities

9.2.2   Outsourcing Matrix

Company Name	Functions	Responsibilities	Cost

9.3.0   Employee Requirements

1. **Recruitment**

   Experience suggests that personal referrals from contractors and distributor reps are an excellent source for experienced associates We will also place newspaper ads and use our Yellow Page Ad to indicate what types of staff we use and what types of customers we serve. We will also make effective use of our newsletter to post positions available and contact local technical trade schools for possible job candidates. We will give a referral bonus to existing employees.

2. **Training and Supervision**

   Training is largely accomplished through hands-on experience and by manufacturer product reps with supplemental instruction. Additional knowledge is gained through our policy and Operations Manuals and attending manufacturer and trade association seminars. We will foster professional development and independence in all phases of our business. Supervision is task-oriented and the quantity is dependent on the complexity of the job assignment. Employees are called team members because they are part of Team _____ (company name). To help them succeed and confidently handle customer questions, employees will receive assistance with our internal certification program. They will also participate in our written training modules and receive regular samples to evaluate.

3. **Salaries and Benefits**

   Staff will be basically paid a salary plus commission basis on product sales. Good training and incentives, such as cash bonuses handed out monthly to everyone for reaching goals, will serve to retain good employees. An employee discount of __ percent on personal sales is offered. As business warrants, we hope to put together a benefit package that includes insurance, and paid vacations. The personnel plan also assumes a 5% annual increase in salaries.

9.4.0   Job Descriptions

Job Description -- Background Check Specialist (Compliance Coordinator)
Key Responsibilities:
1. Process Background Check and Drug Screens according to each client's requirement.
2. Responsible for performance of Quality System procedures in relation to job

description.

3. Abide by company regulations, policies, work procedures, and instructions.
4. Responsible for completion of new hire sign-up paperwork to Human Resources.
5. Collect missing paperwork.
6. Special projects as assigned.
7. Other duties as assigned.

Job Description -- Chief Technology Officer

Under administrative direction, the CTO is responsible for the management of multiple R&D and production projects. This position reports to and provides the CEO a technical voice in the strategic planning for the company and works collaboratively to assist in the determination of the types of products and services the company should focus on. The CTO also works collaboratively with the President, Network Manager and their teams to increase functionality, product development and implementation of plans and production.

Essential Job Functions
1. Coordinates efforts of executive management to ensure successful design, production, and testing of prototypes.
2. Plays a key role in defining the company's technology and product roadmap; executes approved development efforts.
3. Identifies, taps and coordinates external sources of expertise (e.g. suppliers, industry partners, industry experts, academia).
4. Recognized externally as the key technical voice of the company.
5. Possesses a solid understanding of the management practices relating to IT service delivery.
6. Ability to build solid relationships with all involved team members to develop a clear understanding of the company's needs; ability to lead the implementation of plans which meet those needs.
7. Displays capability to champion the processes, tools and commitment to provide quality products and client service.
8. Possesses the capability to create visions and strategies; communicates a clear sense of direction; builds a strong sense of teamwork, purpose and group identity; ability to recognize and use trends and projections to predict the future needs of clients.
9. Performs other duties as assigned by the supervisor.

Job Description -- Affiliate Program Manager

Under general supervision, the Affiliate Program Manage is responsible for online marketing management of daily activities of the affiliate marketing program. The Affiliate Program Manager will participate in product development and merchant relations.

Essential Job Functions
1. Daily affiliate management including ongoing development and deployment of marketing and creative affiliate communications such as e-Newsletters and blog posts, offers, affiliate payments and dispute resolution.

2. Monitor affiliate activity, analyze performance, identify areas of improvement and recommend ways to increase affiliate-generated revenues.
3. Recruit new affiliates, joint venture partners and strategic partners.
4. Oversee development and distribution of marketing tools and creative sales to affiliates.
5. Establish channels of communication to ensure all affiliates and joint venture partners have access to marketing tools.
6. Develop custom marketing material as required.
7. Work closely with Director of Marketing to build and expand the affiliate program.
8. Initiate new campaign ideas, incentives and bonus offers.
9. Develop annual campaign calendar and rollout offers.
10. Contact merchants and networks to establish co-marketing relationships and proactively manage these relationships on an ongoing basis.
11. Develop, track and manage offers to merchant partners. Including establishing benchmarks and reporting relevant metrics.
12. Work directly with IT to develop tracking, monitoring, reporting and other technological integration with existing systems.
13. Performs other related duties as assigned by the supervisor.

9.4.1 Job Description Format

Our job descriptions will adhere to the following format guidelines:

1.	Job Title	2.	Reports to:
3.	Pay Rate	4.	Job Responsibilities
5.	Travel Requirements	5.	Supervisory Responsibilities
6.	Qualifications	7.	Work Experience
8.	Required Skills	10.	Salary Range
11.	Benefits	12.	Opportunities

9.5 Personnel Plan

1. We will develop a system for recruiting, screening and interviewing employees.
2. Background checks will be performed as well as reference checks and drug tests.
3. We will develop an assistant training course.
4. We will keep track of staff scheduling.
5. We will develop client satisfaction surveys to provide feedback and ideas.
6. We will develop and perform semi-annual employee evaluations.
7. We will "coach" all of our employees to improve their abilities and range of skills.
8. We will employ temporary employees via a local staffing agency to assist with one-time special projects.
9. Each employee will be provided an Employee Handbook, which will include detailed job descriptions and list of business policies, and be asked to sign these documents as a form of employment contract.
10. Incentives will be offered for reaching quarterly financial and enrollment goals, completing the probationary period and passing county inspections.

11. Customer service awards will be presented to those employees who best exemplify our stated mission and exceed customer expectations.
12. Independent Contractors will be utilized to perform the following functions in compliance with IRS rules: _____
13. We will help employees to develop career paths within our organization, developing new skills or enhancing existing ones.
14. We will keep employees in the loop through honest and transparent communication.
15. We will make use of noncash awards because noncash incentives are more memorable for employees from all generations.
16. We will schedule planned culture event experiences to improve team spirit.

Our Employee Handbook will include the following sections:
1. Overview
2. Introduction to the Company
3. Organizational Structure
4. Employment and Hiring Policies
5. Performance Evaluation and Promotion Policies
6. Compensation Policies
7. Time Off Policies
8. Training Programs and Reimbursement Policies
9. General Rules and Policies
10. Termination Policies.

9.6 Staffing Plan

The following table summarizes our personnel expenditures for the first three years, with compensation costs increasing from $_____ in the first year to about $_____ in the third year, based on ____ (5?) % payroll increases each year. The payroll includes tuition reimbursement, pay increases, vacation pay, bonuses and state required certifications.

Table: Personnel Plan

	Number of Employees	Hourly Rate	Annual Salaries 2018	2019	2020
Owner/Director					
Operations Manager					
Affiliate Program Manager					
Chief Technology Officer					
Background Check Specialist					
Account managers					
Client services specialists					
Human resource recruiter					
Marketing manager					

Criminal court researchers _____

Software developer _____

Software engineer _____

Sales Associate _____

Customer Service Rep. _____

Marketing Coordinator _____

Accountant/Controller _____

Bookkeeper _____

Janitor _____

Other _____

Total People: Headcount _____

Total Annual Payroll _____

Payroll Burden (Fringe Benefits)   (+) _____

Total Payroll Expense   (=) _____

10.0   Risk Factors

Risk management is the identification, assessment, and prioritization of risks, followed by the coordinated and economical application of resources to minimize, monitor, and control the probability and/or impact of unfortunate events or to maximize the realization of opportunities. For the most part, our risk management methods will consist of the following elements, performed, more or less, in the following order.

1. Identify, characterize, and assess threats
2. Assess the vulnerability of critical assets to specific threats
3. Determine the risk (i.e. the expected consequences of specific types of attacks on specific assets)
4. Identify ways to reduce those risks
5. Prioritize risk reduction measures based on a strategy

Types of Risks:

_____ (company name) faces the following kinds of risks:

1. **Financial Risks**

   Our quarterly revenues and operating results are difficult to predict and may fluctuate significantly from quarter to quarter as a result of a variety of factors. Among these factors are:

   -Changes in our own or competitors' pricing policies.
   - Recession pressures.
   - Fluctuations in expected revenues from advertisers, sponsors and strategic relationships.
   - Timing of costs related to acquisitions or payments.

2. **Legislative / Legal Landscape.**

   Our participation in the background checking arena presents unique risks:

   - Professional liability.
   - Federal and State regulations on licensing, privacy and insurance.

3. **Operational Risks**

   For the past __ (#) years the owner has been dealing with computers, so he is comfortable with technology and understands a wide array of software applications. However, the biggest potential problem will be equipment malfunction. To minimize the potential for problems, the owner will be taking equipment repair training from the manufacturer and will deal with basic troubleshooting and minor repairs. Beyond that, we have identified a service technician who is located close-by.

   To attract and retain client to the _____ (company name) community, we must continue to provide differentiated and quality services. This confers certain risks including the failure to:

   - Anticipate and respond to consumer preferences for partnerships and service.
   - Attract, excite and retain a large audience of customers to our

community.
- Create and maintain successful strategic alliances with quality partners.
- Deliver high quality, customer service.
- Build our brand rapidly and cost-effectively.
- Compete effectively against better-established background check companies.

4. Human Resource Risks

The most serious human resource risk to our business, at least in the initial stages, would be my inability to operate the business due to illness or disability. The owner is currently in exceptional health and would eventually seek to replace himself on a day-to-day level by developing systems to support the growth of the business.

5. Marketing Risks

Advertising is our most expensive form of promotion and there will be a period of testing headlines and offers to find the one that works the best. The risk, of course, is that we will exhaust our advertising budget before we find an ad that works. Placing greater emphases on sunk-cost marketing, such as our storefront and on existing relationships through direct selling will minimize our initial reliance on advertising to bring in a large percentage of business in the first year.

6. Business Risks

A major risk to retail service businesses is the performance of the economy and the small business sector. Since economists are predicting this as the fastest growing sector of the economy, our risk of a downturn in the short-term is minimized. The entrance of one of the major chains into our marketplace is a risk. They offer more of the latest equipment, provide a wider array of products and services, competitive prices and 24-hour service. This situation would force us to lower our prices in the short-term until we could develop an offering of higher margin, value-added services not provided by the large chains. It does not seem likely that the relative size of our market today could support the overhead of one of those operations. Projections indicate that this will not be the case in the future and that leaves a window of opportunity for ___ (company name) to aggressively build a loyal client base. We will also not pursue big-leap, radical change misadventures, but rather strive to hit stepwise performance benchmarks, with a planned consistency over a long period of time.

To combat the usual start-up risks we will do the following:
1. Utilize our industry experience to quickly establish desired strategic relationships.
2. Pursue business outside of our immediate market area.
3. Diversify our range of product and service offerings.
4. Develop multiple distribution channels.
5. Monitor our competitor actions.
6. Stay in touch with our customers and database suppliers.
7. Watch for trends which could potentially impact our business.

8. Continuously optimize and scrutinize all business processes.
9. Institute daily financial controls using Business Ratio Analysis.
10. Create pay-for-performance compensation and training programs to reduce employee turnover.

Further, to attract and retain customers the Company will need to continue to expand its market offerings, utilizing third party strategic relationships. This could lead to difficulties in the management of relationships, competition for specific services and products, and/or adverse market conditions affecting a particular partner.
The Company will take active steps to mitigate risks. In preparation of the Company's pricing, many factors will be considered. The Company will closely track the activities of all third parties and will hold monthly review meetings to resolve issues and review and update the terms associated with strategic alliances.

Additionally, we will develop the following kinds of contingency plans:
Disaster Recovery Plan
Business Continuity Plan
Business Impact and Gap Analysis
Testing & Maintenance

The Company will utilize marketing and advertising campaigns to promote brand identity and will coordinate all expectations with internal and third-party resources prior to release. This strategy should maximize customer satisfaction while minimizing potential costs associated with unplanned expenditures and quality control issues.

10.1   Business Risk Reduction Strategy

We plan to implement the following strategies to reduce our start-up business risk:
1. Implement our business plan based on go, no-go stage criteria.
2. Develop employee cross-training programs.
3. Regularly back-up all computer files/Install ant-virus software.
4. Arrange adequate insurance coverage with higher deductibles.
5. Develop a limited number of prototype samples.
6. Test market offerings to determine level of market demand and appropriate pricing strategy.
7. Thoroughly investigate and benchmark to competitor offerings.
8. Research similar franchised businesses for insights into successful prototype business/operations models.
9. Reduce operation risks and costs by flowcharting all structured systems & standardized manual processes.
10. Use market surveys to listen to customer needs and priorities.
11. Purchase used equipment to reduce capital outlays.
12. Use leasing to reduce financial risk.
13. Outsource manufacturing to job shops to reduce capital at risk.
14. Use subcontractors to limit fixed overhead salary expenses.

15. Ask manufacturers about profit sharing arrangements.
16. Pay advertisers with a percent of revenues generated.
17. Develop contingency plans for identified risks.
18. Set-up procedures to control employee theft.
19. Do criminal background checks on potential employees.
20. Take immediate action on delinquent accounts.
21. Only extend credit to established account with D&B rating
22. Get regular competitive bids from alternative suppliers.
23. Check that operating costs as a percent of rising sales are lower as a result of productivity improvements.
24. Request bulk rate pricing on fast moving supplies.
25. Don't tie up cash in slow moving inventory to qualify for bigger discounts.
26. Reduce financial risk by practicing cash flow policies.
27. Reduce hazard risk by installing safety procedures.
28. Use financial management ratios to monitor business vitals.
29. Make business decisions after brainstorming sessions.
30. Focus on the products with biggest return on investment.
31. Where possible, purchase off-the-shelf components.
32. Request manufacturer samples and assistance to build prototypes.
33. Design production facilities to be flexible and easy to change.
34. Develop a network of suppliers with outsourcing capabilities.
35. Analyze and shorten every cycle time, including product development.
36. Develop multiple sources for every important input.
37. Treat the business plan as a living document and update it frequently.
38. Conduct a SWOT analysis and use determined strengths to pursue opportunities.
39. Conduct regular customer satisfaction surveys to evaluate performance.

10.2   Reduce Customer Perceived Risk Tactics

We will utilize the following tactics to help reduce the new customer's perceived risk of starting to do business with our company.

Status

1. Publish a page of testimonials. _____
2. Secure Opinion Leader written endorsements. _____
3. Offer an Unconditional Satisfaction Money Back Guarantee. _____
4. Long-term Performance Guarantee (Financial Risk). _____
5. Guaranteed Buy Back (Obsolete time risk) _____
6. Offer free trials and samples. _____
7. Brand Image (consistent marketing image and performance) _____
8. Patents/Trademarks/Copyrights _____
9. Publish case studies _____
10. Share your expertise (Articles, Seminars, etc.) _____
11. Get recognized Certification _____
12. Conduct responsive customer service _____
13. Accept Installment Payments _____
14. Display product materials composition or ingredients. _____

15. Publish product test results. _____
16. Publish sales record milestones. _____
17. Foster word-of-mouth by offering an unexpected extra. _____
18. Distribute factual, pre-purchase info. _____
19. Reduce consumer search costs with online directories. _____
20. Reduce customer transaction costs. _____
21. Facilitate in-depth comparisons to alternative services. _____
22. Make available prior customer ratings and comments. _____
23. Provide customized info based on prior transactions. _____
24. Become a Better Business Bureau member. _____
25. Publish overall customer satisfaction survey results. _____
26. Offer plan options that match niche segment needs. _____
27. Require client sign-off before proceeding to next phase. _____
28. Document procedures for dispute resolution. _____
29. Offer the equivalent of open source code. _____
30. Stress your compatibility features (avoid lock-in fear). _____
31. Create detailed checklists & flowcharts to show processes _____
32. Publish a list of frequently asked questions/answers. _____
33. Create a community that enables clients to connect with
    each other and share common interests. _____
34. Inform customers as to your stay-in-touch methods. _____
35. Conduct and handover a detailed needs analysis worksheet. _____
36. Offer to pay all return shipping charges and/or refund all
    original shipping and handling fees. _____
37. Describe your product testing procedures prior to shipping. _____
38. Highlight your competitive advantages in all marketing materials. _____

11.0　　　Financial Plan

The over-all financial plan for growth allows for use of the significant cash flow generated by operations. We are basing projected sales on the market research, industry analysis and competitive environment. ___ (company name) expects a profit margin of over __ % starting with year one. By year two, that number should slowly increase as the law of diminishing costs takes hold, and the day-to-day activities of the business become less expensive. Sales are expected to grow at __% per year, and level off by year _____. Our financial statements will show consistent growth in earnings, which provides notice of the durability of our company's competitive advantage.

The initial investment in _____ (company name) will be provided by _____ (owner name) in the amount of $ _____. The owner will also seek a ___ (#) year bank loan in the amount of $ _____ to provide the remainder of the required initial funding. The funds will be used to renovate the space and to cover initial operating expenses. The owner financing will become a return on equity, paid in the form of dividends to the owner. We expect to finance steady growth through cash flow. The owners do not intend to take any profits out of the business until the long-term debt has been satisfied.

Our financial plan includes:
　Moderate growth rate with a steady cash flow.
　Investing residual profits into company expansion.
　Company expansion will be an option if sales projections are met.
　Marketing costs will remain below ___ (5?) % of sales.
　Repayment of our loan calculated at a high A.P.R. of ___ (10?) percent and at a
　　　　　5-year-payback on our $_____ loan.

11.1　　　Important Assumptions

Since this is a start-up operation, a steady increase in sales is forecast over three years, as consumer awareness and regular repeat business grows with a strong and consistent increase in the local population, from an initial _____ residents to about _____ residents upon completion. A solid business plan and the management skills and experience of the managing partners should be sufficient to orchestrate the necessary growth to make this a successful launch with steady increases in sales over the first three years.

Operating expenses are based on an assessment of operational needs for an office space of this size. Observations of _____ (city) competitor staffing, direct experience at _____ , and interviews with competitor owners and suppliers are the basis for these projections. Rent is based on negotiated lease agreement with the landlord. Other estimates are based on experience in operating a _____ (#) square foot _____ (city) office and on vendor quotes and estimates. Collection days should remain fairly short, given the substantial cash revenues, and standard credit card collection periods.

Financial Plan Assumptions

1. All operating costs are based on the management's research of similar operating companies.
2. Automated informational systems will reduce the staff requirements.
3. Developmental start-up costs are amortized over a five-year period.
4. Home office or other apartment expenses are not included.
5. Overhead and operations costs are calculated on an annual basis.
6. The founders' salary is based on a fixed monthly salary expense basis.
7. All fixed and variable labor costs are scheduled to rise annually at ___ (5?) percent.
8. All revenues are figured to rise annually at ___ (10?) percent.
9. Administrative and office expenses rise at an annual rate of 2.5 percent.
10. Operating costs increase at ___ (5) percent annually.
11. Loan amount interest rate at ___ (10) percent.

Other Assumptions:

1. The economy will grow at a steady slow pace, without another major recession.
2. There will be no major changes in the industry, other than those discussed in the trends section of this document.
3. The State will not enact 'impact' legislation on our industry.
4. Sales are estimated at minimum to average values, while expenses are estimated at above average to maximum values.
5. Staffing and payroll expansions will be driven by increased sales.
6. Materials expenses will not increase dramatically over the next several years, but will grow at a rate that matches increasing consumption.
7. We assume access to equity capital and financing sufficient to maintain our financial plan as shown in the tables.
8. The amount of the financing needed from the bank will be approximately $_____ and this will be repaid over the next 10 years at $_____ per month.
9. We assume that the area will continue to grow at present rate of ___ % per year.
10. Interest rates and tax rates are based on conservative assumptions.

Revenue Assumptions:

	Year	Sales/Month	Growth Rate
1.			
2.			
3.			

Resource:
www.score.org/resources/business-plans-financial-statements-template-gallery

11.2   Break-even Analysis

Break-Even Analysis will be performed to determine the point at which revenue received equals the costs associated with receiving the revenue. Break-even analysis calculates what is known as a margin of safety, the amount that revenues exceed the break-even point. This is the amount that revenues can fall while still staying above the break-even point. The two main purposes of using the break-even analysis for marketing is to (1) determine the minimum number of sales that is required to avoid a loss at a designated sales price and (2) it is an exercise tool so that we can tweak the sales price to determine the minimum volume of sales we can reasonably expect to sell in order to avoid a loss.

Definition: Break-Even Is the Volume Where All Fixed Expenses Are Covered.

Three important definitions used in break-even analysis are:
- **Variable Costs** (Expenses) are costs that change directly in proportion to changes in activity (volume), such as raw materials, labor and packaging.

- **Fixed Costs** (Expenses) are costs that remain constant (fixed) for a given time period despite wide fluctuations in activity (volume), such as rent, loan payments, insurance, payroll and utilities.

- **Unit Contribution Margin** is the difference between your product's unit selling price and its unit variable cost.
  Unit Contribution Margin = Unit Sales Price - Unit Variable Cost

For the purposes of this breakeven analysis, the assumed fixed operating costs will be approximately $ _____ per month, as shown in the following table.

Averaged Monthly Fixed Costs:		**Variable Costs:**	
Payroll	_____	Cost of Inventory Sold	_____
Rent	_____	Labor	_____
Insurance	_____	Supplies	_____
Utilities	_____	Direct Costs per Patient	_____
Security.	_____	Other	_____
Legal/Technical Help	_____		
Other	_____		
Total:	_____	Total	_____

A break-even analysis table has been completed on the basis of average costs/prices. With monthly fixed costs averaging $_____ , $_____ in average sales and $_____ in average variable costs, we need approximately $_____ in sales per month to break-even.

Based on our assumed ____ % variable cost, we estimate our breakeven sales volume at around $ _____ per month. We expect to reach that sales volume by our

_____ month of operations. Our break-even analysis is shown in further detail in the following table.

Breakeven Formulas:

Break Even Units = Total Fixed Costs / (Unit Selling Price - Variable Unit Cost)

.   _____ = _____ / (_____ - _____)
.

·**BE Dollars = (Total Fixed Costs / (Unit Price – Variable Unit Costs))/ Unit Price**

_____ = (_____ / (_____ - _____)) / _____

·**BE Sales = Annual Fixed Costs / (1- Unit Variable costs / Unit Sales Price)**

_____ = _____ / (1 - _____ / _____)

Table: Break-even Analysis

Monthly Units Break-even	_____
Monthly Revenue Break-even	$ _____
Assumptions:	
Average Per-Unit Revenue	$ _____
Average Per-Unit Variable Cost	$ _____
Estimated monthly Fixed Cost	$ _____

Ways to Improve Breakeven Point:

1. Reduce Fixed Costs via Cost Controls
2. Raise unit sales prices.
3. Lower Variable Costs by improving employee productivity or getting lower competitive bids from suppliers.
4. Broaden product/service line to generate multiple revenue streams.

11.3   Projected Profit and Loss

Pro forma income statements are an important tool for planning our future business operations. If the projections predict a downturn in profitability, we can make operational changes such as increasing prices or decreasing costs before these projections become reality. Our monthly profit for the first year varies significantly, as we aggressively seek improvements and begin to implement our marketing plan. However, after the first ____ months, profitability should be established. We predict advertising costs will go down in the next three years as word-of-mouth about   our business gets out to the public and we are able to find what has worked well for us and concentrate on those advertising methods, and corporate affiliations generate sales without the need for extra advertising. Our net profit/sales ratio will be low the first year. We expect this ratio to rise at least _____ (15?) percent the second year. Normally, a startup concern will operate with negative profits through the first two years. We will avoid that kind of operating loss on our second year by knowing our competitors and having a full understanding of our target markets. Our projected profit and loss is indicated in the following table. From our research of the background check industry, our annual projections are quite realistic and conservative, and we prefer this approach so that we can ensure an adequate cash flow.

Key P & L Formulas:

Gross Profit Margin = Total Sales Revenue - Cost of Goods Sold

Gross Margin % = (Total Sales Revenue - Cost of Goods Sold) / Total Sales Revenue

Represents the proportion of each dollar of revenue the company retains as gross profit.

EBITDA =Revenue - Expenses (exclude int., taxes, depreciation & amortization)

PBIT = Profit (Earnings) Before Interest and Taxes = EBIT

A profitability measure that looks at a company's profits before the company pays corporate income tax and interest expenses. This measure deducts all operating expenses from revenue, but it leaves out the payment of interest and tax.

Net Profit = Total Sales Revenues - Total Expenses

Pro Forma Profit and Loss

	Formula	2018	2019	2020
Gross Revenue:				
Employment Screening				
Tenant Screening				
Custom Screening Solutions				
Drug Testing				
Fingerprinting				
DMV Driving Records				
DOT Drug and Alcohol Verification				
Employment Credit Reports				
Tenant Credit Reports				
SSN Verification				
Employment Verification				
Professional Reference Checks				
License and Credential Verification				

Education Verification	_____
Skills and Behavioral Testing	_____
Criminal County Court Check	_____
Form I-9 and E-Verify	_____
Electronic Application Process	_____
Screening Consulting Services	_____
Volunteer Background Checks	_____
Business Background Checks	_____
Misc.	_____
Total Revenue A	_____
Cost of Sales	
Cost of Goods Sold	_____
Other	_____
Total Costs of Sales D	_____
Gross Margin A-D=E	_____
Gross Margin % E / A	_____
Operating Expenses:	
Payroll	_____
Payroll Taxes	_____
Sales & Marketing	_____
Conventions/Trade Shows	_____
Depreciation	_____
License/Permit Fees	_____
Dues and Subscriptions	_____
Rent	_____
Utilities	_____
Deposits	_____
Repairs and Maintenance	_____
Janitorial Supplies	_____
Office Supplies	_____
Classroom Supplies	_____
Leased Equipment	_____
Buildout Costs	_____
Insurance	_____
Professional Development	_____
Resource Library	_____
Merchant Fees	_____
Bad Debts	_____
Miscellaneous	_____
Total Operating Expenses F	_____
Profit Before Int. & Taxes E - F = G	_____
Interest Expenses H	_____
Taxes Incurred I	_____
Net Profit G - H - I = J	_____
Net Profit / Sales J / A = K	_____

11.4 Projected Cash Flow

The Cash Flow Statement shows how the company is paying for its operations and future growth, by detailing the "flow" of cash between the company and the outside world. Positive numbers represent cash flowing in, negative numbers represent cash flowing out. We are positioning ourselves in the market as a medium-risk concern with steady cash flows. Accounts payable is paid at the end of each month while sales are in cash and short-term credit card collectibles. Cash balances will be used to reduce outstanding line of credit balances or will be invested in a low-risk liquid money market fund to decrease the opportunity cost of cash held. Surplus cash balances during the critical first year of operations will function as protection against unforeseen changes in the timing of disbursements required to fund operations.

The first year's monthly cash flows are will vary significantly, but we do expect a solid cash balance from day one. We expect that the majority of our sales will be done in cash or by credit card and that will be good for our cash flow position. Additionally, we will stock only slightly more than one month's inventory at any time. Consequently, we do not anticipate any problems with cash flow, once we have obtained sufficient start-up funds.

A __ year commercial loan in the amount of $_____, sought by the owner will be used to cover our working capital requirement. Our projected cash flow is summarized in the following table and is expected to meet our needs. In the following years, excess cash will be used to finance our growth plans.

Cash Flow Management:

We will use the following practices to improve our cash flow position:
1. Perform credit checks and become more selective when granting credit.
2. Seek deposits or multiple stage payments.
3. Reduce the amount/time of credit given to clients.
4. Reduce direct and indirect costs and overhead expenses.
5. Use the 80/20 rule to manage inventories, receivables and payables.
6. Invoice as soon as the project has been completed.
7. Generate regular reports on receivable ratios and aging.
8. Establish and adhere to sound credit practices.
9. Use more pro-active collection techniques.
10. Add late payment fees where possible.
11. Increase the credit taken from suppliers.
12. Negotiate purchase prices and extended credit terms from vendors.
13. Use some barter arrangements to acquire goods and service.
14. Use leasing to gain access to the use of productive assets.
15. Covert debt into equity.
16. Regularly update cash flow forecasts.
17. Defer projects which cannot achieve acceptable cash paybacks.
18. Require a 50% deposit upon the signing of the contract and the balance in full, due five days before the event.
19. Speed-up the completion of projects to get paid faster.

20. Ask for extended credit terms from major suppliers.
21. Put ideal bank balances into interest-bearing (sweep) accounts.
22. Charge interest on client installment payments.
23. Check the accuracy of invoices to avoid unnecessary rework delays.
24. Include stop-work clauses in contracts to address delinquent payments.

Cash Flow Formulas:

Net Cash Flow = Incoming Cash Receipts - Outgoing Cash Payments

Equivalently, net profit plus amounts charged off for depreciation, depletion, and amortization. (also called cash flow).

Cash Balance = Opening Cash Balance + Net Cash Flow

We are positioning ourselves in the market as a medium risk concern with steady cash flows. Accounts payable is paid at the end of each month, while sales are in cash, giving our company an excellent cash structure.

Pro Forma Cash Flow

	Formula	2018	2019	2020

Cash Received

Cash from Operations

	Formula
Cash Sales	A
Cash from Receivables	B
Subtotal Cash from Operations	A + B = C

	Formula
Additional Cash Received	
Non-Operating (Other) Income	
Sales Tax, VAT, HST/GST Received	
New Current Borrowing	
New Other Liabilities (interest fee)	
New Long-term Liabilities	
Sales of Other Current Assets	
Sales of Long-term Assets	
New Investment Received	
Total Additional Cash Received	D
Subtotal Cash Received	C + D = E

Expenditures

	Formula
Expenditures from Operations	
Cash Spending	F
Payment of Accounts Payable	G
Subtotal Spent on Operations	F+G = H
Additional Cash Spent	
Non-Operating (Other) Expenses	
Sales Tax, VAT, HST/GST Paid Out	
Principal Repayment Current Borrowing	
Other Liabilities Principal Repayment	
Long-term Liabilities Principal Repayment	
Purchase Other Current Assets	
Dividends	
Total Additional Cash Spent	I
Subtotal Cash Spent	H + I = J
Net Cash Flow	**E - J = K**
Cash Balance	

11.5   Projected Balance Sheet

Pro forma Balance Sheets are used to project how the business will be managing its assets in the future. As a pure start-up business, the opening balance sheet may contain no values. As the business grows, our investment in inventory increases. This reflects sales volume increases and the commensurate ability to secure favorable volume discount terms with our distributors. The projected accounts receivable position is relatively low and steady due to the nature of the business, in which up to 50% of our sales are cash, and the balance are consumer credit card purchases. No other consumer credit terms are envisioned or necessary for the operation of this business.

Capital assets of $\_\_\_\_\_$ are comprised of a quoted $_____$ for the build-out of the store (depreciating straight line over the 15-year term of the lease), $\_\_\_\_\_$ for start-up costs (amortized over five years), and $\_\_\_\_\_$ for the landlord's security deposit (about eight months rent). Long-term liabilities are projected to decrease steadily, reflecting re-payment of the original seven-year term loan required to finance the business. It is important to note that part of the retained earnings may become a distribution of capital to the owners, while the balance would be reinvested in the business to replenish depreciated assets and to support further growth.

Note: The projected balance sheets must link back into the projected income statements and cash flow projections.

___ (company name) does not project any real trouble meeting its debt obligations, provided the revenue predictions are met. We are very confident that we will meet or exceed all our objectives in the Business Plan and produce a slow but steady increase in net worth. All our tables will be updated monthly to reflect past performance and future assumptions. Future assumptions will not be based on past performance but rather on economic cycle activity, regional industry strength, and future cash flow possibilities. We expect a solid growth in net worth by the year ___. The Balance Sheet table for fiscal years 2018, 2019, and 2020 follows. It shows managed but sufficient growth of net worth, and a sufficiently healthy financial position.

Excel Resource:
www.unioncity.org/ED/Finance%20Tools/Projected%20Balance%20Sheet.xls

Key Formulas:

Paid-in Capital = Capital contributed to the corporation by investors on top of the par value of the capital stock.

Retained Earnings = The portion of net income which is retained by the corporation and used to grow its net worth, rather than distributed to the owners as dividends.

Retained Earnings = After-tax net earnings - (Dividends + Stock Buybacks)

Earnings = Revenues - (Cost of Sales + Operating Expenses + Taxes)

Net Worth = Total Assets - Total Liabilities
         Also known as 'Owner's Equity'.

Resources:
business.com/articles/power-of-profitability-the-financial-ratios-you-need-to-check/

Pro Forma Balance Sheet

	Formulas	2018	2019	2020
Assets				
Current Assets				
Cash				
Accounts Receivable				
Inventory				
Other Current Assets				
Total Current Assets	A			
Long-term Assets				
Long-term Assets	B			
Accumulated Depreciation	C			
Total Long-term Assets	B - C = D			
Total Assets	**A + D = E**			

Liabilities and Capital

	Formulas	2018	2019	2020
Current Liabilities				
Accounts Payable				
Current Borrowing				
Other Current Liabilities				
Subtotal Current Liabilities	**F**			
Long-term Liabilities				
Notes Payable				
Other Long-term Liabilities				
Subtotal Long-term Liabilities	**G**			
Total Liabilities	**F + G = H**			
Capital				
Paid-in Capital	I			
Retained Earnings	J			
Earnings	K			
Total Capital	I - J + K = L			
Total Liabilities and Capital	**H + L = M**			
Net Worth	**E - H = N**			

11.6   Business Ratios

The following financial ratios will be used to assist in determining the actual meaning of our financial statements and comparing the performance of similar businesses. The below table provides significant ratios for the ____ industry. Our comparisons to the SIC Industry profile are very favorable and we expect to maintain healthy ratios for profitability, risk and return.   Use Business Ratio Formulas provided to assist in calculations.

Key Business Ratio Formulas:

EBIT = Earnings Before Interest and Taxes
EBITA = Earnings Before Interest, Taxes & Amortization. (Operating Profit Margin)

Sales Growth Rate =((Current Year Sales - Last Year Sales)/(Last Year Sales)) x 100
Ex: Percent of Sales = (Advertising Expense / Sales) x 100

Net Worth = Total Assets - Total Liabilities

Acid Test Ratio = Liquid Assets / Current Liabilities
Measures how much money business has immediately available. A ratio of 2:1 is good.

Net Profit Margin = Net Profit / Net Revenues
The higher the net profit margin is, the more effective the company is at converting revenue into actual profit.

Return on Equity (ROE) = Net Income / Shareholder's Equity
The ROE is useful for comparing the profitability of a company to that of other firms in the same industry. Also known as "return on net worth" (RONW).

Debt to Shareholder's Equity = Total Liabilities / Shareholder's Equity
A ratio below 0.80 indicates there is a good chance the company has a durable competitive advantage, with the exception of financial institutions, which are highly leveraged institutions.

Current Ratio = Current Assets / Current Liabilities
The higher the current ratio, the more capable the company is of paying its obligations. A ratio under 1 suggests that the company would be unable to pay off its obligations if they came due at that point.

Quick Ratio = Current Assets - Inventories / Current Liabilities
The quick ratio is more conservative than the current ratio, because it excludes inventory from current assets.

Pre-Tax Return on Net Worth = Pre-Tax Income / Net Worth
Indicates stockholders' earnings before taxes for each dollar of investment.

Pre-Tax Return on Assets = (EBIT / Assets) x 100
Indicates much profit the firm is generating from the use of its assets.

Accounts Receivable Turnover = Net Credit Sales / Average Accounts Receivable
A low ratio implies the company should re-assess its credit policies in order to ensure the timely collection of imparted credit that is not earning interest for the firm.

Net Working Capital = Current Assets - Current Liabilities
Positive working capital means that the company is able to pay off its short-term liabilities. Negative working capital means that a company currently is unable to meet its short-term liabilities with its current assets (cash, accounts receivable and inventory).

Interest Coverage Ratio = Earnings Before Interest & Taxes /Total Interest Expense
The lower the ratio, the more the company is burdened by debt expense. When a company's interest coverage ratio is 1.5 or lower, its ability to meet interest expenses may be questionable. An interest coverage ratio below 1 indicates the company is not generating sufficient revenues to satisfy interest expenses.

Collection Days = Accounts Receivables / (Revenues/365)
A high ratio indicates that the company is having problems getting paid for services.

Accounts Payable Turnover = Total Supplier Purchases/Average Accounts Payable
If the turnover ratio is falling from one period to another, this is a sign that the company is taking longer to pay off its suppliers than previously. The opposite is true when the turnover ratio is increasing, which means the firm is paying of suppliers at a faster rate.

Payment Days = (Accounts Payable Balance x 360) / (No. of Accounts Payable x 12)
The average number of days between receiving an invoice and paying it off.

Total Asset Turnover = Revenue / Assets
Asset turnover measures a firm's efficiency at using its assets in generating sales or revenue - the higher the number the better.

Sales / Net Worth = Total Sales / Net Worth

Dividend Payout = Dividends / Net Profit
Assets to Sales = Assets / Sales
Current Debt / Totals Assets = Current Liabilities / Total Assets

Current Liabilities to Liabilities = Current Liabilities / Total Liabilities

Business Ratio Analysis

	2018	2019	2020
Sales Growth			
Percent of Total Assets			
Accounts Receivable			
Inventory			
Other Current Assets			
Total Current Assets			
Long-term Assets			
Total Assets			
Current Liabilities			
Long-term Liabilities			
Total Liabilities			
Net Worth			
Percent of Sales			
Sales			
Gross Margin			
Selling G& A Expenses			
Advertising Expenses			
Profit Before Interest & Taxes			
Solvency (Main) Ratios			
Current Ratio			
Quick Ratio			
Total Debt to Total Assets			
Profitability Ratios			
Pre-tax Return on Net Worth			
Pre-tax Return on Assets			
Net Profit Margin			
Return on Equity			
Efficiency (Activity) Ratios			
Accounts Receivable Turnover			
Collection Days			
Inventory Turnover			
Accounts Payable Turnover			
Payment Days			
Total Asset Turnover			
Inventory Productivity			
Sales per sq/ft.			
Gross Margin Return on Inventory (GMROI)			

Leverage (Debt) Ratios
Debt to Net Worth   _____
Current Liabilities to Liabilities   _____

Liquidity Ratios
Net Working Capital   _____
Interest Coverage   _____

Additional Ratios
Assets to Sales   _____
Current Debt / Total Assets   _____
Acid Test   _____
Sales / Net Worth   _____
Dividend Payout   _____

Business Vitality Profile
Sales per Employee   _____
Survival Rate   _____

We will also track the following Performance Metrics:

1. Customer service: response time, one-call resolution, and dedicated account support
2. Reporting services: verification rates and criminal record rates
3. Turnaround time: turnaround time measurement corporate and by location
4. Technology: system uptime, security, performance.
5.   Cost control: cost alignment, monitoring, consistency
6. Compliance: adverse action monitoring and support.

12.0   Summary

_____ (company name) will be successful. This business plan has documented that the establishment of _____ (company name) is feasible. All of the critical factors, such as industry trends, marketing analysis, competitive analysis, management expertise and financial analysis support this conclusion.

Project Description: (Give a brief summary of the product, service or program.)

_____

Description of Favorable Industry and Market Conditions.
(Summarize why this business is viable.)

_____

Summary of Earnings Projections and Potential Return to Investors:

_____

Summary of Capital Requirements:

_____

Security for Investors & Loaning Institutions:

_____

Summary of expected benefits for people in the community beyond the immediate business concern:

_____

Means of Financing:
A. Loan Requirements: $_____
B. Owner's Contribution: $ $_____
C. Other Sources of Income: $_____
Total Funds Available: $_____

13.0   Potential Exit Scenarios

Two potential exit strategies exist for the investor:

1. **Initial Public Offering. (IPO)**
    We seek to go public within ____ (#) years of operations. The funds used will both help create liquidity for investors as well as allow for additional capital to develop our _____ (international/national?) roll out strategy.

2. **Acquisition Merger with Private or Public Company.**
    Our most desirable option for exit is a merger or buyout by a large corporation. We believe with substantial cash flows and a loyal customer base our company will be attractive to potential corporate investors within five years. Real value has been created through the novel combination of home health care services as well as partnering with key referral groups.

APPENDIX

Purpose: Supporting documents used to enhance your business proposal.

Tax returns of principals for the last three years, if the plan is for new business

A personal financial statement, which should include life insurance and endowment policies, if applicable

A copy of the proposed lease or purchase agreement for building space, or zoning information for in-home businesses, with layouts, maps, and blueprints

A copy of licenses and other legal documents including partnership, association, or shareholders' agreements and copyrights, trademarks, and patents applications

A copy of résumés of all principals in a consistent format, if possible

Copies of letters of intent from suppliers, contracts, orders, and miscellaneous.

In the case of a franchised business, a copy of the franchise contract and all supporting documents provided by the franchisor

Newspaper clippings that support the business or the owner, including something about you, your achievements, business idea, or region

Promotional literature for your company or your competitors

Product/Service Brochures of your company or competitors

Photographs of your product. equipment, facilities, etc.

Market research to support the marketing section of the plan

Trade and industry publications when they support your intentions

Quotations or pro-forma invoices for capital items to be purchased, including a list of fixed assets, company vehicles, and proposed renovations

References/Letters of Recommendation

All insurance policies in place, both business and personal

Operation Schedules

Organizational Charts

Job Descriptions

Additional Financial Projections by Month

Customer Needs Analysis Worksheet

Sample Sales Letters

Copies of Software Management Reports

Copies of Standard Business Forms

Equipment List

Personal Survival Budget

Background Check Form

Helpful Resources:

Associations:

American Society for Industrial Security (ASIS)   www.asisonline.org/
National Association of Professional Background Screeners   www.napbs.com

Publications:

The Background Investigator   www.thebackgroundinvestigator.com

Miscellaneous:

Vista Print Free Business Cards   www.vistaprint.com
Free Business Guides   www.smbtn.com/businessplanguides/
Open Office   http://download.openoffice.org/
US Census Bureau   www.census.gov
Federal Government   www.business.gov
US Patent & Trademark Office   www.uspto.gov
US Small Business Administration   www.sba.gov
National Association for the Self-Employed   www.nase.org
International Franchise Association   www.franchise.org
Center for Women's Business Research   www.cfwbr.org

http://sbinformation.about.com/
http://www.business.gov/
http://www.sba.gov/regions/states.html
http://freeadvice.com/
http://www.government-grants-101.com/
http://www.pueblo.gsa.gov/
http://www.smallbusinessnotes.com/sitemap.html

Source:
http://www.sba.gov/content/pre-employment-background-checks

How to Get Started Marketing on Twitter

1. **Import Your Contacts**
    Import contacts from Gmail, Hotmail and your own address book.

2. **Make Sure that Your Profile is Complete**
    Fill in all the fields (both required and optional) and include your website URL.
    Personalize your Twitter page to match your company's branding.

3. **Understand the Dynamics of Twitter**
    Use Twitter as a social tool, not a classifieds site and follow these tips:
    - Don't spam others about your specials.
    - Follow other users.
    - Don't promote your company directly.
    - Tweet about an informative blog posting.

4. **Build Your Followers Base**
    - Put a link to "Follow Me on Twitter" everywhere (your email signature, forums, website, and business cards)
    - Every time you post on your blog, invite people to follow you on Twitter

5. **Balance Your Followers/Following Ratio**
    - Strike a balance between people you follow and people that follow you.
    - Grow slowly by adding 30 friends at a time, and then wait for them to follow you back.

6. **Make it Worthwhile to Follow You**
    - Tweet only interesting stuff.

7. **Learn from the Best**
    - Find users with several hundred followers and learn their best practices.

8. **Twitter Uses**
    - Use twitter to extend the reach of an existing blogging strategy and to deepen or further ties. Ex: Carnival Cruise Lines.
    - Use to announce sales and deals. Ex: Amazon.
    - Increase the ability for frequent updates to blogs or web sites or news.
    - Build consensus or a community of supporters.
    - Build buzz for a new blog.
    - Update breaking news at conferences or events.

Advertising Plan Worksheet

Ad Campaign Title: _____

Ad Campaign Start Date: _____ End Date: _____

What are the features (what product has) and hidden benefits (what product does for consumer) of my products/services?

Who is the targeted audience?

What problems are faced by this targeted audience?

What solutions do you offer?

Who is the competition and how do they advertise?

What is your differentiation strategy?

What are your bullet point competitive advantages?

What are the objectives of this advertising campaign?

What are your general assumptions?

What positioning image do you want to project?

__ Exclusiveness	___ Low Cost	____ High Quality
__ Speedy Service	___ Convenient	____ Innovative

What is the ad headline?

What is the advertising budget for this advertising campaign?

What advertising methods will be used?

__ Radio	___ TV/Cable	__ Yellow Pages
__ Coupons	___ Telemarketing	__ Flyers
__ Direct Mail	___ Magazines	__ Newspapers
__ Press Release	___ Brochures	__ Billboards
__ Other		

When will each advertising method start and what will it cost?

Method	Start Date	Frequency	Cost

Indicate how you will measure the cost-effectiveness of the advertising plan?
Formula: Return on Investment (ROI) = Generated Sales / Ad Costs.

Marketing Action Plan

Month: _____

Target Market: _____

Responsibilities: _____

Allocated Budget: _____

Objectives _____

Strategies _____

Implementation _____

Tactics _____

Results
Evaluation _____
_____

_____
_____
_____
_____
_____
_____
_____
_____
_____
_____
_____
_____
_____
_____

Lessons Learned:

_____
_____
_____

Viral Marketing

Definition: Also known as word-of-mouth advertising.
Objective: To prompt your customers to deliver your sales message to others.
Strategy: Encourage and enable communication recipients to pass the offer or message along to others.
Benefit: Provides an excellent advertising return on investment and builds the trust factor.

Methodologies:
1. Encourage blog comments and two-way dialogue.
2. Use surveys to solicit feedback.
3. Use refer-a-friend forms or scripts.
4. Provide discount coupon or logo imprinted giveaway rewards for telling a friend.
5. Utilize pre-existing social networks.
6. Participate in message boards or forums.
7. Add a signature line with a refer-a-friend tagline to all posts and emails.
8. Enable unrestricted access.
9. Facilitate website content sharing.
10. Write articles and e-books and encourage free reprints with byline mention.
11. Submit articles with 'about the author' box to article directories, such as www.articlecity.com.
12. Develop attention-grabbing product line extensions to stay connected.
13. Do the unexpected by offering a surprise benefit.
14. Deliver a remarkable offering that exceeds customer expectations.
15. Provoke a strong emotional response by getting involved with a cause that is important to your customers.
16. Provide referral incentives.
17. Get free samples into the hands of respected opinion leaders.
18. Educate customers, as to your product benefits and competitive advantages, to act as spokespersons for your company.

Explain Your Viral Marketing Program

_____
_____
_____
_____
_____

Integrate Marketing into Daily Operations

Objective: To seamlessly integrate marketing processes into daily, routine operations.

Strategies:
1. Develop form to ask for referrals upon new customer registration and annual renewal.
2. Present a sales presentation folder upon registration or contract sign-up with needs analysis worksheets, testimonials, new product introduction flyers, innovative application ideas, etc.
3. Develop a second sales presentation folder version for presentation upon job completion or sale, with referral program details, warranty service contract blank, and accessory suggestions.
4. Include business cards and coupons with all product deliverables.
5. Install company yard signs during job set-up.
6. Include a thank you note/comment card with all deliverables.
7. Include flyers and helpful articles in all customer correspondence, especially mailed invoices and statements.
8. Attach logo and contact info to all finished products.
9. Conduct customer satisfaction surveys while clients are waiting to be served.
10. Develop enclosed warranty card to build customer database and feed drip marketing program.
11. Provide competitor product/service comparisons that highlight your strengths.
12. Incorporate feedback cards into merchandise displays.
13. Train all employees to also be sales and customer service agents.
14. Print your Mission Statement or slogan on all forms and correspondence.
15. _____
16. _____

Indicate how you will incorporate marketing into daily operations.

Sales Stage	Business Processes	Opportunities to Incorporate Marketing Techniques
Pre-sale		
Transaction		
Post Sale		

Monthly Marketing Calendar

Instruction: Use to plan your monthly marketing events or activities and evaluate individual event results and marketing lessons learned for the month.

Month/Year: _____

Event/ Activity	Responsibility	Cost	Comments	Date	Results Evaluation

Monthly Evaluation of Lessons Learned:

_____

_____

_____

Form Strategic Marketing Alliances

Definition: A collaborative relationship between two or more non-competing firms with the intent of accomplishing mutually compatible and beneficial goals that would be difficult for each to accomplish alone. Also referred to as 'Collaboration Marketing'.

Note: Usually, potential alliance partners sell distinct or complementary products and/or services to the same target market audience.

Advantages: Improve marketing efficiency by achieving synergy in resource allocation with strategic partners.
Improve marketing effectiveness by creating a one-stop or wraparound shopping experience.
A way to inexpensively test the market for growth potential.

Types of Co-Ventures:
1. Informal Strategic Alliances
2. Contractual Relationships (Attorney review recommended)
3. New Business Entity (Set-up by attorney)

Informal Strategic Alliances
1. Most involve consultations regarding:
   a. Mutual Referrals
   b. Research for product improvements
   c. Promotion of products or services (affiliate programs).
   d. Creative product bundling arrangements.
2. May or may not require a written agreement.
3. May or may not require compensation.

Topics to be Covered:
1. The specific strategic goals and objectives of the alliance.
2. The performance expectations of the parties.
3. The scope of the alliance.
4. The period of performance.
5. Termination and renewal procedures.
6. Strategic marketing plan to promote the alliance.
7. Dispute resolution procedures.
8. Performance tracking methods.
9. Periodic evaluation of reciprocal benefits realized.
10. Website pages/links to promote alliance partners.

Example: The mutual referral relationship between a sports bar and a fitness club or physical fitness trainer.

Strategic Marketing Alliance Worksheet

Methodology:
1. Identify the assets and capabilities you can provide to the alliance.
2. Identify the assets and capabilities that the proposed partner will bring to the alliance.
3. Determine the benefits you are seeking from the alliance.
4. Determine the gaps in your offerings that the alliance partner can fill.
5. List any conflicting relationships with other businesses and benefits received.
6. Research the potential alliance for strategic fit and other opportunities.
7. List the ways in which your customers will benefit from this alliance.
8. Assess any alliance risks.
9. Determine the ongoing actions needed to maintain the alliance.
10. Design a marketing plan to promote the alliance.
11. Develop a Mission Statement for the alliance.
12. Develop the Management Plan for the alliance.
13. Design the alliance appraisal and renewal procedures.

Potential Alliance Partner	Partner Strengths Offered	Your Offering Gaps Filled	Customer Benefits	Alliance Risks

Referral Program Tips

Objective: To formalize your referral program so that it can be easily and consistently integrated into your operating processes.

1. Define the stages in the sales process when you will ask for a referral. Ex: Registration, Renewals, Annual Drive, etc.)

2. Document your referral asking script (include objection handling responses).

3. Include a request for referrals in your customer satisfaction survey and your registration forms.

4. Stress the dependence of your business on referrals in all your marketing communications.

5. Set-up a follow-up procedure and tracking form to convert referral leads into actual customers.

6. Publish your referral incentives, awards criteria and timetable for settlement.

7. Customize your referral program to the motivational needs of a select number of potential 'Bird Dogs' or 'Big Hitters'.

8. Educate potential referral agents as to the characteristics of your ideal prospect. (Develop Ideal Prospect Profile)

9. Set-up special, mutual referral arrangements with strategic business alliance partners and track the reciprocity of efforts.

10. Join or start a local lead group.

11. Set-up 'thank-you note' templates to facilitate your expression of gratitude.

12. Use logo imprinted giveaways, such as T-sheets, as referral thank you expressions.

Seminar Outline Worksheet

Objective: To establish your expertise on the subject matter and produce future possible networking contacts by offering a newsletter sign-up and/or business card exchange.

Warning: Make seminar information rich and not a sales presentation.

1. Start with Attention-Grabbing Headline
   Ex: Hard-hitting Quotation, Thought Provoking Question, Startling Fact

   _____

2. Introduce Yourself and Establish Your Credentials

   _____

3. Present Seminar Overview

   _____

4. Discuss Attendee Participation Guidelines

   _____

5. Solicit a sampling of attendee interests, backgrounds and concerns.

   _____

6. Establish Learning Objectives

   _____

7. Preview the Bulleted Topics To be Covered

   _____

8. Share a Relevant Success Story (Case Study).

   _____

9. Use analogies and comparisons to create reference points.

   _____

10. Use statistics to support your position.

    _____

11. Conclusion: - Summarize Benefits for Attendees / Appeal to Action

    _____

    _____

    _____

12. Hold Question and Answer Session

13. Final Thoughts
    - Appreciation for Help Received
    - Indicate after-seminar availability

14. Handout A Remembrance
    - Business Cards   - Glossary of Terms
    - Seminar Outline   - Feedback Survey

YouTube Marketing Tips

Definition: An online video destination to watch and share original video clips. (World-wide approx. 55 million unique users/month)

1. Focus on something that is funny or humorous, so that people will feel compelled to share it with friends and family.
2. Make the video begin and end with a black screen and include the URL of your originating website to bring traffic to your site.
3. Put your URL at the bottom of the entire video.
4. Clearly demonstrate how your product works.
5. Create how-to videos to share your expertise and develop a following.
6. Build contests and events around special holidays and occasions.
7. Run a search on similar content by keyword and use the info to choose the right category and tags for your video.
8. Make sure the video is real, with no gimmicks or tricks.
9. Add as many keywords as you can.
10. Make sure that your running time is five minutes or less.
11. Break longer videos into several clips, each with a clear title, so that they can be selectively viewed.
12. Encourage viewer participation and support.
13. Take advantage of YouTube tags, use adjectives to target people searching based on interests, and match your title and description to the tags.
14. Use the flexibility provided by the medium to experiment.
15. Use the 'Guru Account' sign-up designation to highlight info videos and how-to guides.
16. Create 'Playlists' to gather individual clips into niche-targeted context so viewers can easily find related content.
17. Use 'Bulletins' to broadcast short messages to the world via Your YouTube Channel.
18. Email 'The Robin Good YouTube Channel' to promote a new video release.
19. Join a 'YouTube Group' to post videos or comments to the group discussion area and build your network of contacts.
20. Use 'YouTube Streams' to join or create a room where videos are shared and discussed in real-time.
21. Use 'Active Sharing' to broadcast the videos that you are currently watching, and drive traffic to your profile.
22. Use the 'Share Video' link found under each video you submit and then check the box 'Friends' to send your video to all your friends.
23. Create your own YouTube Channel when you sign-up for a new YouTube account.

Basic Monthly Marketing Plan Checklist

1. Send birthday greetings to existing clients. _____
2. Contact referral sources and express appreciation for their referrals. _____
3. Implement program to develop new referral sources. _____
4. Research new ways to solve more problems of your target clients. _____
5. Research possible new target audience needs. _____
6. Make your friends/family/associates/social contacts aware of your expanding capabilities. _____
7. Train all employees to assist in marketing efforts. _____
8. Conduct selected client interviews to assess performance, changing needs and suggestions. _____
9. Forward copies of articles of interest to contacts. _____
10. Take contact to breakfast, lunch or dinner. _____
11. Invite contact to sporting or cultural event. _____
12. Distribute articles that demonstrate your expertise. _____
13. Invite contacts to an informative seminar. _____
14. Send personal notes of congratulation. _____
15. Join organizations important to your contacts. _____
16. Update your mailing list. _____
17. Issue a press release on a firm accomplishment or planned marketing event. _____
18. Update your firm's list of competitive advantages. _____
19. Attend a networking event. _____
20. Update the helpful content on your website. _____
21. Arrange to speak on your area of expertise. _____
22. Become actively involved in the community. _____
23. Track your ad results to determine resource focus. _____
24. Develop alliances with complementary businesses. _____
25. Conduct customer satisfaction surveys. _____
26. Implement client needs analysis checklist. _____
27. Distribute newsletter featuring clients. _____
28. _____ _____
29. _____ _____
30. _____ _____

Networking Insights

Definition: A reciprocal process in which you share ideas, leads, information, and advice to build mutually beneficial relationships.

Networking Tips:

1. Start your own local referral group with other business owners.
2. Understand your long-term networking goals.
3. Become a helpful resource to networking members.
4. Research people and companies to know their goals and interests.
5. Offer referrals, resources and recommendations to receive same in return.
6. Consistently try to meet new people and make new friends.
7. Develop good listening skills.
8. Frequently express your gratitude for assistance.
9. Know what interests, strengths and availability you bring to the table.
10. Stay in touch with a newsletter, blog, postcards or email messages.
11. Keep asking questions to get others to tell you more about themselves.
12. Show warmth, display confidence, smile and shake hands firmly.
13. Explore organizations that offer accreditation and directory listings.

Entrepreneur Networking Possibilities

1. Meet Up — www.meetup.com
2. FaceBook, Friendster, Myspace — www.facebook.com
3. LinkedIn — www.linkedIn.com
4. Ryze — www.ryze.com
5. Int'l Virtual Women's Chamber of Commerce — www.ivwcc.org
6. Business Network International — www.BNI.com
7. Club E Network — www.clubENetwork.com
8. Local Chamber of Commerce
9. Rotary Club — www.rotary.org
10. Lion's Club — www.lionsclubs.org
11. Jaycees
12. Toastmasters — www.toastmasters.com
13. Woman Owned Network — wwwwomanowned.com
14. Alumni Associations
15. Parent Teacher Associations (PTA)
16. Trade Shows — www.tsnn.com
17. Trade Associations — www.associationscentral.com
18. EONetwork — www.eonetwork.org
19. Prof. Organizations, Economic Clubs, Charities, Churches, Museums, etc.

Perfect Your Elevator Pitch

A brief, focused message aimed at a particular person or niche segment that summarizes why they should be interested in your products and/or services.

I am a/we are _____(profession) and we help _____ (target market description) to_____(primary problem solved).

Press Release Cover Letter Worksheet

Instructions: Use this form to build a ready-to-use cover letter.

Your Letterhead.

Date

Dear _____ ,

As a company located in your coverage area, we thought the attached Press Release would be of special concern to your readers/viewers, as it touches upon something that we all have in common, an interest in

_____ .

Brief overview purpose of the press release.

_____

I have also enclosed a media kit to give you background information on _____ Company and myself. I hope to follow-up with you shortly.

I also possess expertise in the following related areas:
- _____
- _____
- _____

Should you wish to speak to me or require additional information, I can be reached at _____ or via email at _____ .
Additional assistance with company supplied photos can be requested at the same number. This Press Release can also be downloaded from my company website at www. _____ .

Thank you for your time and attention,

Contact Name
Company Title
Phone Number
Email Address

New Release Template

News Release

For Immediate Release
(Or Hold for Release Until …(date)….)

Contact:
Contact Person _____
Contact Title _____
Company Name _____
Phone Number _____
Fax Number _____
Email Address _____
Website Address _____

Date: _____
Attention: _____ (Target Type of Editor)

Headline: Summarize Your Key Message:
_____

Sub-Headline: Optional: _____

Location of the Firm and Date.
_____

Lead Paragraph: A summary of the newsworthy content.
_____
Answers the questions:
Who: _____
What: _____
Where: _____
When: _____

Second Paragraph:
Expand upon the first paragraph and elaborate on the purpose of the Press Release.
_____
_____

Third Paragraph:
Further details with additional quotes from staff, industry experts or satisfied clients.
_____
_____

For Additional Information Contact:

_____

_____

About Your Expertise:
Presentation of your expert credentials

_____

_____

About Your Business:
Background company history on the firm and central offerings.

_____

_____

Enclosures: Photographs, charts, brochures, etc.

Special Event Release Format   Notes

1.	Type of Event	_____
2.	Sponsoring Organization	_____
3.	Contact Person Before the Event	_____
4.	Contact Person at the Event	_____
5.	Date and Time of the Event	_____
6.	Location of the Event	_____
7.	Length of Presentation Remarks	_____
8.	Presentation Topic	_____
9.	Question Session (Y/N)	_____
10.	Speaker or Panel	_____
11.	Event Background	_____
12.	Noteworthy Expected Attendees	_____
13.	Estimated Number of Attendees	_____
14.	Why readers s/b interested in event.	_____
15.	Specifics of the Event.	_____
16.	Biographies	_____

Track Ad Return on Investment (ROI)

Objective: To invest in those marketing activities that generate the greatest return on invested funds.

Medium	Cost	Calls Received	Cost/Call	No. Act. New Clients	Cost/New Client
Formula:	A	B	A/B=C	D	A/D=E
Newspaper					
Classified Ads					
Yellow Pages					
Billboards					
Cable TV					
Magazine					
Flyers					
Posters					
Coupons					
Direct Mail					
Brochures					
Business Cards					
Seminars					
Demonstrations					
Sponsored Events					
Sign					
Radio					
Trade Shows					
Specialties					
Cold Calling					
Door Hangers					
T-shirts					
Coupon Books					
Transit Ads					
Press Releases					
Word-of-Mouth					
Totals:					

Made in the USA
Las Vegas, NV
01 October 2024

96100164R00143